'Of the hut I builded'

THE ARCHAEOLOGY OF AUSTRALIA'S HISTORY

Australia
1788-1988

Published for the Australian Bicentennial
with special assistance from the
Australian Bicentennial Authority
as part of the Heritage Program.

By the same author

The archaeology of Benin: excavations and other researches in and around Benin City, Nigeria (Oxford University Press, 1975)

Three thousand years in Africa: Man and his environment in the Lake Chad region of Nigeria (Cambridge University Press, 1981)

Australian field archaeology: A guide to techniques (ed.) (Institute of Aboriginal Studies, Canberra, 1983)

African civilizations: Precolonial cities and states in tropical Africa: an archaeological perspective (Cambridge University Press, 1987)

'Of the hut I builded'

THE ARCHAEOLOGY
OF AUSTRALIA'S HISTORY

Graham Connah

University of New England

Drawings by Douglas Hobbs

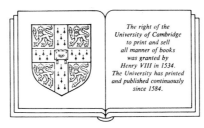

The right of the
University of Cambridge
to print and sell
all manner of books
was granted by
Henry VIII in 1534.
The University has printed
and published continuously
since 1584.

CAMBRIDGE UNIVERSITY PRESS

Cambridge

New York   New Rochelle   Melbourne   Sydney

Published by the Press Syndicate of the University of Cambridge
The Pitt Building, Trumpington Street, Cambridge CB2 1RP
32 East 57th Street, New York, NY 10022, USA
10 Stamford Road, Oakleigh, Melbourne 3166, Australia

First published 1988

Typeset by Love Computer Typesetting, Sydney.
Printed in Australia by MacArthur Press, Parramatta.

National Library of Australia cataloguing in publication data
Connah, Graham.
    Of the hut I builded: the archaeology of Australia's history.
    Includes index.
    1. Archaeology — Australia.
    2. Archaeology and history — Australia.
    I. Hobbs, Douglas.
    II. Title.
930.1'0994

British Library cataloguing in publication data
Connah, Graham.
    Of the hut I builded: the archaeology of Australia's history.
    1. Australia. Archaeology.
    I. Title
994

Library of Congress cataloguing in publication data
Connah, Graham.
    Of the hut I builded: the archaeology of Australia's history/
        Graham Connah: drawings by Douglas Hobbs.
        p. cm.
    Bibliography: p.
    Includes index.
    ISBN 0 521 34567 7.
    1. Australia — Antiquities. 2. Australia — History — 1788–1900.
    3. Archaeology — Australia. I. Hobbs, Douglas. II. Title.
DU106.C66 1988
994 — dc 19

ISBN 0 521 34567 7

To Alan, Sarah and Ian

Ten miles from Ryan's Crossing
  And five below the peak,
I built a little homestead
  On the banks of Rocky Creek;
I cleared the land and fenced it
  And ploughed the rich red loam;
And my first crop was golden
  When I brought Mary home.

Now still down Reedy River
  The grassy sheoaks sigh;
The waterholes still mirror
  The pictures in the sky;
The golden sand is drifting
  Across the rocky bars;
And over all for ever
  Go sun and moon and stars.

But of the hut I builded
  There are no traces now,
And many rains have levelled
  The furrows of my plough.
The glad bright days have vanished;
  For sombre branches wave
Their wattle-blossom golden
  Above my Mary's grave.

Extract from Henry Lawson, *Reedy River*

Contents

Illustrations

Foreword

More than sixty years ago, an English economic historian attempted to divert reluctant historians away from their documents into utilizing the material evidence available for enriching medieval history. 'It is the greatest error to suppose that history must needs be something written down', Eileen Power urged readers of her *Medieval people* in 1924, 'for it may just as well be something built up, and churches, houses, bridges, or amphitheatres can tell their story as plainly as print for those who have eyes to read.'

That is precisely the message of this timely book about the sources of Australian historical archaeology, written in popular terms for lay readers, but of particular relevance to historians or to prospective university students. Graham Connah succeeds in explaining the purpose of historical archaeology and in synthesizing discoveries during the past twenty years. Not attempting an exhaustive coverage of places or publications, he selects illuminating examples of sites, structures or objects. His philosophy is humanistic, so the people and their particular societies, rather than mere material relics, are the focus of attention.

The scope of historical archaeology in Australia is broad, for it includes shipwrecks ('maritime archaeology'), the investigation of past industries ('industrial archaeology', as it is termed in Britain), excavations on British frontier posts ('colonial archaeology', in the United States) and the traces of human activities in urban or rural landscapes ('landscape archaeology'). 'It is the business of the archaeologist . . . to extract information from things that were made by human beings in the past', Connah explains (p. 64). 'Surely it would be foolish to limit such studies merely to the remnants that have survived beneath the ground while ignoring complete structures that are still standing? Houses are artefacts . . . why confine oneself to broken or buried examples when there are complete ones around?'

His survey includes some of the grand places and structures, including bridges, and the excavated foundations of Australia's first important house, Governor Arthur Phillip's residence which was commenced in May 1788. Most of the book concerns more humble people, living or working in bush shacks, isolated settlements, convict barracks, or mines, brickworks and shearing sheds. It also examines the evidence from Dutch and British shipwrecks around the coast, and the beach encampments of Indonesian trepang fishermen, involved in Australia's oldest export industry.

Some Australian archaeologists and historians question the worth of historical archaeological data, or its merits as a discipline. Connah faces these doubts squarely. He poses the question, and answers affirmatively (p.105), 'What can the material evidence possibly tell us that we cannot learn more easily from the amazingly rich documentary sources of information that exist?' Mining history is a relevant case. Despite voluminous records, 'they are . . . notable for what they do not tell us. So remote or so small-scale were some mining operations that they never got into the written records at all' (p.106).

xiii

A reading of this book makes it obvious that historical archaeology offers more than a supplementary footnote to documentary records, or a source of pictorial illustration. A less satisfying inference is, however, that Australian practitioners have proved tardy in publishing detailed reports on their field investigations. Information about significant places therefore remains inaccessible. The quality of the flourishing *Australian Journal of Historical Archaeology* indicates, however, that much is being achieved.

It is worth reflecting that academic research and teaching of Australian prehistoric archaeology commenced only about thirty years ago, while systematic historical archaeology is of even more recent origin. This book indicates that much has been achieved. While all states now have protective legislation for Aboriginal sites and artefacts (although the will to implement these laws varies), however, many states ignore the protection of post-1788 places, structures or movable relics. This book should assist a better understanding of, and the need for, positive legislative action.

The pioneering mentality survives strongly in Australia. In the environment, woodchippers have succeeded ringbarkers as agents of progress, based upon criteria of present economic need. Private enterprise exploitation of single resources still produces fleeting settlements which soon become archaeological. The large Mary Kathleen uranium mining town in Queensland was established in the mid-1950s. It was abandoned some years ago, when all the buildings and structures were removed bodily. Today, its paved streets, tree plantings and building footings are as ghostly as any abandoned gold-mining era township.

Some introspection is desirable at this time of bicentennial retrospection. There surely is a logical contradiction inherent in those developers who see Australia as a 'new' society, yet who promote the demolition of buildings or townscapes because they are 'old' and uneconomic. This wholesale demolition for the sake of presumed economic progress, contrasts oddly with European cultural traditions. The patina of age in Europe is an economic asset, a source of community pride and a cultural benefit. In addition to legislation on historic places, therefore, Australia needs forms of economic diversification which consider the long-term future employment of the many, instead of the immediate enrichment of the few.

It must be inferred from this study, that the intelligent conservation of the past, informed by historical archaeological research, could assist both the cause of regional tourism and a greater community maturity in the perception of its built environment. Graham Connah correctly observes (p.109), that 'Sometimes imagination is more important to society than practicality'.

D.J. Mulvaney

Preface

The aim of this book is to provide an introduction to the archaeology of the last two centuries in Australia. An increasing number of people are interested in the material evidence for the European colonization of this continent, but historical archaeologists have been somewhat reluctant to explain to the general reading public how such evidence can be studied. Although there have been some notable exceptions, there is a general lack of introductory books on this subject. There seem to be two possible reasons for this situation. First, the idea of studying the archaeology of the recent past is very new, being virtually unknown in Australia prior to the late 1960s. Second, in recent years the most pressing need in Australian historical archaeology has been conservation, so that far more effort has gone into descriptive recording than into research publication. As a consequence of these two factors, we do not yet have a large body of published material for the synthesizing author to draw on. To some extent, therefore, it can be argued that any general book on this subject is premature at the present time. I do not fully believe this, but I would ask readers to regard this book as an 'essay', in the original sense of that word, as used by the sixteenth-century French writer, Montaigne. It is intended as a trial, a test, an attempt, meanings that the French word *essai* has retained. In a few years time it may be possible to write a more comprehensive and a more definitive account of Australian historical archaeology. Until that time comes we can only make progress by making the best attempt possible.

This book was written on the suggestion of Dr Robin Derricourt of Cambridge University Press, and I am grateful to him for his encouragement and help throughout its preparation. I am also grateful to the following, who provided helpful advice and information during the course of writing: Dr Michael Pearson of the Australian Heritage Commission, Canberra; Associate Professor Ian Jack of the Department of History, University of Sydney; Associate Professor Dennis Jeans of the Department of Geography, University of Sydney; and Dr Aedeen Cremin of the Department of History, University of Sydney. In addition, I would like to thank Professor John Mulvaney of the Australian National University, Canberra, for consenting to write the Foreword.

As with most books, there are many other people whose help has been essential. Douglas Hobbs of the Department of Archaeology and Palaeoanthropology, University of New England, prepared most of the line drawings, and Rudi Boskovic and Steve Clarke of the Department of Geography of the same university did the photography of those drawings. Graham Macdonald of Armidale drew the illustration on p. vii. Noelene Kachel and Di Watson, also of the University of New England, looked after the word processing of the text, and the Department of Photography at the same university solved a variety of photographic problems.

The line illustrations come from many different places, most of them having been redrawn specially for this book. Their sources are indicated in the individual captions, usually in an abbreviated form that can be understood by examining the notes at the end of each chapter. Similarly, the photographs have a variety of origins, and acknowledgements will be found in the individual captions. I am most grateful to all the individuals and institutions who have supplied this illustration material, in some cases putting themselves to considerable inconvenience to be helpful. Without their goodwill, the book would have been very much the poorer.

Finally, this book was written whilst attempting to run a university department, meet my obligations to undergraduate and postgraduate students and cope with the multifarious other demands made on one's time in a modern university. It is a tribute to the forbearance of my colleagues and students that I was able to complete a book during such a busy period. It is also a tribute to the stoic patience of my family, to the younger members of which I have dedicated the result. To my wife Beryl I have merely promised that I will not write another book — for a little while.

Chapter 1

'There are no traces now'

THE MATERIAL HERITAGE OF AUSTRALIAN HISTORY

To many people, Australia is a 'new' country. The idea that it is really an 'old' country is taking some getting used to. The first shock came in the 1960s and 1970s, when research workers demonstrated that the original Australians, the Aboriginal people, had been in this continent for fifty thousand years or so. The second shock is occurring now, with the realization that two hundred years have elapsed since the beginnings of European settlement. Two centuries is a tiny piece of time compared with fifty thousand years, but a great many things have happened during that period and the whole appearance of this land has been changed. The territories of highly adapted hunter-gatherers have become sheep runs, cattle stations and cultivation paddocks; have been torn apart by mining; have been covered by massive cities and scattered with country towns and rural dwellings; have been seamed with railways, roads and land divisions, and altered in countless other ways. This has not been a simple process of transformation: in those two hundred years land-use has changed several times in some areas; the mines have flourished and died; cities have continuously modified their appearance, while whole towns have been abandoned and thousands of rural dwellings have vanished; and roads, railways and fences have changed their course or been dismantled. As a result the Australian landscape is like a drawing to which each generation has added a few lines, whilst erasing a few others. Our land is patterned with its past and it is a pattern of great complexity that grows daily more complex. This pattern tells us not only about our country but also about ourselves.

Some of the faintest parts of the pattern belong to the Aboriginal settlement that pre-dates European colonization. Interpreting those traces has become the task of the prehistoric archaeologist. There is much that has now been published on this subject, including some general books.[1] Most of the pattern, however, relates to European settlement and study of that part of the pattern is relatively new in Australia. Whose task is it to interpret such evidence?

In the first instance, the investigation of Australia's last two hundred years is obviously the task of Australianist historians.[2] However, historians are specialists in interpreting the contemporary written records of the past, or the subsequent written commentaries on those records, and have enough to do puzzling over documents in the various archives without worrying about a heap of bricks in the middle of a paddock or an unusual pattern on an aerial photograph. They have usually regarded such material evidence as not really their business, although some remarkable exceptions exist.[3] Also, historians have tended to be more interested in political and constitutional developments and in the activities of the more notable individuals of the past. To say this is to do a grave injustice to the social and economic historians, but they seem to have been in the minority, and even they have been

1

more interested in general trends than in particular elements of the landscape. The study and writing of *local* history has remained largely in the hands of interested amateurs. Nevertheless, it is clear that a detailed knowledge of Australia's history is essential for anyone seeking to understand the material evidence scattered across its landscape.

Landscapes are of interest to geographers and, in so far as landscapes are created by humans, they are of particular interest to historical geographers. As a result, scholars studying the historical geography of Australia have contributed substantially to our understanding of the impact of European colonization on this continent.[4] Indeed, because of the technological complexity of that impact, there have also been other specialists who have played an essential role in its study. A very obvious part of the human contribution to landscapes are buildings which, in some places, virtually obliterate any natural features. Because of this, architects and architectural historians have much to tell us about the material evidence for Australia's last two hundred years.[5] That evidence also includes bridges and tunnels, roads and railways, mines, factories and machines. In order to understand things of that sort we need the expertise of engineers, and some of them have indeed turned their attention to the study of such material evidence for the past.[6] Others who can help us to understand the very varied evidence that exists include metallurgists, soil scientists, agronomists, botanists, photogrammetrists, industrial chemists and many more.

All these many contributions are essential if we are to comprehend the very complex material evidence that we have for the European settlement of Australia. However, the people who really specialize in extracting information about the past from *material* evidence are archaeologists. It is a common belief that they are interested only in remote antiquity, and much has been published on the prehistory of Australia. However this is not true, things don't have to be very old before archaeologists are interested in them. Nor is it the case that archaeologists only study societies that did not have the capacity to write their own histories. Some of the most famous research done by archaeologists during the last century or so has been on the historical civilizations of Mesopotamia, Egypt, Greece and Italy. Indeed, in Western Europe, archaeologists have extended their interests to include sites belonging to the Middle Ages and even to the post-medieval period. Particularly in Britain, the main interest of archaeologists studying this most recent period has been in the technology of the so-called Industrial Revolution, and so the archaeological investigation of the last two to three hundred years is often referred to as 'industrial archaeology'. However in several parts of the world that were colonized by Europeans after A.D. 1500 there has developed a far broader interest in the archaeology of recent centuries. In the United States of America, Canada, South Africa, New Zealand and in Australia, interest and concern has grown for what has come to be known by its American title: 'historical archaeology'. In Australia this development is a very recent one, it originated no earlier than the late 1960s. The Australian Society for Historical Archaeology, for instance, was not founded until 1970,[7] and it was 1983 before it was able to publish its own scholarly journal *The Australian Journal of Historical Archaeology*. This now appears once a year, but the fact remains that many people in Australia have not yet heard about historical archaeology. It is the purpose of this book to provide a brief introduction to the subject. The intention is to do this not by a general survey, which would be impossible in a book of this size, but by looking at a selection of studies that historical archaeologists have done in Australia. This selection has been mostly based on published sources so that those readers who wish to do so can read more by consulting the Suggested Reading section at the end of the book.

2

We have already examined two common but incorrect ideas about archaeology: first, that it only studies things that are very old, and second, that it only concerns itself with prehistoric societies. Before going further it is important to dispose of a third common misconception. This is that archaeologists spend all their time digging holes or, to give it its more polite name, excavating. This is just not true. Even for periods of quite remote antiquity there are landscape features of human origin that can be studied from their surface characteristics. Although most of the evidence for such periods is buried beneath the ground, not all of it is. In the case of Australian historical archaeology, concerned as it is with relatively recent times, a very large amount of the evidence is in the form of standing structures that survive as part of the visible environment in which we live. Because of this there are many useful investigations that do not involve excavation. However, much of the earliest colonial settlement, and many of the later activities, have not left visible remains. To all intents and purposes they have vanished. It is in these instances that archaeological excavation can sometimes be appropriate and can give us information that would not otherwise be obtainable. Modern archaeologists, however, regard excavation rather as modern medicine regards surgery: it is something you do if you cannot fix your problem any other way. Excavation is 'the unrepeatable experiment',[8] you have only one chance to get it right; once a site has been excavated it is virtually useless for further investigations.

Along with popular misconceptions about archaeology go doubts about its value for studying recent periods. What is the point, many people ask, in conducting archaeological inquiries when there are such huge quantities of historical records? There are several answers to this question. First, even very recent archaeological sites can tell us things that contemporary documents have not recorded. For instance, many of Australia's earliest European settlers were illiterate or of limited literacy, such people have not left us accounts of what they did. Contemporary records that describe the activities of such people were usually written by their social and economic superiors who were often ill-informed, if not prejudiced, witnesses. The role of convicts in the early settlement of Australia is a case in point. Other early settlers who would have been well able to write about themselves were often too busy carving out a new life to have either the time or the inclination. Tragically, such letters and diaries that were written by them were, in many cases, destroyed by their descendants who thought that they were of no value. In many ways it is a miracle that so many contemporary documents have survived, but it is a fact that the ordinary people and the underprivileged are not as well represented in those records as they might be. With archaeology, however, we can reconstruct the way that such people lived and appreciate some of the things that they achieved. This is important because it was they who made modern Australia, with their own hands.

Another frequent limitation of contemporary written records is that they will often tell us that something was done, but will be uninformative about how it was done. Thus a document may tell us that a certain person built a homestead in a particular place at a specified date, but it may tell us nothing about how that building was constructed. If the building survives, either intact or as a ruin, an archaeological structural analysis can provide quite a lot of information even if it has been subsequently modified by later additions. If it does not survive, archaeological excavation can inform us of its plan, and give some indication of the materials used and the building technique employed, even if all that remains are stains on the surface of the subsoil.

Contemporary documents, in spite of their enormous value for any understanding of the past, have one other shortcoming that every historian is aware of. The information they contain is what the writer says happened — this may not be the same as what actually happened. The writer may have been deliberately dishonest, prejudiced, poorly informed, mistaken, or may merely have made a slip of the pen. In contrast, relevant archaeological evidence may be able to show us what really happened. Thus the historical document gives us evidence comparable to that of a witness in a court of law; archaeology provides evidence similar to that of the forensic scientist.

A second reason for studying the archaeology of the recent past is that archaeologists are interested in an aspect that historians have not usually concerned themselves with. This is the study of human 'culture'. This word is used here in a specialized anthropological sense, and is not intended to have anything to do with either the Sydney Opera House or with the things that interest bacteriologists! The best definition of the anthropological use of the word is that of James Deetz, who defined 'culture' as 'learned behavior', or 'everything a person would not do were he [or she] to grow up completely isolated on a desert island'.[9] Anthropologists know that human cultures vary from place to place, and archaeologists can show that they also change with time. The learned behaviour of a past human group can be studied by archaeologists through the agency of surviving parts of its 'material culture', that is, the things that the group made. Anthropologists tell us that human culture is patterned, and they have argued that it is possible to infer non-material aspects of a culture from the material aspects that archaeologists study. For the archaeologist, one of the most intriguing questions about past human societies is to understand how and why their cultures change. And so we come back to Australian historical archaeology. The European colonization of this continent was one of the longest-range mass migrations in human history, involving the transplanting of large numbers of people from one side of the world to the other and from one group of environments to a completely different group. Those people brought with them the cultures of their own societies in Western Europe, but their descendants in Australia evolved a culture of their own. Just as the historian is fascinated by the process by which the English, Irish, Scots, Germans and others became Australians, so is the archaeologist. All around us, in the Australian landscape, there is material evidence that can help us to understand more about this most remarkable example of cultural adaptation and change. Such an understanding could improve our knowledge of how human societies function in general, and that is relevant, not merely to the study of the past, but also to our present and to our future.

There is a third reason for archaeologists investigating the material remains of the recent past and it is an unashamedly selfish reason: it helps *them*. As has already been stated, it is the business of archaeologists to extract information from the material remains so as to discover how people lived in the past. The difficulty is to know how to do it. As the American archaeologist Lewis Binford has pointed out, archaeological evidence is 'a sort of untranslated language, something that we need to "decode" in order to move from simple statements about matter and its arrangement to statements of behavioral interest about the past'.[10] Another American archaeologist, William Rathje, has defined archaeology as 'a focus on the interaction between material culture and human behavior and ideas, regardless of time or space'.[11] Clearly, the only place where archaeologists can discover the detailed linkages between material culture and human behaviour is in the present time or in the recent past. Historical archaeology therefore provides a wonderful testing ground for archaeologists to try out their theories and their methods. This is because the documentary record, and sometimes the oral record, can provide the experimental control. For example, if one wants to know more about how archaeological sites form, one can excavate the sites of structures for which there is detailed historical information.[12] Or, to give another example, if one wishes to test the validity of an archaeological dating method such as the technique known as 'seriation', which provides dates from changing fashions in artefacts, one can try it out on historical remains where all the dates are provided, such as the tombstones of an eighteenth- or nineteenth-century cemetery.[13] In short, it is being increasingly realized that the archaeology of the recent past can help us to understand the archaeology of the remote past. With Australian historical archaeology there are some particularly exciting possibilities of this sort. One of the most interesting of these has been perceived by the historian David Denholm, a scholar with a lively appreciation of the value of historical archaeology. 'Our unique situation when we look at Colonial Australia', he has written, 'is that we can actually see and study disappearance in the process of happening, for the act of disappearing is taking place in front of our eyes.'[14] Perhaps Denholm should have been an archaeologist!

This brings us back to the pattern of Australia's past which is scrawled across its landscape. The quotation in the title of this chapter is taken from a poem of Henry Lawson's, three stanzas of which are printed at the beginning of this book. Some of the other chapters also have titles which include extracts from this poem and the title of the book has the same origin. Lawson was called, by one of his contemporaries, 'the first articulate voice of the real Australia'.[15] His poem *Reedy River* is evocative of a past that is lost beyond recovery. Yet perhaps he was too pessimistic; Australia's colonial achievement has not vanished without leaving traces, those traces are all around us, and it is the archaeologist's task to recover from them an understanding of past life.

Notes

[1] For example: J. Flood, 1983. *Archaeology of the Dreamtime*, Collins, Sydney, and J.P. White and J.F. O'Connell, 1982. *A prehistory of Australia, New Guinea and Sahul*, Academic Press, Sydney.

[2] For example: C.M.H. Clark, 1962-1987. *A history of Australia* (6 vols), Melbourne University Press, Carlton, and R. Ward, 1978. *The Australian legend* (New edn), Oxford University Press, Melbourne.

[3] For example: L.A. Gilbert, W.P. Driscoll and A. Sutherland, 1974. *History around us: An enquiry approach to local history*, Hicks Smith, Sydney, second edition 1984, Methuen, North Ryde, and R.I. Jack, 1986. *Exploring the Hawkesbury*, Kangaroo Press, Kenthurst. Also D. Denholm, 1979. *The Colonial Australians*, Penguin, Harmondsworth.

[4] For example: D.N. Jeans (ed.), 1984. *Australian historical landscapes*, Allen & Unwin, North Sydney; D.N. Jeans and P. Spearritt, 1980. *The open air museum: The cultural landscape of New South Wales*, Allen & Unwin, North Sydney; J.M.R. Cameron, 1981. *Ambition's fire: The agricultural colonization of pre-convict Western Australia*, University of Western Australia Press, Nedlands; M. Williams, 1974. *The making of the South Australian landscape: A study in the historical geography of Australia*, Academic Press, London and New York; J.M. Powell, 1970. *The public lands of Australia Felix: Settlement and land appraisal in Victoria 1834-91 with special reference to the Western Plains*, Oxford University Press, Melbourne.

[5] For example: J.M. Freeland, 1968. *Architecture in Australia: A history*, Cheshire, Melbourne, and M. Herman, 1970. *The early Australian architects and their work* (2nd edn), Angus & Robertson, Sydney.

[6] For example: Institution of Engineers, Australia, 1982. *The protection of the engineering heritage, Brisbane, May 1982*, Institution of Engineers, Australia, National Conference Publication No. 82/2, and C. O'Connor, 1985. *Spanning two centuries — historic bridges of Australia*, University of Queensland Press, St Lucia, Brisbane.

[7] Judy Birmingham, of the Department of Archaeology in the University of Sydney, was the prime mover in this development.

[8] P. Barker, 1982. *Techniques of archaeological excavation* (2nd edn), Batsford, London, pp.11-12.

[9] J. Deetz, 1967. *Invitation to archaeology*, Natural History Press, Garden City, New York, p.6.

[10] L.R. Binford, 1983. *In pursuit of the past: Decoding the archaeological record*, Thames & Hudson, pp.19-20.

[11] W.L. Rathje, 1979. Modern material culture studies. In M.B. Schiffer (ed.), *Advances in archaeological method and theory*, Vol. 2, Academic Press, New York, p.2.

[12] For example: G. Connah, 1986. Historical reality: archaeological reality. Excavations at Regentville, Penrith, New South Wales, 1985. *Australian Journal of Historical Archaeology* 4, pp.29-42.

[13] For example: J.F. Deetz and E.S. Dethlefson, 1978. Death's head, cherub, urn and willow. In R.L. Schuyler (ed.), *Historical archaeology: A guide to substantive and theoretical contributions*, Baywood, Farmingdale, New York, pp.83-9. (Originally published in *Natural History* 76(3), pp.29-37, in 1967.)

[14] D. Denholm, 1979, p.111.

[15] D.M. Wright, 1980. *In the days when the world was wide: The poetical works of Henry Lawson*, Currey O'Neil, Windsor, Victoria, p.viii.

Chapter 2

They came by sea

THE HISTORICAL ARCHAEOLOGY OF PRECOLONIAL CONTACT

In the last chapter there was some discussion of Australia's archaeological landscape and of the things that we can learn from its study. It needs to be emphasized, however, that this 'landscape' includes not only the surface of the continent but also its coastal margins and the seabed in its vicinity. Indeed, research by maritime archaeologists over the last two decades has made important and exciting contributions to the field of Australian historical archaeology. All human settlement in Australia had to cross the sea to get here. This was as true for the earliest Aboriginal settlers, who are thought to have arrived from southeast Asia about fifty thousand years ago, as it was for the groups of Europeans and others who have settled here since 1788. From this arises important implications: first, that the Aboriginal arrival is the oldest evidence in the world for such a sea-crossing, and second, that the success and growth of European settlement required the maintenance of strong maritime contacts with the rest of the world. It is hardly surprising, therefore, that the shores and seas around Australia are a vital source of archaeological evidence about our past. The last two centuries have seen several thousands of vessels wrecked in Australian waters. Convict ships, immigrant ships, general traders, whalers, even warships, are all represented. Some of this post-settlement maritime archaeological evidence will be considered, where appropriate, in later chapters. In this chapter it is the pre-settlement evidence that will be examined for it provides the only indications of contact with other societies with a written history prior to the commencement of European colonization at the end of the eighteenth century A.D. In short, the earliest study material available to Australian historical archaeologists is provided by maritime archaeology, taking that word to mean 'anything connected with seafaring' whether the evidence is situated 'underwater or on land'.[1]

Before examining this evidence it is necessary to dismiss the numerous legends that have grown up about the existence of shipwrecks or other archaeological data said to demonstrate the presence in Australia of the Portuguese, Spanish, or even the Chinese during the fifteenth and sixteenth centuries. Whatever the historical possibilities might have been, there are no material remains available for archaeological analysis that can be attributed with certainty to those people at that time. Our earliest certain evidence consists of one English and several Dutch shipwrecks, dating from the seventeenth and eighteenth centuries, that have been found on the Western Australian coast. Almost as early, however, are some of the trepang-processing sites scattered around parts of the northern Australian shoreline that represent seasonal visits by southeast Asian fishermen from about 1700 to about 1900 (Figure 2.1). These seafarers came from the Macassar region of the southern Celebes (now known as Sulawesi, and forming part of Indonesia). The average time for this voyage seems to have been about fourteen days, of which the longest piece of open-sea

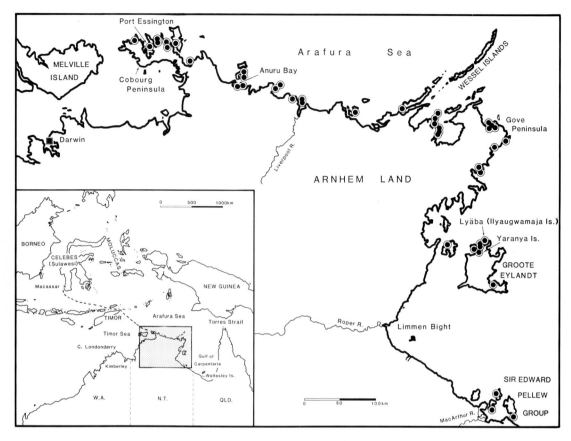

Figure 2.1   Trepang-processing sites in northern Australia. Inset
shows the route sailed from Macassar. (After Macknight 1976.)

sailing (between Timor and Melville Island) took only four days.[2] The Macassans were
equipped with very seaworthy boats known as 'praus', and when one considers that
Madagascar, on the far side of the Indian Ocean, was colonized by Indonesians about
fifteen hundred years ago, it is difficult to believe that the northern Australian coast was not
visited until the end of the seventeenth century. Indeed, Macassan sites on the Australian
coast have produced radiocarbon dates back to about eight hundred years ago, although
historical and artefactual evidence has led to the rejection of these early dates.[3] In Australia
the Macassan sites are amongst the earliest historical sites and, because they may be only
the latest manifestation of a very much older contact, it is perhaps appropriate to consider
them first.

The Macassan visitors[4] came to the northern Australian coast to collect trepang, which is
a generalized name for a range of edible sea slugs otherwise known as sea cucumbers, or by
the French name *bêche-de-mer*. These sea cucumbers are to be found in very large numbers
in the shallow inshore waters of island southeast Asia and adjacent areas. Only some of the
many species are both edible and easy to collect, however, and it seems that the Macassans
regarded northern Australia as a good place to find these varieties. It is the Chinese that ate,
and still eat, most of the trepang from southeast Asia. It comes in the same exotic food

category as birds' nests and sharks' fin, and is valued for its jelly-like texture after cooking, for its supposed ability to bring out the flavour of other foods, and as a stimulant and aphrodisiac. The main problem with trepang was to get a highly perishable commodity to a relatively distant market. Because of this it was necessary to process the catch immediately, and this was done on the beach adjacent to the area of collection. The trepang were washed, gutted and boiled. The boiling process sometimes included tree bark, which not only dyed the trepang but also assisted in its preservation. Following this, the trepang were often buried in the beach sand for some hours, or perhaps several days, in order to remove calcareous deposits from the skins of certain species. Finally, they were thoroughly dried, and usually smoked over a slow fire. We know about the details of this complex processing from historical sources (Figure 2.2), but it is clear that such activities must have left archaeological traces on suitable parts of the northern coast of Australia.

This is indeed the case. To reach Australia, the Macassans relied on the northwest monsoon that blew steadily during the summer months. To return home, they depended on the southeast monsoon that was equally reliable during the winter months. This meant that it was the northern Australian coast between Bathurst Island and the Wellesley Islands that was the easiest to exploit, although a stretch of the northwestern coast, southwest of Cape Londonderry, was also visited. From the archaeological evidence it would seem that the northern and eastern coasts of Arnhem Land were the most important, and C.C. Macknight has recorded the existence of Macassan trepang-processing sites from the Cobourg Peninsula in the west, to the islands known as the Sir Edward Pellew Group in the east. The Macassans spent only a few months on the Australian coast during each year, roughly from January to April, and they moved regularly as the trepang became temporarily depleted in each place. Their utilization of individual processing sites was, therefore, often brief, but a suitable site would be revisited year after year. The most favoured places seem to have been sandy beaches adjacent to shallow inlets that provided both large numbers of trepang and a

Figure 2.2   Trepangers at Port Essington in 1845. (Drawing by
H.S. Melville originally published in *The Queen*, 8 February 1862.)

sheltered anchorage for the praus. There also needed to be mangroves nearby to provide the large quantities of firewood needed for boiling and smoking the trepang, and adequate supplies of fresh water.

Archaeologically, the Macassan sites are usually indicated by the existence of several lines of stones, which mark the place where the trepang-boiling fireplaces were situated, and by a surface scatter of broken pottery and other artefacts. One or more tamarind trees are also often present. These magnificent trees have grown from the seeds in the tamarind fruit that the Macassans brought with them for flavouring their rice. Although having been introduced in this way, the tamarind tree now naturally propagates in favourable places. During the 1960s, Macknight carried out surface collections on some of the sites and was able to excavate at several of them.

The most informative of the excavations was at the Anuru Bay site, situated on the northern coast of Arnhem Land adjacent to South Goulburn Island. This site seems to have been frequently used, and is marked by a prominent tamarind tree, by twenty-one stonelines, by several shallow depressions indicating the location of former smokehouses, and by a rectangular arrangement of stones over a double grave (Figure 2.3). Prior to excavation there was also a substantial scatter of artefacts, and the surface sand was discoloured by the charcoal from the Macassans' fires. The preservation of the stonelines varied, suggesting that some were older than others, and the lack of glass fragments associated with the separate group of structures at the eastern end of the site indicated that this was the scene of the earliest activity. Excavation threw considerable light on the way in which the site had been used, revealing the fireplaces represented by the stonelines, the pits in which the trepang had been buried briefly, and the ash-filled depressions that were all that remained of the smokehouses. The grave proved to contain the skeletons of two Macassan men, one about thirty-two years old and the other in his early twenties. They had

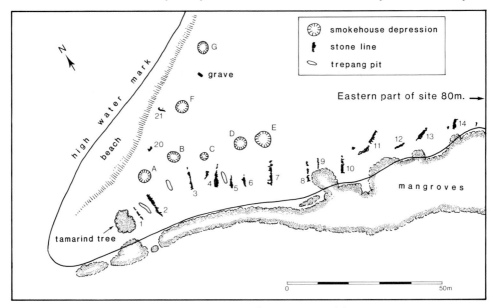

Figure 2.3 Anuru Bay trepang site showing some of the twenty-one stonelines. The eastern part of the site has been omitted. (After Macknight 1976.)

been buried at different times, with the second one disturbing the first. Both had dental problems, either caused or aggravated by chewing betel-nut and lime, and their teeth had been filed down in accordance with the cultural practice of their people. The second burial had been arranged according to Islamic practice, the body being placed on its right side facing west towards Mecca. Macassan graves are also known from other sites.

Excavations and surface collection at the Anuru Bay site also revealed the sophistication of Macassan material culture. The most common artefactual evidence were potsherds (broken pieces of pottery) of plain earthenware cooking pots, all of which were brought to the site in the praus, and most of which had been made in the southern Celebes. There was also a small number of fragments of glazed wares, made in both mainland Asia and Europe, usually from decorated rice bowls. In addition there were numerous fragments of glass, most commonly of Dutch gin bottles. Other evidence included metal fish-hooks, a bronze needle and various other fragments of metal. Some indication of the impact of Macassan material culture on the local environment was visible in the vicinity of the site, where numerous old stumps of mangroves chopped off with a rather blunt axe could be seen among fully grown mangroves. These serve as a reminder of the large quantities of firewood that must have been consumed at this site.

Given the ephemeral character of the structures on Macassan sites, and the technical difficulties of excavating in beach sand, the Anuru Bay excavations were remarkably successful in explaining the activities that went on. They also managed to give some indication of the way in which different parts of the site had been used at different times.

Judging from historical sources, the most impressive features of Macassan sites must have been the smokehouses, but as they were most likely constructed from only mats and bamboo poles it is not surprising that they have left little to excavate. The traces of the smokehouses at Anuru Bay were slight, but at Lyäba, on the island of Ilyaugwamaja at the northern end of Groote Eylandt, a looser sand with a high proportion of quartz meant that the only sign of a smokehouse was a band of white ash in the deposit. Nevertheless, excavations at this site confirmed many of the conclusions reached at Anuru Bay. Lyäba has several large tamarinds and fifteen stonelines, and excavation revealed the presence of a number of trepang pits and traces of several smokehouses. The artefactual evidence was similar to that from Anuru Bay but, in addition, included a musket ball, a lead sinker, and a copper coin of the Dutch East India Company that was probably minted in Dordrecht in 1742. At least five other coins have been recovered from Macassan trepang-processing sites and they are all small copper coins issued by the Dutch East India Company or successor governments. Their dates range from the late eighteenth to the early nineteenth century.

One of the most difficult things about interpreting Macassan sites is the confusion that is caused by most of them having been used on so many separate occasions and for periods of such short duration. Parts of older stone fireplaces, for instance, were often removed to make new ones. In these circumstances, a site which has only been used a few times can give a far clearer impression of the way in which it functioned, and the structures on such a site will be easier to understand. It seems likely that Macknight found such a site on Yaranya Island in Northwest Bay, Groote Eylandt (Figure 2.4). This island is rather dry and barren, and the site has only a small quantity of potsherds on its surface. Its features, however, are well preserved, and include four stonelines and six clear smokehouse depressions. A trench excavated through part of one of these smokehouses gave more structural information than had been available on other sites. It was clear that the depression had been formed by digging out sand that was then dumped on the ground surface immediately outside of the

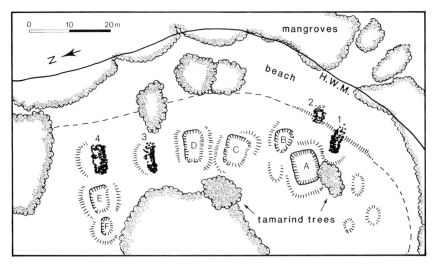

Figure 2.4 Yaranya Island trepang site. Numbers indicate stonelines
and letters indicate smokehouse depressions. (After Macknight 1976.)

building. A possible posthole was located at the point where one of the smokehouse walls
would have stood. Once in use, the depression gradually accumulated ash from the slow
fires kept burning within the building. Periodically the ash was shovelled out and dumped
outside the building, on top of the sand which had been thrown there when the depression
was originally dug. Macknight concluded that it was very probable that all the features at
the site had been in use at the same time. He was of the opinion that the site was late in date,
and may only have been used on relatively few occasions.

   Macknight has called the collection and processing of trepang: 'Australia's first modern
industry'. He has also emphasized that the visits of the Macassans to the northern
Australian coastline were only a part of a complex trading network within island southeast
Asia and beyond. Certainly the glazed wares found on Australian Macassan sites are vivid
reminders that these visitors had extensive international contacts. How long their ancestors
may have been coming to Australia prior to the development of the trepang industry is
unknown. What is clear, however, is that the Macassan trepangers were the first voluntary
historical visitors to have left substantial archaeological evidence that we can study.

   In contrast, the earliest European visitors to leave substantial archaeological traces in
Australia had no choice in the matter, they hit it accidentally. During the seventeenth and
eighteenth centuries, at least four Dutch ships and one English ship were wrecked on the
Western Australian coast.[5] To understand why this happened it is necessary to appreciate
the limitations of geographical knowledge and of navigational technology at that time. All
of these ships were on their way to Batavia (the present day Djakarta), the centre of Dutch
trading interests in island southeast Asia. Prior to 1610, ships making this journey from
Europe had been accustomed to sail from the Cape of Good Hope via the Mozambique
Channel to India, or via the east coast of Madagascar and Mauritius directly to the Sunda
Strait. Because of the prevailing winds these were slow and unhealthy routes on which
there was considerable danger of being becalmed. In 1611, the Dutchman Hendrick
Brouwer demonstrated that by sailing south to beyond latitude 36° it was possible to take
advantage of the strong westerly winds that blew in those cooler and healthier latitudes. He

was then able to sail due east, and turned north when he estimated that he was in the same longitude as the Sunda Strait. He was the first captain to exploit what sailors came to know as the 'Roaring Forties', and he halved the length of time that it took to get from Holland to Java. Others quickly followed because the Dutch East India Company instructed its commanders to follow a course between 35° and 40° south after leaving the Cape of Good Hope. They were to sail east for at least a thousand Dutch miles before turning north. The problem was that, although latitude could be obtained by observation of the sun using an instrument known as an astrolabe, longitude could only be estimated by dead reckoning. This was the determination of a ship's position from distance and course, involving the use of log and sand glass and of the compass, with estimated corrections for such factors as current and leeway. On a long voyage the error in longitude was bound to accumulate, and with their new eastern course from South Africa it was only a matter of time before ships came within sight of the Western Australian coast. This first happened in 1616. It was equally inevitable that, sooner or later, ships would be wrecked on this dangerous and unknown coast. The first known was the English ship *Trial* in 1622, followed by the Dutch East Indiamen *Batavia* in 1629, the *Vergulde Draeck* in 1656, the *Zuytdorp* in 1712, and the *Zeewijk* in 1726. In the circumstances it is surprising that so few vessels were wrecked, and indeed it is possible that other ships were lost on this coast during the seventeenth and eighteenth centuries. Certainly there were others that left the Cape of Good Hope and were never seen again.

The wreck sites of all five of these vessels have now been located by maritime archaeologists (Figure 2.5). Investigations have been carried out at all of the sites, but two of them, those of the *Batavia* and the *Vergulde Draeck*, have been subjected to extensive excavation. Such underwater wreck sites are of very great importance in the archaeological investigation of the past. This is because they are an archaeologist's dream: a massive collection of

Figure 2.5   Early shipwrecks in Australian waters. (After Henderson 1986.)

13

associated evidence that must belong together and cannot be later than a certain date. A shipwreck lying on the bed of the sea is, literally, a time capsule, an incredibly rich source of information providing the proper techniques of investigation are employed. This is in stark contrast with dry-land archaeology, where many sites have continued to be modified by subsequent human activity. In the case of most of the Macassan sites, for instance, it is difficult, if not impossible, to identify the separate occasions of activity that are represented by the archaeological evidence.

What are some of the things that shipwrecks can tell us? First, if portions of the hull have survived we can study the way in which the ship was built and perhaps the manner in which it was repaired or modified during its life. Prior to the eighteenth century few records were kept of shipbuilding and, even for periods where we have extensive documentation, shipwrecks can still augment and correct our knowledge. Second, most ships were carrying a cargo of some sort when they sank and, although parts of this might have been salvaged (either at the time or since), it would be most unlikely that it had all been removed. In some instances it is virtually complete, and there is much that can be learned from ships' cargoes. They can tell us about trade patterns and technology and, because all the items belong to the same period, they can help us to date things found on dry-land sites and to check archaeological typologies. Even ships that were only in ballast when they sank can be informative, because ballast sometimes consisted of bricks or slates or other marketable materials. Third, whether or not they carried a cargo, ships had to carry an extensive and varied amount of stores and equipment. The crew and passengers, if they were carried, had to be fed, and this required substantial quantities of food, drinking water and other beverages — the containers of which at least might survive for study. In addition a ship needed cooking equipment, furniture, navigational instruments, spare fittings and ship's chandlery, tools and a host of other things. In the past even merchant ships were usually armed and so there would also be ship's guns and firearms, and all the equipment and supplies to enable them to be used. All this varied evidence clearly has considerable potential as a source of information about life and work on a ship at sea. Fourth, passengers and crew had personal possessions which often had to be abandoned at the time of sinking — these have the capacity to throw light on personal lifestyle, and even on individual interests and aspirations. Fifth, the location and characteristics of a wreck site can also be informative. From these matters can be learned something of the sailing and navigational skill of the crew (or the lack of such skill). It is also possible to study the mechanics of wreck formation and to understand better the various things that can happen to a ship when it sinks.

The extent to which any one shipwreck can provide all this varied evidence will, of course, depend on the circumstances of the sinking, on the conditions of preservation at the site, and on the degree of subsequent interference by salvage workers or looters. Whatever their individual limitations, however, the seventeenth- and eighteenth-century wrecks off the Western Australian coast have a unique contribution to make to Australian archaeology; together with later shipwrecks, they provide us with our longest historical archaeological sequence. It is fortunate, indeed, that their investigation has been a model of archaeological endeavour. This work has been organized by the Western Australian Museum, and it has achieved world-wide recognition not only because of its discoveries, but also because of the sophisticated survey, excavation, recording, recovery, conservation and display techniques that have been used. Many people have contributed to this work, but it is the name of Jeremy Green which has become particularly associated with it.

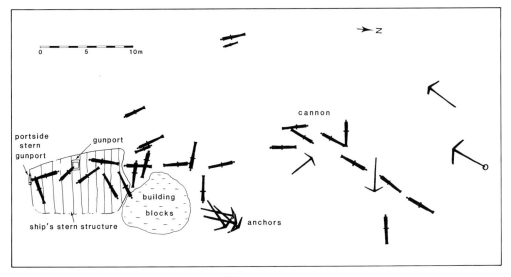

Figure 2.6 Wreck site of the *Batavia*, off the coast of Western Australia. (After Green 1975.)

Perhaps the most important excavation was that conducted on the wreck of the *Batavia*, which lies in 5 metres of water on a reef in the Abrolhos Islands.[6] The excavation occupied four seasons between 1973 and 1976, but the conservation and display of the evidence recovered took many more years to complete. The wreck covered an area of 50 by 15 metres and consisted of a slight depression in the surface of the coral littered with twenty-eight cannon, nine anchors, heaps of ballast bricks, sandstone building blocks and fragments of lead and ceramic (Figure 2.6). Hidden beneath the coral, however, was a section of the wooden hull belonging to the stern part of the ship. Constructed in 1628, the *Batavia* was only a year old when she was wrecked, and the surviving timbers are the earliest known substantial remains of an East Indiaman — the hull section measured some 12 by 6 metres, and weighed about 30 tonnes. The sides of the ship had been extremely thick, being composed of two layers of planking on the inside of the frames, and no less than four layers of planking and a layer of tar and cow hair on the outside. Careful excavation allowed the piecemeal recovery of the surviving section of the hull, which has now been reconstructed and put on display at the Western Australian Maritime Museum in Fremantle.

Before the section of hull could be investigated, however, it was necessary to excavate the deposits that covered it, and these proved to contain an enormous amount of evidence. Not only were there the anchors and cannon already mentioned, but there were also firearms and other weapons and an astonishing quantity and variety of projectiles and other equipment for the cannons. In addition there was a remarkable collection of navigational instruments, and the sandstone building blocks provided perhaps the greatest surprise of all. These blocks, of which there were 128 in all, had been carefully shaped and carved. When removed, it was found that they comprised the two columns and the pediment of a tasteful arched entrance. This had been prefabricated in Holland, and many of the blocks numbered to indicate their position in the intended structure. It is thought that this portico, which measured 7.5 metres high, was to have been erected at the Dutch fort in Batavia. It never got there; instead, after a delay of some 350 years, it was erected in the Western Australian Maritime Museum (Figure 2.7).

15

Figure 2.7 Sandstone portico from the wreck of the *Batavia*, erected
in the Western Australian Maritime Museum. (Photograph by
Patrick Baker, courtesy Western Australian Maritime Museum.)

The *Batavia* also yielded a varied collection of other artefacts, but it was nearby Beacon
Island that produced evidence of the fate of some of its crew and passengers. Several
skeletons were excavated on this uninhabited island and these confirmed the historical
record of the grisly events that took place there. Following the shipwreck, a large number of
survivors camped for some time on this and other adjacent islands, but a mutiny of some of
the crew led to the massacre of 125 people. Although those responsible were eventually
punished, and the residue of the survivors rescued, the name of the *Batavia* became
associated with one of the worst horror stories of maritime history.

Another important excavation of an early shipwreck off the Western Australian coast was that of the *Vergulde Draeck*, which lies in 7 metres of water on a limestone reef about 100 kilometres north of Perth. This ship had broken up almost immediately upon striking the reef and no parts of the ship's structure were found during excavation. Nevertheless the wreck did provide a wide range of domestic items, equipment, provisions and cargo. These included about fifty Rhenish stoneware jugs, of the sort known to archaeologists as the Bellarmine jug because of the face that decorates it. There were also eight types of clay smoking pipes, including a box of 250 pipes all of the same type. It is rare, indeed, to find so many pipes of such antiquity that are complete. Other finds included a tool box, still full of tools, the bones of what had once been salt beef and pork, and even the bones of rats which had, on this occasion, gone down with the sinking ship. The *Vergulde Draeck* had been carrying a vast number of ballast bricks; 8 tonnes of these bricks were removed during the excavation which was limited to one season in 1972. There was also a heap of elephant tusks from African elephants which had formed part of the cargo of trade goods known to have been aboard (Figure 2.8). In addition there had been eight chests of silver coins amongst the cargo and the excavation recovered about 8000 of these. Others had previously been looted from the wreck after its accidental discovery in 1963. There was an astonishing variety of evidence at this site, not forgetting the fourteen cannon and the six anchors that were obvious features of the wreck even before excavation began. Most appealing of all, perhaps, were two bronze mortars, that is to say, vessels used for grinding up ingredients for food or medicine. Both were inscribed in Latin: 'AMOR VINCIT OMNIA', meaning, 'love

Figure 2.8 Excavating one of the elephant tusks at the wreck site of the *Vergulde Draeck*, Western Australia. (Photograph by Brian Richards, courtesy Western Australian Maritime Museum.)

conquers all'.[7] Not quite, it would seem, as something more than love would have been needed to save the *Vergulde Draeck* from the perils of the Western Australian coast.

An early shipwreck from another coast is that of H.M.S. *Pandora*, which sank in 30 metres of water on the Great Barrier Reef in 1791 while returning to Britain after capturing fourteen of the *Bounty* mutineers on Tahiti. Excavation of this site commenced only in 1983, and is still continuing at the time of writing (Figures 2.9 and 2.10). Technically, the *Pandora* is a post-settlement shipwreck but again, like the Western Australian shipwrecks that have already been discussed, its presence in Australian waters has nothing to do with the history of Australia; it just happened to be passing and it hit a reef. Nevertheless, all these seventeenth- and eighteenth-century wrecks are of enormous archaeological signifiance. They are a most important part of the historical archaeology of Australia, even although they inform us about Dutch trading activities or the development of the British Navy rather than about our own history. They are a reminder that Australian historical archaeology has a contribution to make to other parts of the world as well as to its own country.

Figure 2.9 Excavating at the wreck site of H.M.S. *Pandora*, off the coast of northern Queensland. One of the great advantages of underwater excavation is that you do not have to stand on the work that you are doing. (Photograph by courtesy of Ronald Coleman, Queensland Museum.)

Figure 2.10 Glass bottles from the wreck site of H.M.S. *Pandora*. The central bottle is 243mm high. (Photograph by Brian Richards, courtesy of Ronald Coleman, Queensland Museum.)

This chapter has looked at some of the archaeology of the historical forerunners of European colonization. It has been concerned with maritime archaeology, using that term in its broadest sense. Both the Macassans and the Dutch came by sea, the first for only brief visits, the second by accident. Yet they left archaeological traces on our shores and in our seas. Any investigation of those traces hints at the unbelievable diversity of historical archaeological evidence in Australia, for trepang-processing sites are very different from submerged shipwrecks. Furthermore, perusal of the work that has been done on the Macassans and the early shipwrecks demonstrates very clearly the dependence on both historical documents and archaeological data that characterizes the study of historical archaeology.

Notes

[1] G. Henderson, 1986. *Maritime archaeology in Australia*, University of Western Australia Press, Nedlands, p.6. In this definition Henderson followed K. Muckelroy, 1977. *Maritime archaeology*, Cambridge University Press, Cambridge.

[2] C.C. Macknight, 1976. *The voyage to Marege': Macassan trepangers in northern Australia*, Melbourne University Press, Carlton, pp.34-5.

[3] C.C. Macknight, 1976, pp.98-9.

[4] The discussion of Macassan trepangers is based on C.C. Macknight, 1976.

[5] The discussion of seventeenth- and eighteenth-century European shipwrecks is based on G. Henderson, 1986.

[6] J.N. Green, 1975. The VOC ship *Batavia* wrecked in 1629 on the Houtman Abrolhos, Western Australia. *International Journal of Nautical Archaeology and Underwater Exploration* 4(1), pp.43-63.

[7] J.N. Green, 1973. The wreck of the Dutch East Indiaman the *Vergulde Draeck, 1656. International Journal of Nautical Archaeology and Underwater Exploration* 2(2), pp.267-89. Also J.N. Green (ed.), 1977. *The A.V.O.C. jacht 'Vergulde Draeck' wrecked Western Australia 1656*, BAR Supplementary Series 36(i) & (ii), Oxford.

Chapter 3

The birth of a nation

SEEKING THE REMAINS OF EARLY SYDNEY

The area of Sydney known as 'The Rocks', west of Circular Quay, now calls itself 'the birthplace of Australia'. Its claim is not strictly accurate, but it is very nearly true, for it was on the shores of Sydney Cove, of which The Rocks forms one side, that the first European settlers officially landed on 26 January 1788 (it was actually on 24 January: the landing took several days). Some days earlier they had gone ashore in Botany Bay, but had decided that it was not a suitable place to begin a new settlement, whereas Port Jackson offered a protected, deep-water harbour of enormous extent. Of the many bays, coves and inlets that exist in what we now call Sydney Harbour, the one selected as the starting point of the new colony had two marked advantages: a depth of water that allowed ships to anchor close to the shore, and a small stream or creek that could provide fresh, clean, drinking water. It was on the banks of the 'Tank Stream', as it became known, that Sydney Town grew up. It was here that a new nation was born.

Historians and many others have written endlessly about the early years of Sydney and the origins of the colony of New South Wales. It is not appropriate here to attempt to contribute further to those efforts. The task for the archaeologist is to wonder where the material evidence for the early years of Sydney has gone. As one walks through the concrete canyons of high-rise buildings that now characterize the old part of the city, one questions whether anything can have survived from that first unpretentious settlement. The quick answer is that nothing has, but like most quick answers it isn't true.

As always, it is a good idea to start by defining one's terms: for instance, what is meant by 'the early years of Sydney' or by 'the first settlement'? Clearly, Sydney still has a very large number of nineteenth-century buildings and other standing structures that the archaeologist can study. Admittedly, the further one goes back in time the less there is that has survived, but from quite an early date there is an impressive range of public buildings that demand attention and admiration. These include the 'Rum Hospital', the Government House Stables, St James's Church, Hyde Park Barracks, part of the Supreme Court and the obelisk in Macquarie Place. However, these result from the ambitious building programme of Governor Lachlan Macquarie (1810-1821) and, in most cases, from the architectural genius of Francis Greenway,[1] who had been transported for forgery but now has his picture on the Australian ten dollar note. This remarkable collaboration of Macquarie and Greenway represents a period of consolidation rather than of first settlement. For the latter it is necessary to look to the years before 1810, to the first twenty-two years of Sydney's existence, and to ask what has survived from that period. Unfortunately it is not possible to give archaeological evidence such a close chronological definition as historical data, and there will be cases when it is difficult to date physical remains more accurately than to some time within the first fifty years of settlement. Nevertheless it is the archaeology of the pre-Macquarie period that is the most relevant for the investigation of Sydney's early years.

One difficulty is that most of the first settlement consisted of tents and wooden huts. These were gradually replaced by brick or stone buildings, many of which were so poorly constructed that their durability was little better. As a result, as early as 1829, a contemporary description of Sydney could record that: 'The original buildings, which were of soft wood of the cabbage palm, have long since decayed; indeed, but very few of the earliest brick buildings remain.'[2] Small wonder that, over a century and a half later, one gets the impression that all traces of the first settlement have vanished for ever. The closer one looks, however, the more it appears that this impression is incorrect.

There are two ways in which archaeological evidence of the first settlement has indeed survived. The first way can be most readily appreciated by comparing a map of Sydney in the early 1800s (Figure 3.1) with a modern map of the older part of the city of Sydney — the area between the Town Hall and the Harbour Bridge and between the Botanic Gardens and Darling Harbour (Figure 3.2). It is immediately apparent that the tiny early town, that grew from a little over 1000 people in 1788 to only about 6000 people in 1810 (and this figure included the outlying districts), has largely determined the basic layout of the heartland of an urban giant. A city that, in 1983, contained an estimated population of nearly 3½ million. Looking at the modern map one can, as it were, see the ghost of old Sydney; its substance has gone but much of the basic layout of the streets and the open spaces survives to remind us of what it once looked like. True, the Sydney Harbour Bridge and the highways that feed into it have stamped a modern pattern on top of the old one, but even they have not obliterated it. George Street, for example, north of the Town Hall, remains on much of its original line, even though before 1810 it had several different names. With justice, it has been called the oldest street in Australia, first appearing on a map in July 1788.[3] In addition, the location of the major open spaces in the old part of Sydney also dates from the beginnings of settlement. It was Governor Arthur Phillip (1788-1792) who set aside a large area of land for parks and gardens, much of which has survived as the Inner Domain, the Outer Domain, the Botanic Gardens and Hyde Park. Certainly they have changed in appearance over the years, but their very existence as open spaces that have never been built on is because of decisions made during the first few years of European colonization. Indeed, both Australian agriculture and Australian horticulture had their origins in what became the Sydney Botanic Gardens. It was here, by the aptly named Farm Cove, that cereal crops were sown in 1788 and, when these failed, that the many garden plants introduced to Australia were first grown.[4]

The second way in which archaeological evidence of Sydney's early years has survived is as specific physical remains, nearly always located beneath the present ground surface. The only exceptions known to the author are the two sandstone walls of the incomplete Fort Phillip that still stand on Observatory Hill. These date from 1804-8, and throw light on the attempts to fortify Sydney rather than on the town itself.[5] All other remains are underneath the ground, although the deep foundations of high-rise buildings constructed over the last few decades would have destroyed much of the evidence. The problem with interpreting the early deposits that do survive is to disentangle them from the often extensive remains of subsequent periods. In addition, much has been obliterated, truncated, or cut through by the provision or replacement of the complex underground services without which no modern city can function — the underground railways, sewers, water mains, gas pipes, electricity cables of several different kinds and telephone cables. Nevertheless there is evidence of Sydney's earliest years down there, although not much has yet been studied, it is difficult to locate, and some of it is probably being unknowingly destroyed even as you read this. However there is a growing interest in the archaeology of the city of Sydney and it is quite likely that further specific evidence of the first settlement will be forthcoming over the next few years.

In the meantime let us consider some of the archaeological data that we already have. What about the Tank Stream, the central feature around which Sydney Town grew up? This stream rose in marshy ground on the edge of Hyde Park between Market and Park Streets, assuming a definite channel within the block bounded by Market, King, George and Pitt Streets. From there it flowed between Pitt and George Streets and ran into Sydney Cove just below Bridge Street, much of the land from that point to the modern Circular Quay having been reclaimed. The Tank Stream provided Sydney's first water supply, although it soon had to be supplemented with wells. Indeed, it was in an attempt to husband its water that tanks were cut into the rock north of Hunter Street thus giving the stream its distinctive name. Where has the Tank Stream gone? Nowadays there is no sign of it in the busy streets of central Sydney. The answer is that in the 1830s it ceased to matter as a water supply because of the excavation of 'Busby's Bore', a rock-cut tunnel that brought water into Sydney from the Lachlan Swamps (now Centennial Park). The provision of this tunnel, much of which still exists for archaeologists to study, meant that the Tank Stream, which already had pollution problems, rapidly became merely an open sewer. During the second half of the nineteenth century, therefore, it was gradually enclosed so that it ran through pipes and a tunnel to empty into the developing underground sewerage system. Thus in one sense the Tank Stream was destroyed, but in another sense it is still there beneath the pavements we walk on, a reminder of the origins of Sydney.[6]

Also hidden beneath the present ground surface is evidence of the substantial changes to the shape of Sydney Cove since 1788. From Bridge Street to Circular Quay, land reclamation has gradually encroached on the cove, so that it is now considerably shorter than it was originally. An opportunity to examine part of the original shoreline came in 1986, when archaeologist Ted Higginbotham was able to inspect the foundation excavations for the Gateway Plaza office-block development, situated near Circular Quay. The sandstone bedrock was found to slope down into where the cove had originally been, and it was possible to see the extent of harbour silts, sands and gravels, the area occupied by the beach sand, and the limits of the topsoil where the dry land had at one time ended. There was also archaeological evidence present from the period of first settlement. Fragments of sandstock roofing tiles and of either plain or lead-glazed earthenware pottery appeared to be of early date and, significantly, their occurrence was restricted to the shore and area above high-water mark prior to 1823. The Gateway Site is an interesting example of occupation evidence surviving where none might have been expected (Figure 3.3).[7]

A type of evidence that we might have expected to survive, however, has in general not done so. Judging by the old burial grounds to be found in Britain or in the eastern parts of the United States, one would think that the earliest graveyards in Sydney would still be available for us to study. Sadly, this is not the case. Quite early in Sydney's history land values became too high for the first settlers to be left undisturbed in their last resting places. The earliest burial grounds have disappeared without trace, although it is known that two of them were situated in or near The Rocks. It was from the site of one of these that

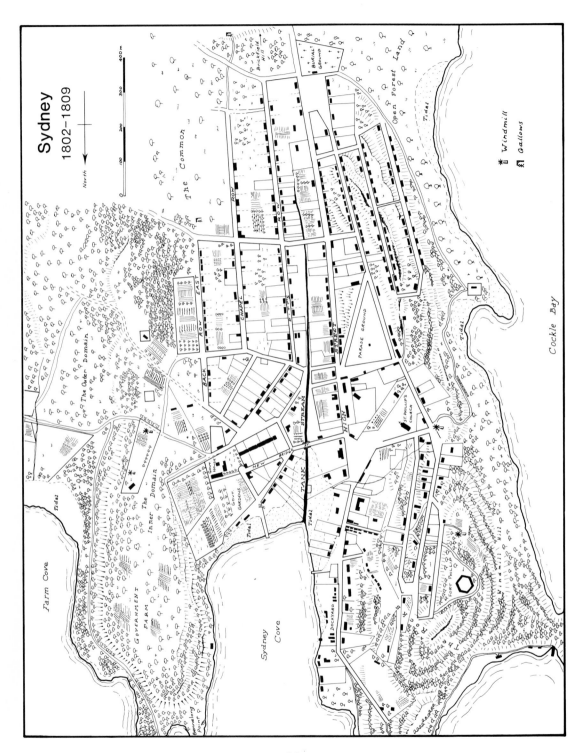

opposite: *Figure 3.1* Sydney 1802-1809 showing the origins of its layout. (Based on a modern composite map by Bryan Thomas, published in N.A.W. Ashton, 1984. *Sydney: Village to metropolis*, Department of Environment and Planning, New South Wales.)

below: *Figure 3.2* The centre of modern Sydney.

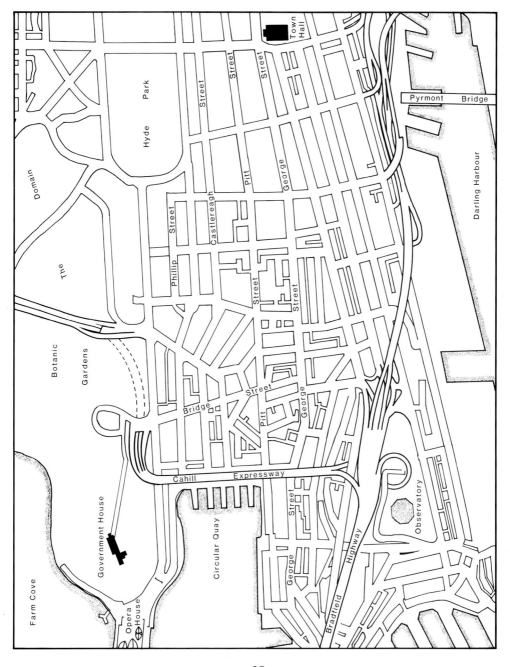

Alfred St.

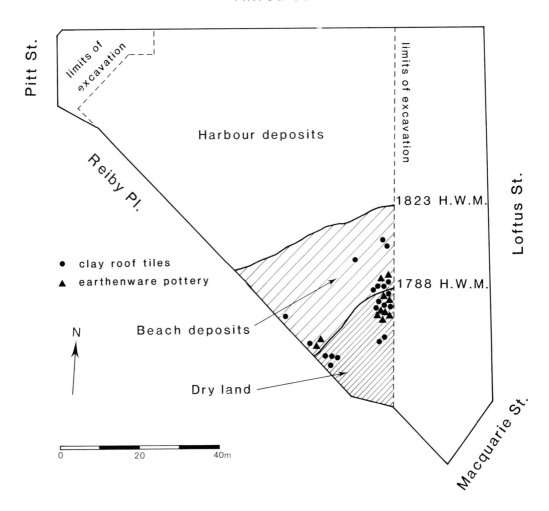

Figure 3.3 Plan of the Gateway Site, Sydney, showing early occupation evidence. (After Higginbotham 1987.)

Australia's oldest extant gravestone came. This stone is inscribed 'In memory of George Graves late boatswains yeoman of His Majesty's Ship Sirius. Who departed this [life] ye 10 July 178[8] aged 48 years.' After a chequered career this stone has survived, although in a damaged condition, and may be seen at Vaucluse House in Sydney. A third graveyard was situated in Clarence Street and, in 1912, a coffin was unearthed here during building operations. Rather more is known about the burial ground that was in use between 1792 and 1820. Its site is now marked by the Town Hall, just as the cemetery that replaced it is now occupied by Sydney's Central Railway Station. An opportunity for some archaeological investigation, of what was sometimes called the Town Hall Cemetery, occurred in 1974, when demolition work uncovered the remains of several brick vaults. The best preserved of these still contained a cedar coffin in which was found the remains of a skeleton. It was thought that this burial dated to before 1812. The excavation of these vaults, by Judy Birmingham of the University of Sydney, was one of the earliest attempts to examine the archaeology of Sydney's history.[8]

The best preserved archaeological evidence that has survived from Sydney's earliest years is the site of First Government House, the first settlement's most important building.[9] This site is of particular archaeological significance because it contains, amongst other things, the only *in situ* archaeological evidence from the first year of European occupation. Located on the corner of Phillip Street and Bridge Street, this was the site of the official residence of the Governor of New South Wales and the centre of government administration from 1789 till 1845, when it was demolished. During that time it grew from a relatively modest, two-storeyed house of only eight rooms and a stairwell, to what Mortimer Lewis, the Colonial Architect, described in 1845 as 'an incongruous mass of Buildings built at different periods'. It was Mortimer Lewis who recommended that the house be demolished, a task that took over a year to accomplish, but it was also Lewis who left us a plan of First Government House in its final form (Figure 3.4). This plan gives a clear impression of the rambling pile that the house had become and, together with the numerous contemporary illustrations of the house at different dates, has allowed architectural historians to work out its complex structural history. There were many additions and modifications made over time both to the house and to its outbuildings, which (after 1795)

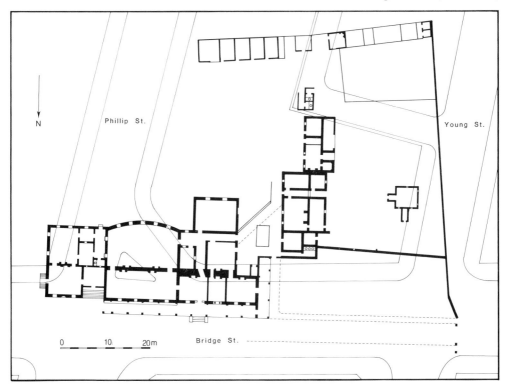

Figure 3.4 Plan of First Government House, Sydney, in 1845 just
before its demolition. This plan shows the ground floor
superimposed onto a modern street layout. (After Bickford and
others, 1983.)

27

housed the Government Printery as well as the kitchen and other domestic facilities. There seem to have been four major building phases, each equatable with a particular governor: first, that of Phillip in 1788; second, that of King in 1800; third, that of Macquarie in 1811; and fourth, that of Darling in the late 1820s and early 1830s. Following demolition, the site of First Government House was used for a variety of purposes as the years went by. As a result the site now presents a range of structures and deposits which comprise the longest continuous historical archaeological sequence to be found on any one site in Australia. Although it can be debated as to whether this site is, as it has been called, 'the most exciting archaeological find of European civilization in this country',[10] it is without any doubt a site of very considerable importance.

For the purposes of this discussion, it is the early part of the site's history that is of most interest. The research of historians and of architects enables us to appreciate in detail the plan and appearance of the house that Governor Phillip built (Figure 3.5). It is clear that

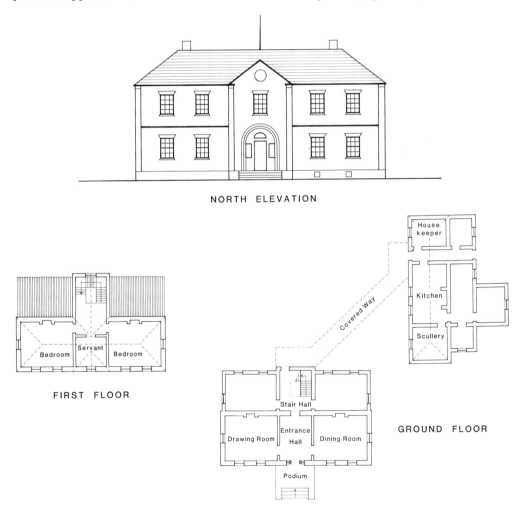

Figure 3.5 Front elevation and plans of First Government House, Sydney, in 1789. (After Conybeare Morrison & Partners 1985.)

Phillip's house, in both plan and elevation, was a model of Georgian correctness. True, later occupants had to increase its size, improve its facilities and put verandahs on it to keep it cool, but it is still quite remarkable that such a building could be constructed of stone and brick and be available for occupation within eighteen months of the first settlers struggling ashore. Modern construction projects do not seem to do so well!

The First Government House site produced significant archaeological evidence as long ago as 1899, when a trench, being dug for telephone cables, cut through its foundations. This yielded a number of bricks and a fine copper plate that is thought to have been fixed originally to the foundations of the house. The plate records the landing of the first settlers and the laying of the foundation stone of the house by Governor Phillip on 15 May 1788 (Figure 3.6). This was one of those lucky finds that undoubtedly occur, but most of our

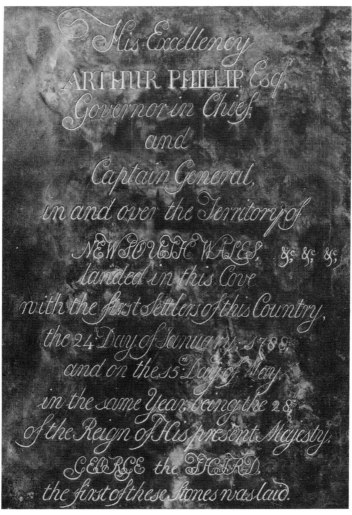

Figure 3.6   Engraved copper foundation plate from the site of First Government House, Sydney; found in 1899 by a workman digging a trench for telephone cables along the Bridge Street footpath. (By courtesy of Mitchell Library, Sydney.)

29

knowledge of the archaeology of First Government House has come not from luck but from a great deal of very hard work by Anne Bickford and her excavation team. Archaeological excavations were carried out in 1983 and 1984, following a proposal, in 1982, to build a tower block on the site which would have destroyed it completely. As a result of those excavations, the site is to be conserved, and it is intended that parts of it will be made available for public inspection. The work was primarily of an exploratory nature in connection with the conservation of the site, but it was also remarkably informative about some of the details of the structure. The excavations confirmed that the greater part of the house itself is underneath Bridge Street, Phillip Street and their intersection. Thus, service trenches of various sorts must have cut through the foundations, and at one time two tram routes ran across the site of the building. In view of the considerable cultural significance of First Government House, it is to be hoped that parts of these streets can eventually be closed to enable the archaeological investigation of these important areas of the house. The work done so far has had to be restricted to a former car park on the corner of the two streets and has demonstrated that substantial remains of foundations survive, together with associated deposits. Parts of the footings of the western, southern and eastern walls of Phillip's house have been revealed. Similarly, some of the footings of the walls of the outbuildings have been uncovered, including evidence of a bread oven. Part of a privy has also been excavated, and two drains have been found, one of which had many pieces of printer's lead type amongst its fill which presumably originated from the printery that was located for some time in part of the outbuildings. Other excavated structures belonged to later phases of the site, but enough has been uncovered to give a picture of the manner in which the most important man of the early colony was housed. Adding the archaeological evidence to the historical record, we can get a clearer impression of how the Governor lived and worked. First Government House represents one extreme of the social and economic spectrum. What was going on at the other extreme? Can the archaeological record also inform us about the manner of life of the less fortunate?

Archaeologists the world over have always had a tendency to excavate structures that tell us about the lives and deaths of the powerful and the famous. It is rather unfair for other archaeologists to blame them for this, because such structures are usually easier to find than those connected with ordinary people. They also tend to produce a far wider and a far more attractive range of evidence, especially movable evidence that looks well in a museum. This tendency is particularly unfortunate for historical periods, because it merely tells us more about people for whom we already have extensive documentation and fails to exploit the potential of archaeology to tell us about those people for whom the written records are limited or absent. The society of Australia's earliest colony was characterized both by social separation and by social interdependence. There were those who were convicts, and there were those who were free, and within both categories there was a complex social stratification. Thus there were social and economic gulfs between people who could not do without one another in the struggle for survival of the early years of settlement. It is particularly interesting, therefore, to explore the impact that this interaction has had on the archaeological record.

The 1788 attempt to grow wheat at Sydney Cove was a failure and, at the end of that year, an agricultural settlement was established at Rose Hill where it was thought that the soil would be more suitable. This proved to be the case and, in December 1789, the convict workers of Rose Hill produced Australia's first successful grain harvest thus staving off for a while the threat of starvation. It was this achievement, together with the arrival of the

Figure 3.7   Parramatta in the 1790s. A row of convict huts can be
seen to the left. This drawing was originally published in D. Collins,
1798. *An account of the English colony in New South Wales*, Cadell
and Davies, London. (Photograph by David McClenaghan, courtesy
of the Armidale College of Advanced Education Library.)

Second Fleet in June 1790, that seems to have made Governor Phillip decide to establish a township at Rose Hill, which he renamed Parramatta. We are fortunate to possess a contemporary illustration of this settlement in the 1790s (Figure 3.7), and a plan of the township that grew up, dated to about 1813. From these, and from contemporary descriptions, it is known that the largely convict population lived in single-storeyed, two-roomed huts which were built of wattle-and-daub with thatched roofs. These buildings measured 7.3 by 3.7 metres and although designed for ten men each, accommodated in some cases up to fourteen. By the end of 1791 there were at least a hundred of these structures, but the materials from which they were made created substantial maintenance problems over subsequent years. Also, as time went on, the convict population of Parramatta was gradually replaced by free settlers, but little is known of this process or of how the mean convict huts were succeeded by more substantial dwellings.

The archaeological excavation of some of these convict huts should tell us something about life at the bottom end of the society that was being governed from First Government House. The problem is to find them! It was most fortunate that Ted Higginbotham was able to locate and excavate one of them during 1985.[11]

As is so often the case in urban environments, the opportunity for this excavation only occurred because of a major building development on a substantial part of a Parramatta city block bounded by George, Marsden, Macquarie and O'Connell Streets which then became available for investigation. From the available historical documentation Ted Higginbotham was able to reconstruct the town plan for the period 1790 to 1792 and to relate it accurately to the modern plan. This showed where the convict huts and their allotments had been. Other historical and archaeological evidence was combined to indicate the part of the site most likely to have escaped subsequent disturbance. Attention was thus focussed on the George Street frontage where it was thought that it might be possible to locate two of the huts. In a bold move, mechanical excavation was employed to remove demolition rubble and most of the topsoil layer from an area of approximately 915 square metres. This mechanical excavation also included a trial trench across the area which revealed that the site of one of the huts had been destroyed by later disturbance. Work was therefore concentrated on an area of approximately 540 square metres, where the lower part of the topsoil and the surface of the subsoil sand were meticulously excavated by manual methods using shovels and trowels. These remarkably well-planned efforts paid off. The archaeological traces of one hut were found, almost exactly where they should have been, and, quite unexpectedly, the remains of another contemporary structure were located immediately behind it. The structural evidence consisted of a confused jumble of postholes, pits, shallow depressions and trenches or slots, all cut into the natural sand, and mixed up with these were numerous modern disturbances (Figure 3.8). If the latter are excluded, then a plan emerges that tells us something about the living conditions of the Parramatta convict labourers (Figure 3.9). In the northern part of the plan can be seen an oblong of postholes oriented approximately northwest to southeast. This is thought to be one of the convict huts

Figure 3.8 Excavation in 1985 of the site of early timber buildings at Parramatta. View to north, compare with Figure 3.9. Scale of 1m in 500mm divisions. (Photograph by Edward Higginbotham.)

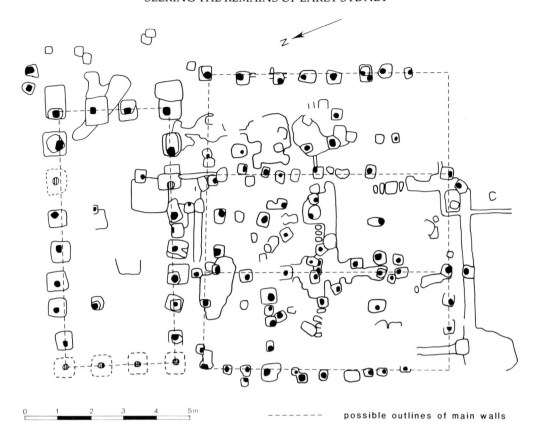

0   1   2   3   4   5m   --------   possible outlines of main walls

Figure 3.9   Plan of traces of early timber buildings excavated at
Parramatta in 1985. The oblong of postholes to the north is thought
to be the remains of one of the convict huts of the 1790s. (After
Higginbotham 1987.)

of the early 1790s, and it is clear that it was a cruder structure than the historical records
might have led us to believe. It consisted of a timber framework in which the upright posts
were set straight into the ground rather than into ground-plates. Grey clay that was foreign
to the site occurred in the posthole fills, confirming the use of the wattle-and-daub
technique. The archaeological evidence is unable to indicate what form of flooring was
present, but it seems likely that this was merely an earth floor or, at best, one consisting of
timber laid directly on the ground. A general scatter of sandstock brick fragments and a
depression at the eastern end of the hut suggest the existence of the chimney which
historical records indicate. Postholes within the building do not confirm the existence of
two rooms, as the historical records claim, but they suggest that a hammock-bar may have
run from one end of the structure to the other, leaving a narrow access space along the side
in which the door was situated. It would appear that the only way in which ten to fourteen
men could have slept in such a small space would have been by using hammocks, which
was apparently the common practice for convicts in the Sydney area. Sleeping in hammocks, each individual needs a minimum of about 0.5 metres width, although alternate

hammocks will have to be slung slightly lower and slightly higher to achieve such overcrowding. The excavated Parramatta hut would have had a hammock-space of 7.3 by 2.4 metres, certainly sufficient space for fourteen men in an emergency, and quite adequate for only ten men. Not only would hammocks have been more comfortable and far healthier than sleeping on an earth floor, but during the day they could have been lashed and stowed in a corner, leaving the inside of the small hut free for eating and other activities. There is even a posthole in the Parramatta hut, near its southeast corner, that could have been the corner-post of a hammock-rack in which the lashed hammocks would have been stowed upright when not in use. Much of this is supposition, but the hut was of the size claimed in the historical records and it was constructed of simple cheap materials using primitive construction techniques. With the building sitting straight on the ground, and a framework of earthfast posts, it is no wonder that deterioration was rapid as is claimed in the surviving documentation. A convict hut in Parramatta on a winter's night was a long way removed from the comfort and stylistic correctness of First Government House. People were housed according to their station, and there would have been few who would have expected it to have been otherwise.

Parallel with the traces of the convict hut and close to them were indications of another structure, rather larger in size. It is possible that this was a stockyard rather than a roofed building, but if it was indeed a building then the four lines of postholes running from northeast to southwest would suggest some sort of farm building like a stable or a barn, with a skillion on each side. It seems likely that the hut was built first and that the other structure was a little later in date, although built at a time when the hut was still standing. The excavator has concluded that the hut was erected in 1790, and rebuilt by 1800, and that the structure behind it was probably built in 1800. It is thought that both would have collapsed and been abandoned by 1815-23.

The range and number of artefacts recovered from the excavation of these two structures was very limited. This contrasted with the variety and quality of artefacts from later contexts on the site and is thought to be due to social and economic factors, not merely to a bias in the archaeological sample. The first structural phase of the hut had very few artefacts associated with it, while the second phase had appreciably more, and the structure behind the hut yet more again. The excavator's tentative suggestion was that the hut had first been occupied by convicts but then by free persons, who were also responsible for the structure behind it. Certainly, there is an interesting increase in iron nails from the three contexts: 1 to 13 to 47. Similarly, bottle glass increases from 1 to 9 to 23 fragments, and imported porcelain (only 12 fragments in all) was only found in the third context. It is also significant that even in the third context a glass tumbler and a porcelain tea bowl had been crudely repaired by piercing holes in them through which either wire or rivets could be fastened. These had obviously been items that the owner either was not able or could not afford to replace. The overall impression gained from the artefacts was that the later occupants had relatively few possessions and the original occupants, the convicts, had virtually none. So far as the date is concerned, the artefactual material was in broad agreement with the historical record, but it is particularly interesting to note that this site produced unglazed and lead-glazed earthenware that is broadly comparable with that from the Gateway Site which has been discussed above. This material is thought to represent Australia's first attempts at indigenous pottery production.

Within this chapter I have examined the findings, and the questions they raise, from some of the work already undertaken. There is, of course, much more that could be discussed concerning the archaeology of the early years of Australia's first European colony. For instance, maritime archaeology undoubtedly has an important contribution to make to this subject just as to so many others. H.M.S. *Sirius*, the principal ship of war escorting the First Fleet, that raced round the world in 1788-9 in order to bring essential supplies of food to the new colony from Cape Town, lies wrecked at Norfolk Island where she ran onto a reef in 1790. Similarly, the *Sydney Cove* lies in Bass Strait, where she met her end, in 1797, carrying a cargo of 32,000 litres of alcohol and a quantity of general merchandise. There were even a number of convict ships that sank in Australian waters, usually after having landed their convicts, but on two occasions, off Tasmania, substantial numbers of convicts were in fact drowned.[12] Some research has been conducted on the wreck sites of the *Sirius* and the *Sydney Cove* and it is obvious that such sites can tell us quite a lot about the beginnings of European settlement in Australia.

The topics selected for discussion in this chapter demonstrate the manner in which the archaeological record reflects the character of the times. The problems, the aspirations and the achievements of the first European settlers, convict and free, can be perceived in such material evidence as the street layout of the old part of Sydney, the Botanic Gardens, the Town Hall Cemetery, the site of First Government House and the traces of the Parramatta convict hut. The birth of a new nation can be observed from the archaeological evidence, just as it has so often been from the historical records. From such a study can emerge a new appreciation and a fuller understanding of those men and women who attended that birth.

Notes

[1] M. Dupain, 1980. *Francis Greenway: A celebration*, Cassell, North Ryde.

[2] R. Burford, 1829. *Description of the Town of Sydney*. Cited in D.N. Jeans and P. Spearritt, 1980. *The open air museum: The cultural landscape of New South Wales*, Allen & Unwin, North Sydney, p.100.

[3] M. Kelly, 1979. Roads to yesterday. In P. Stanbury (ed.), *10,000 years of Sydney life: A guide to archaeological discovery*, Macleay Museum, University of Sydney, pp.2-9.

[4] P. Valder, 1979. Gardens of the past. In P. Stanbury (ed.), *10,000 years of Sydney life: A guide to archaeological discovery*, Macleay Museum, University of Sydney, pp.28-37.

[5] J.S. Kerr, 1986. *Fort Denison*, National Trust (N.S.W.), Sydney, p.5.

[6] J.F. Campbell, 1924. The valley of the Tank Stream. *Journal and Proceedings of the Royal Australian Historical Society* 10(2), pp.63-103.

[7] E. Higginbotham, 1987. The excavation of buildings in the early township of Parramatta, New South Wales, 1790 – 1820s. *Australian Journal of Historical Archaeology* 5, pp. 3–20.

[8] On Sydney burial grounds see: K. Johnson, 1979. The historical grave. In P. Stanbury (ed.), *10,000 years of Sydney life: A guide to archaeological discovery*, Macleay Museum, University of Sydney, pp.10-19. For a photograph of the gravestone of George Graves see: L. Gilbert, 1980. *A grave look at history*, Ferguson, Sydney, p.19. Concerning the Town Hall Cemetery excavation see: J. Birmingham and C. Liston, 1976. *Old Sydney Burial Ground*, Studies in Historical Archaeology 5, Australian Society for Historical Archaeology, University of Sydney.

[9] Detailed archaeological studies have yet to be published on First Government House. The discussion in this book is based on the following: D.J. Mulvaney, 1985. *'A good foundation': Reflections on the heritage of the First Government House, Sydney*, Australian Heritage Commission Special Australian Heritage Publication Series No.5, Australian Government Publishing Service, Canberra, and H. Proudfoot, 1983. The First Government House, Sydney. *Heritage Australia* 2(2), pp.21-5. Also H. Temple and S. Sullivan (eds), 1985. *First Government House Site, Sydney: Its significance and its future*, Proceedings of Seminar No.2, 2 May 1984, Department of Environment and Planning, Sydney. Also A. Bickford and others, 1983. *First Government House Site, Sydney, Australia: Statement of cultural significance*, Australian Archaeological Association, Sydney. Also Conybeare Morrison & Partners, 1985. Conservation plan for First Government House, 2 vols, unpublished report for Department of Environment and Planning, Sydney.

[10] H. Proudfoot, 1983, p.21.

[11] The discussion of the Parramatta excavation is based on E. Higginbotham, 1987.

[12] G. Henderson, 1986. *Maritime archaeology in Australia*, University of Western Australia Press, Nedlands.

Chapter 4

It didn't always work

INVESTIGATING THE SITES OF FAILED SETTLEMENTS

Perhaps the most astonishing thing about the first European settlement at Sydney Cove is that it succeeded at all. It is quite remarkable that a thousand people, taken half-way round the world and dumped on an alien shore, were able to found a new city and a new country. It is even more remarkable when you consider that the greater number of those people did not make the journey because they wished to. To appreciate this achievement it is necessary to see it in context, a context in which Sydney was the only case of successful primary settlement in eastern Australia and one of the very few in the continent as a whole. Australia is littered with the sites of abandoned settlements and 'ghost towns' where all or almost all of the population has departed. Most of these date from well after the beginnings of settlement, however, and many of them result from demographic changes brought about by the fluctuating fortunes of mining, pastoralism or agriculture. There are some early settlement sites which represent instances of colonization failure. These are cases where primary settlement was attempted, as it had been in Sydney Cove, but did not succeed. It is instructive to examine such failures in order to throw light on the circumstances that were necessary for colonization to succeed. This is a task to which archaeological evidence can make an important contribution because the sites of these early failures are usually on land which has had comparatively little subsequent development. Thus it is possible to investigate the earliest evidence of settlement just because it did fail. Such traces have not been destroyed or hidden by the multi-storeyed growth of a modern city.

Not all of the sites of early settlement failure have yet been studied archaeologically, but six examples have been investigated to some extent and of these no less than four have been subjected to limited excavation. The six sites are widely dispersed around Australia: one in Tasmania, two in Victoria, two in the Northern Territory and one in South Australia (Figure 4.1). As a result, they provide a variety of environmental and geographical circumstances. All these settlements were located on the coast or on a river giving ready access to the coast, for in all cases the subsequently unsuccessful settlers arrived by sea, just as the eventually successful ones had done at Sydney Cove. Furthermore, when these settlements were abandoned, evacuation was effected by water transport. Perhaps one of the secrets of Sydney's success was that, as the very first settlement, there was nowhere else in Australia to retreat to if things went wrong. Failure in Sydney would have meant return to Britain, where most of the unsuccessful settlers would have been anything but welcome. It might be suggested, therefore, that Sydney succeeded because it *had* to, although in the first crucial years of settlement it came dangerously near to failure. The settlements that are the subject of this chapter did fail, and the question is, why?

Figure 4.1   Sites of early settlement failure discussed in this chapter.

A convenient way to examine these sites is in a roughly chronological order but grouped geographically. The first one to be considered is Risdon Cove, Tasmania, the first site of Hobart, occupied in September 1803 and abandoned in July 1804.[1] Risdon Cove was the location of the first official European settlement in Tasmania and was situated on the northern side of Risdon Brook, which runs into Risdon Cove, on the eastern side of the River Derwent about 15 kilometres from its mouth. Fortunately, this site has escaped modern development, and a programme of archaeological survey and of excavation has been carried out there by Angela McGowan. The surviving documentary evidence and the survey indicated that the settlement was extensive but dispersed, covering at least 38 hectares. A substantial number of archaeological features have been located on the site (Figure 4.2), although many of them are of later nineteenth- or even early-twentieth-century date, and some are of unknown date. McGowan has identified only six features that belong to the first settlement: the storehouse, the storekeeper's house, the Governor's new house, Mountgarrett's house, a hut platform and an enclosed clearing. Historical records show that there were far more structures than this, but the majority of these were small wooden huts for convicts and soldiers and these dwellings have left no apparent surface traces. Indeed, nearly two centuries of cultivation have destroyed almost everything except stone foundations. This illustrates one of the problems faced by archaeologists when investigating a settlement of such short duration and composed of such socially different groups. The greater part of the surviving evidence from Risdon Cove is restricted to its most important buildings.

McGowan carried out partial excavation on eight of the twenty-nine archaeological features located on the site. Only three of these were of particular significance for the 1803-4 settlement: the storehouse, the Governor's new house and Mountgarrett's house. Judging

38

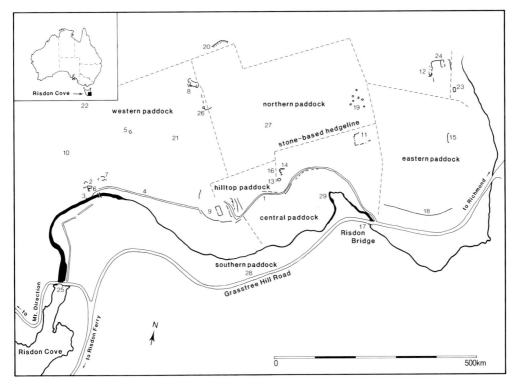

Figure 4.2   The Risdon Cove settlement site. Numbers indicate
archaeological features. For the original settlement, those of
particular significance are: 2: Storehouse. 8: Governor's new house.
12: Mountgarrett's house. (After McGowan 1985.)

from the excavated evidence from these structures it is quite remarkable what had been
achieved in less than a year of occupation. It would appear that, at least originally, there was
every intention of remaining on this site. The storehouse, for instance, was a solidly
constructed stone building about 12.5 metres long and about 5.5 metres wide. It showed
evidence of two building phases, only the first of which belonged to the abandoned
settlement. The earlier phase seems to have terminated with a fire, and the second phase
probably belonged to the subsequent agricultural settlement of the site after its evacuation.
Documentary claims that the building was removed to the new site of Hobart when Risdon
Cove was evacuated are hard to believe, although the excavator compromises by suggesting that only one wall was moved. In all early settlement attempts the building of a store had
a high priority. The supplies which had been dumped on the beach, along with the new
colonists, were absolutely vital for the survival of the settlement, at least up to the time
when it could produce its first harvest. Those supplies had to be protected against
deterioration and against pilfering, and a tent or a flimsy wooden hut was no place for them.
It is therefore no surprise that the most substantial building completed during the brief
occupation of the Risdon Cove settlement was the storehouse.

Also high on the list of building priorities was a suitable house for the governor of the new
settlement, Lieutenant John Bowen, R.N., who at first had to live in a tent made of a ship's
mainsail. Partial excavation of this house revealed lime-mortared stone footings which had

39

been intended to support wooden walls, but the archaeological evidence suggested that the building had never been completed. It was clearly intended to become the largest and most dominant building of the settlement, as befitted its important role. Measuring about 21 metres by about 9.5 metres, and situated on the hillside above Risdon Brook, the house would have had a commanding view of the rest of the settlement and of the River Derwent. In order to make sure that the governor enjoyed this view, it was even provided with two bay-windows on its front.

In contrast, the third structure partly excavated, that of Mountgarrett's house, was primitive and unassuming, but it was the first substantial residential building to be erected in the settlement and it had certainly been lived in. Mountgarrett was a naval surgeon and magistrate to the settlement. He also had considerable property interests at Risdon Cove. His house showed evidence of two periods of construction, of which only the first is certainly associated with him. This building seems to have been only roughly rectangular and to have measured 11.8 by 6.6 metres. Three of its walls were of wattle-and-daub on mud-mortared stone footings, but the wall at the southern end, containing the fireplace and chimney, was built of rammed earth. The chimney was probably of bricks, and at least some of the windows had glass in them. This was not the most impressive of buildings but, compared with other dwellings in the settlement, it must have offered both comfort and convenience. The excavated artefacts included not only the expected domestic items but also two naval buttons, that probably belonged to Mountgarrett himself, and an assortment of munitions including gunflints, lead shot, and a cannonball of about 5 kilograms weight! The latter serves as a reminder that, in May 1804, it was Mountgarrett who was instrumental in having a carronade fired at a large group of Aborigines who were hunting kangaroo near his house. At least two of them were killed, and probably many more, as a result of this overreaction. Mountgarrett must have been a determined individual, rather like the remarkable bone carving of a sailor which was found in the topsoil of his house-site (Figure 4.3).

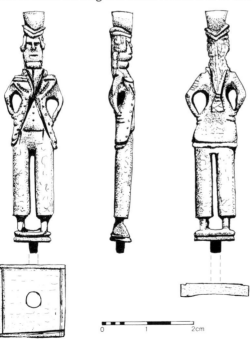

Figure 4.3   Bone carving of a sailor, found on the site of Mountgarrett's house at Risdon Cove. (Drawing by Keith Moon, courtesy Angela McGowan, with permission of the Tasmanian Lands, Parks and Wildlife Department.)

Why was Risdon Cove abandoned after all the hard work that must have been put into it? McGowan merely says that the site was found to be unsuitable, and an examination of its location suggests that this was indeed the case. It was abandoned in favour of Sullivans Cove, around which the future city of Hobart grew up. Sullivans Cove was only about 10 kilometres away on the other side of the Derwent, but it must have had a number of advantages over Risdon Cove. It was nearer to the sea, which provided contact with the outside world, and access by ships was superior to that at Risdon Cove where the settlement had to be approached along the narrow Risdon Brook. In addition, although some of the soils around Risdon Cove were reasonably fertile, the western shores of the River Derwent have a higher rainfall. It must have taken a lot of courage to admit that the settlement had been started in the wrong place and to move it elsewhere. It could be argued that Risdon Cove was not a failure at all: the settlers did not give up, they just moved to a better site. It would appear that one of the major factors in determining whether early settlement succeeded or not was the choice of site. In the case of Hobart, the settlers got it wrong the first time, but they seem to have been right enough the second time.

During the very same months that Risdon Cove was being found to be unsuitable, another disastrous attempt at settlement was occurring across Bass Strait, in what is now Victoria. Victoria's first official European settlement was at Sullivans Bay.[2] This is situated near Sorrento, on the northern side of the long, narrow peninsula that forms the eastern side of the entrance to Port Phillip Bay (Figure 4.4). Thus the settlement looked northeast across Port Phillip Bay: Melbourne later developed at the northern end of the bay. In this case the choice of site was disastrous; fresh water was scarce and the soil was unsuitable for agriculture. The anchorage was also poor, so that ships had to stand almost a kilometre offshore while people and equipment were laboriously landed in longboats, which in turn often had to be unloaded by convicts wading into the water. The settlers, numbering 467 persons and including convicts, marines, free settlers, officers and officials, as well as some wives and children, arrived in October 1803 in two ships. Most of them left, again by sea, at the end of January 1804. Those remaining left by the end of May in that same year. The settlement was evacuated to the Derwent River in Tasmania, but not in time to prevent an outbreak of scurvy brought on by the conditions at Sullivans Bay following the long voyage from Britain. It is easy to condemn Lieutenant-Governor Collins who was in charge of this resounding failure, but he had been given very precise instructions. He had been expressly told to locate the settlement on the coast of Bass Strait; this was in order to prevent the French in any future war from interrupting communications through that strait between Britain and Sydney. Thus the siting of the settlement was for strategic reasons rather than any other, and this proved fatal.

Peter Coutts has painstakingly investigated both the historical sources and the archaeological evidence for the Sullivans Bay settlement. While the site has been subjected to modern suburban development, with consequent land subdivision and house building, Coutts has been able to demonstrate, from studies of the documentation and of the modern landscape, both the exact location of the settlement and some of the details of its layout. However, no traces of archaeological features belonging to the settlement have survived and no excavations have been conducted. Even the several graves that local tradition associates with the early settlement seem more likely to be those of subsequent settlers. Considering the ephemeral materials which the extraordinarily short-lived settlement was mostly constructed of, the extensive coastal erosion that the site has been subject to, and the extent of modern development, Coutts suggests that little archaeological evidence will have

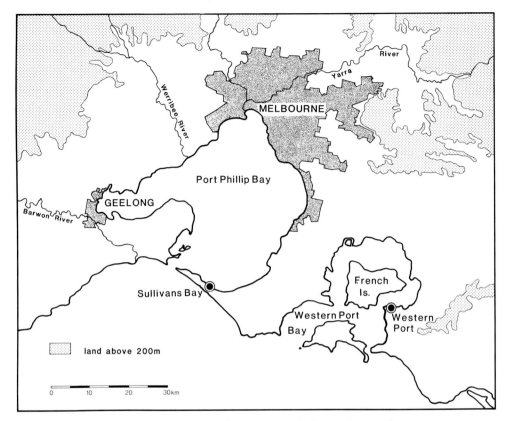

Figure 4.4   Location of the Sullivans Bay and Western Port settlements.

survived other than subsoil features (wells, privies, other pits) and scattered artefacts. Indeed such evidence has come to light accidentally from time to time. The remains of several barrel-wells, sunk into the beach above high-water mark, have been found in this way, and some of the wooden staves from the perforated barrels that lined them are now preserved in local collections. In addition, traces of an early jetty and of a stone-built powder magazine were visible until early this century, and various artefacts, including a fine pair of leg irons, have been discovered over the years. In general, however, Sullivans Bay has provided little archaeological indication of the settlement disaster that took place there.

The second attempt to start a European settlement in Victoria was also a failure, although this time it survived much longer. Again the motive was strategic rather than anything else; on this occasion the aim was to frustrate French colonial ambitions in the area. The settlement was known as Western Port and was located near the present-day township of Corinella, on the eastern side of Western Port Bay.[3] This was less than 50 kilometres in a straight line from Sullivans Bay, although a good deal further by water (Figure 4.4). The settlers, who numbered about forty convicts and soldiers, arrived in December 1826, and only landed at Corinella after a careful exploration of the area. This time the choice of site was rather better, Corinella has reasonable soil and nowadays is quite good pastureland. Nevertheless, water supplies were a problem, just as they had been at Sullivans Bay. For fifteen months the settlers laboured to create their settlement and it looked as if it might succeed. Indeed, more convicts were sent there during 1827. Then it was killed off by a similar government whim to that which had brought it into being. The perceived French threat having ended, Governor Darling ordered the settlement to be evacuated to Sydney; the total population of sixty-three people were removed by sea in March 1828. The story of the Western Port settlement raises the question whether such a small group of people consisting almost entirely of soldiers and convicts could ever have succeeded. It also makes one question the chances of success of government-inspired settlement. It was only seven years later that a successful European colonization of Victoria was inaugurated by a group of Tasmanian pastoralists: a private enterprise effort motivated by economic factors, rather than a strategic move by government.

As with Sullivans Bay, it is again Peter Coutts who has investigated both the history and the archaeology of this short-lived settlement. Although the number of people involved was much smaller than at Sullivans Bay, the longer duration of the settlement at Western Port meant that more building and more modification of the environment occurred. In addition, the level of modern development in the area is not so intense as is the case at Sullivans Bay and, as a result, Coutts was able to establish not only the exact location of the settlement but also the position of some of its main buildings such as the storehouse, the military barracks, the prisoners' barracks, the blacksmith's shop and the commandant's house. He was also able to carry out a number of excavations, but in most cases they revealed more about the subsequent use of the site than about the early settlement. Only one structure that is thought to belong to the 1826-8 period was uncovered. This consisted of an extensive area of depressions and ridges which were interpreted as the marks of floorboards which may have rotted in position. It seems likely that this structure was in some way associated with the commandant's house. The excavations at Western Port again demonstrate the difficulties faced by archaeologists when attempting to investigate a settlement of such a short duration. Indeed, without the very sensitive excavation techniques employed by Coutts, even the little that was discovered would have been missed.

The problems faced by the first attempts at European colonization in Tasmania and Victoria were substantial, but they pale into insignificance when compared with those that were met in what is now the Northern Territory. Between 1824, and the foundation of Darwin in 1869, there was a series of six short-lived settlements along the northern Australian coast, all of which failed. The first of these was Fort Dundas, established in October 1824 on the west coast of Melville Island, facing Apsley Strait, and abandoned in early 1829.[4] Although this settlement survived longer than Risdon Cove, Sullivans Bay or Western Port, it still came to nothing. Again the motive for its foundation has something to do with this. The British government wished to establish a pre-emptive garrison that would discourage Dutch or French interference, would protect British shipping between Sydney and India (that sailed via the Torres Strait), and one that would develop trading contacts with island southeast Asia. The successful foundation of Singapore only a few years earlier must have made these ambitions seem quite reasonable. In the outcome, however, no foreign threat evolved, the shipping lanes were too far away, and very few southeast Asian traders bothered to call at the new settlement.

Fort Dundas is a fascinating site for the archaeologist and it has been subjected to a detailed archaeological survey by Eleanor Crosby, who has also done a small amount of test excavation. The site of the settlement is situated on a low sandstone point which has a fairly dense cover of tropical forest and a fringe of mangrove swamp that is particularly extensive to the north. In spite of these difficult conditions, the survey revealed that a large number of

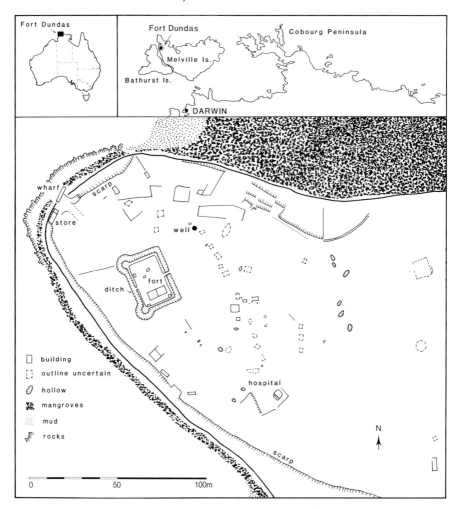

Figure 4.5 Plan of the archaeological features at Fort Dundas. The eastern
part of the site has been omitted. (After Crosby 1978.)

archaeological features could still be seen (Figure 4.5). Dominating these were the ditches
and banks of the stockade, which measured about 70 by 56 metres. This was a veritable fort
— provided with gun emplacements that looked out over the Apsley Strait and entered by a
single gate that was situated on the landward side, adjacent to the centre of the settlement. It
was here that Crosby conducted her limited excavation, sectioning the ditch and bank to
investigate their original form. By this means she was able to demonstrate that the bank had
consisted of earth, stones and timber and had constituted a substantial rampart, providing
both parapet and firing step.

The other archaeological features observed on the site included traces of a wharf, a store,
numerous dwellings and other buildings, a hospital, various enclosures, a well, a number of
rubbish pits, and to the east the convict barracks, the commandant's house and several
graves. Although the remains of most of these features were only slight, it was possible to
see the whole layout of this important settlement. Because of the remoteness of this part of

Australia the site has escaped modern development, and there seems to have been relatively little activity on it since its abandonment.

Why was it abandoned? Both historical sources and archaeological evidence indicate that the choice of site was disastrous. Strong tides and difficult shoals made the settlement awkward to approach by ship. Furthermore, the site had literally to be carved out of the forest in which there were substantial numbers of Aborigines who did not welcome the newcomers and demonstrated their feelings by throwing spears at them from time to time. In addition, the settlement was a very long way from Sydney or, indeed, from anywhere else of any size. Also, its population was small, nearly half of its settlers were convicts and, throughout the four-and-a-half years of its existence, there were never many more than 100 people present. Given all these factors, and the unfamiliar tropical climate, it is remarkable that the settlement lasted so long and that so much building took place. One unwelcome contribution that Fort Dundas did make to northern Australia was the buffalo, which was introduced to the settlement and successfully bred there. There would be many environmentalists who might wish that Fort Dundas had failed more quickly.

In the case of the settlement named Victoria, at Port Essington, failure took very much longer. This settlement, which lasted from 1838 till 1849, is perhaps the best known of all the aborted European colonies in nineteenth-century Australia. Jim Allen, who has re-searched both the documentary sources and the archaeology of the site, has argued that, rather than being seen as a failed attempt at colonization, Victoria should be regarded as a successful strategic manoeuvre.[5] Supporting his view is the fact that this settlement was never more than a military outpost manned by a handful of Royal Marines. There were no free settlers and, except for four months in 1844-5, no convicts. The population seems never to have exceeded a total of seventy-eight, and the deathrate from malaria was high.

Military strategy seems to have been the major reason for establishing this settlement. The overriding concern was that of maintaining British sovereignty over a part of Australia that might otherwise fall under the influence of the French, the Dutch or even the Americans. Thus the choice of site was significant — near the head of the large inlet known as Port Essington, which is situated at the northern end of the Cobourg Peninsula. In such a location this settlement was very roughly half-way between Singapore and Sydney, its two nearest British neighbours. Indeed, there could have been few reasons, other than a strategic one, for the maintenance of this outpost for so long in such a difficult environment. It was only when the British government's fear of foreign intervention in Australia had diminished that Victoria was finally abandoned. By then it had served its purpose, so perhaps Allen is correct in claiming it as a success rather than a failure.

Because this settlement lasted very much longer than any of the other failed settlements discussed in this chapter, its site has more substantial building remains, and includes the standing remnants of some stone structures. Victoria was located on a headland that was higher than the rest of the country around Port Essington, a position clearly selected because of its defensive advantages. The archaeological features found on this headland provide a remarkable insight into the difficulties of life in this remote and lonely outpost (Figure 4.6). The settlement was protected by a gun emplacement and a small defensive earthwork at the end of the headland. Spread across the rest of the headland were a kitchen, a hospital, a sawpit, several limekilns, a number of wells, a smithy, a store, a bakehouse, the officers' mess, married quarters for some of the men, a quartermaster's store, a magazine and a Government House for the commandant, approached by its own roadway. There was also an all-important jetty and, at a respectful distance outside of the settlement, a cemetery

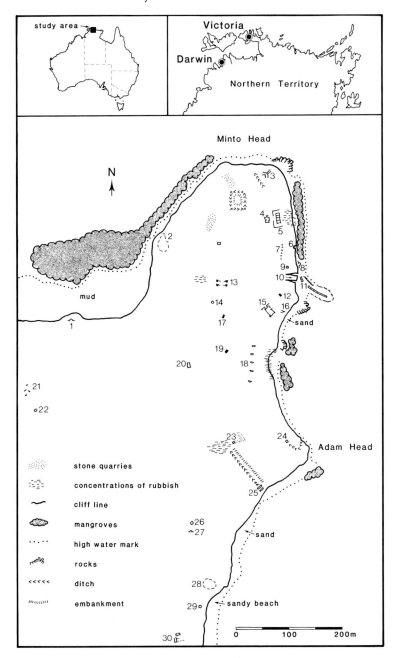

Figure 4.6 Plan of the archaeological features at Victoria, Port Essington. 1: kiln. 2: Aboriginal midden. 3: gun emplacement. 4: kitchen. 5: hospital. 6: sawpit. 7: stoneline. 8: kiln. 9: well. 10: roadway. 11: jetty. 12: smithy. 13: quartermaster's store. 14: well. 15: store. 16: drain. 17: bakehouse. 18: married quarters. 19: stone block. 20: officers' mess. 21: cemetery. 22: well. 23: Government House. 24: magazine. 25: roadway. 26: well. 27: kiln. 28: Aboriginal midden. 29: well. 30: John Lewis' cottage. (After Allen 1967.)

that was to get rather too much use. It is probable that the archaeological features do not represent every aspect of life in this settlement, but they give a fairly good impression.

By combining the historical and archaeological evidence Allen has been able to show the remarkable achievement of the people who lived and worked and, in some cases, died at Victoria. After the first few years, malaria gained an increasing hold over the garrison. Its cause and transmission were not at that time understood and there was no treatment. By 1843, those left alive were described as looking like 'yellow skeletons'. When the garrison was replaced, every man amongst the new arrivals had contracted malaria within the first twelve months and deaths occurred at regular intervals. In addition, the mosquitoes and sandflies were unbearable and their continual biting resulted in painful ulcers. Furthermore, the climate was vile: hot, humid, and without any of the breezes that a location nearer the open coast would have provided. Even the initial clearance of the site was a grim experience, with millions of green tree ants making their presence felt. Water supplies were limited, rats attacked the gardens, cockroaches and flies spoiled food and stores, and termites (white ants) ate the largely wooden buildings almost as fast as they were put up. Also, a year after the commencement of the settlement when a lot of building had already been completed, a cyclone devastated the place and the work had to begin all over again.

In these circumstances, the archaeological features at Victoria are witness to an unbelievable determination amongst its inhabitants. Trees were felled, timber was sawn for buildings, lime was burnt, bricks were made, quarries were dug and stone walls were constructed where necessary. Amongst the latter there are even several round chimneys of a type which has been claimed to originate in west Cornwall in Britain. Attached to the cottages of the married quarters, these still stand as a monument to the undoubted courage of the men who built them. Courage is not too strong a word, anyone who has lived in the humid tropics with the modern benefits of air conditioning, electric fans, refrigerators and cooling showers, can imagine how difficult such an existence must have been, an existence indeed that, without the aid of anti-malarial drugs, could be terminated rather quickly.

Allen not only surveyed the site of Victoria, but also carried out limited excavations that provided additional information about its structures. Furthermore, using the ceramics retrieved from those excavations, he was able to demonstrate that, in spite of its remoteness, even this settlement could enjoy the latest fashions from Britain. More importantly, the same seems to have applied to weaponry, with the excavations producing both gunflints and percussion caps, and thus reflecting an important change in musketry that was taking place in the British forces during the very years that Victoria was occupied.

The peculiar circumstances of Victoria, Port Essington, make it difficult to know whether it should really be treated as an example of failed settlement. There can be no such doubt in the case of our last example, however. This is the site of the settlement known as Kingscote, at Reeves Point on Kangaroo Island, in South Australia.[6] It was occupied by the South Australian Company from July 1836 till the end of 1839, and is regarded as the first formal European settlement in South Australia. The settlement, whose name has been retained by the principal modern township on Kangaroo Island, was occupied in order to engage in various commercial activities — primarily whaling and pastoralism. It was not a success. There was a lack of suitable fresh water, and there was dense vegetation and a poor soil. In addition, the intended commercial developments either failed or were taken over by the new settlement of Adelaide, founded when Kangaroo Island was found to be unsuitable.

Marilyn Truscott has conducted an archaeological survey of the Reeves Point site which has demonstrated that this was undoubtedly the location of the 1836-9 settlement. The

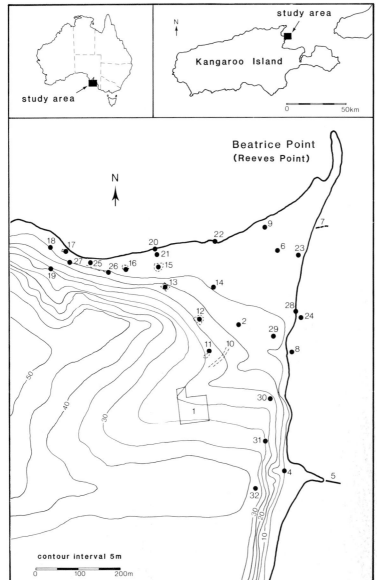

Figure 4.7 Plan of the archaeological features at the Reeves Point site, Kangaroo Island. Probable evidence for the early settlement comprises:

1: certain graves in the cemetery.
2: mulberry tree.
4: quarry.
7 & 8: piles of two jetties.
10: road cutting.
11-13: house hollows.
14: possible house site.
15 & 17: depressions in ground.
20: artefact scatter.
22: charcoal lens in bank.
24: artefact scatter below high-water mark.
(After Truscott 1983.)

report on this work, which is unfortunately not published, gives some indication of the settlement's layout. A substantial number of archaeological features have been located (Figure 4.7), but it is not entirely clear how many of these formed part of the original settlement and how many belonged to subsequent activities. Nevertheless, a number of house sites, a road cutting, a quarry, the remains of at least one jetty, other miscellaneous features and several graves, probably do belong to the failed settlement. There seems to have been no excavation conducted at the site and without this the archaeological features remain difficult to interpret.

Reviewing the six examples of colonization failure that have been discussed, it is apparent that there were a number of factors that helped to bring about those failures.

Perhaps the most obvious, and certainly the one that was common to all six cases, was poor choice of site. Clearly this was a matter of crucial importance. The ideal site needed to be easily accessible by sea-going ships, to have plentiful fresh water supplies, a soil suitable for agriculture, well-drained ground that was not too difficult to clear, a supply of local building materials and a healthy climate. It might be argued that such an ideal site would have been difficult if not impossible to find, but in the case of the sites that have been discussed too many of these basic requirements were absent. Another obvious factor in these instances of settlement failure was the size and composition of the group of settlers involved. In several of the cases the number of people was just too small, and those involved consisted of little more than convicts and their guards. In one settlement the inhabitants were almost entirely military, and in most of the settlements there were few free settlers. This brings us to a third factor that played a part in colony failure: the problem of remoteness. Not only were the settlements small, but they were also a very long way from anywhere, in particular, they were a long way from where both their instructions and their supplies came. In the case of Victoria, Port Essington, for instance, the nearest 'home base' was Sydney, over 4000 kilometres away and at least six weeks sailing. Fort Dundas would have been no better, and the other four examples, although appreciably nearer to Sydney, were still a substantial distance from it in terms of the available communication technology. Finally, there is a basic factor underlying these failures and that is the question of motives. This influenced choice of site, size and composition of settler group and general geographic location. Too often, it would appear, strategic motives were involved, rather than a genuine interest in colonization. In some cases it is not even certain that the settlements were intended to succeed in the long term. Thus, Allen has argued persuasively, Victoria, Port Essington, did succeed in accomplishing all that was required of it. However this may be, strategic and political considerations were not a sufficient basis on their own for colonial success. A good deal more was needed, and it is apparent that the successful colony of Sydney Cove had just that.

Notes

1 A. McGowan, 1985. *Archaeological investigations at Risdon Cove Historic Site: 1978-1980*, National Parks and Wildlife Service, Tasmania, Occasional Paper No.10, Sandy Bay.

2 P.J.F. Coutts, 1981. *Victoria's first official settlement Sullivans Bay, Port Phillip*, Victoria Archaeological Survey, Albert Park.

3 P.J.F. Coutts, 1983. *Corinella: A forgotten episode in Victoria's history*, Victoria Archaeological Survey, Albert Park. Also P.J.F. Coutts, 1985. *Report on the results of archaeological investigations at the 1826 settlement site at Corinella*, Victoria Archaeological Survey, Albert Park.

4 E. Crosby, 1978. *Survey and excavation at Fort Dundas, Melville Island, Northern Territory, 1975*, Australian Society for Historical Archaeology, Occasional Paper No.1, Sydney.

5 On Victoria, Port Essington, see: J. Allen, 1967. The technology of colonial expansion: A nineteenth-century military outpost on the north coast of Australia. *Industrial Archaeology* 4(2), pp.111-37; J. Allen, 1967. The Cornish round chimney in Australia, *Cornish Archaeology* 6, pp.68-73; J. Allen, 1972. Port Essington — A successful limpet port? *Historical Studies* 15(59), pp.341-60; and J. Allen, 1978. The archaeology of nineteenth-century British imperialism: An Australian case study. In R.L. Schuyler (ed.), *Historical archaeology: A guide to substantive and theoretical contributions*, Baywood, Farmingdale, New York, pp.139-48. (Originally published in *World Archaeology* 5(1), pp.44-59, in 1973.)

6 M.C. Truscott, 1983. Archaeological survey of the Reeves Point site — place of the South Australian Company's settlement of Kingscote, Kangaroo Island. Unpublished report for Heritage Conservation Branch, Department of Environment and Planning, Adelaide.

Chapter 5

The convict contribution

VESTIGES OF THE PENAL SYSTEM

Australia started as a convict colony, and the most significant common factor of the settlements whose archaeology has been considered in Chapters 3 and 4 is the presence, in almost all cases, of convicts. Subsequent generations of Australians have varied in their attitude to this convict element in their origins. For a long time it was considered a shameful thing, best forgotten, and certainly played down. In more recent times, however, it has become a matter of pride that so much has been achieved from such apparently inauspicious beginnings. Along with these changes in opinion have gone wildly conflicting views about the character of those who were sentenced to be transported. These have oscillated between the extremes — on the one hand, of believing all convicts to be the vilest of criminals and, on the other hand, of thinking of them as unfortunate minor offenders who were brutalized by a repressive penal system. The reality was probably a complex intermixture of the two. Whatever the public or even the historians' view of the convicts, however, the fact remains that 'convictism' made a significant and sometimes quite distinctive contribution to the archaeological record of Australia's history. Whether we like it or not, some of our most important historic monuments, and probably a good many of the lesser important ones, were built or created for, or by, convicts.

To the historical archaeologist, the convict contribution to Australia's archaeological record provides a very special opportunity. Perhaps in no other country in the world did convicts play such a crucial role in the origins of a nation. Yet contemporary documentation, because of its substantial input from penal authorities, was often somewhat less than appreciative of that role. As suggested in Chapter 1, archaeological evidence has the power to redress the balance a little. By looking at what convicts did, or at what was done for them, we can begin to see things from their point of view. Unfortunately, there has, as yet, been no real attempt made to carry out a comprehensive study of the archaeological evidence for Australian convictism, although there are some remarkable individual investigations that have taken place. James S. Kerr, an architectural historian, has begun with an important book that examines the design of convict establishments throughout the Australian colonies during the transportation era.[1] His work is based almost totally on documentary sources but, significantly, the very last paragraph of his book makes a plea for the recording of the archaeological evidence that is 'still being mutilated, quarried or neglected'.

Kerr's interest, however, is in only one of the two kinds of contribution that convictism has made to the archaeological record. It is obvious that an important part of the material remains consist of the ruins or sites of prisons and associated buildings, and it is with these that Kerr is concerned. These were a convict 'contribution' in the sense that they had to be built to house the convicts and often, but not always, they seem to have been built by the convicts themselves. A less obvious contribution made by convicts, and one that is rather more difficult to study, consists of physical evidence resulting from their activities in society at large. For instance, they cleared land, worked as agricultural labourers, built roads, constructed bridges and performed many other essential functions. Even those of them that remained locked up in penal settlements undertook a variety of tasks: sawing timber, building ships, making salt, producing bricks, mining coal, to mention but a few. To understand why the convict contribution to the archaeological record should be so varied it is necessary to understand something of the convict system. This changed, of course, through time, because convicts were sent to one part of Australia or another for a total of eighty years. For the late 1820s and the 1830s, however, Kerr has provided us with a useful diagram which explains the system during one of the most important periods of convictism (Figure 5.1).

As this diagram shows, the convict system can be thought of as a stairway on which the individual could move either upwards or downwards. Although the details of that stairway changed as time went on, the essential point remained: that status varied (theoretically) with behaviour. In the period to which the diagram refers, the convict arriving from Britain might either be retained in government service or 'assigned' as labour to a private landholder. From either situation he or she might obtain a 'ticket of leave', which was a limited form of freedom that restricted residence to a named area. Eventually a 'conditional pardon' might be granted, conditional, that is to say, on never returning to the British Isles. For the fortunate few even an 'absolute pardon' might ultimately be obtained or the time of their sentence might expire. All of these steps constituted the way up, a series of carefully graded incentives. The way down consisted of a series of disincentives graded with equal care. The convict might be put out on a labour gang, undertaking a variety of tasks on public works such as road building. The more recalcitrant might be placed in an 'iron gang' and forced to labour while wearing chains which were fastened to both ankles and waist. If this failed to modify behaviour the individual could be sent to a special penal settlement which

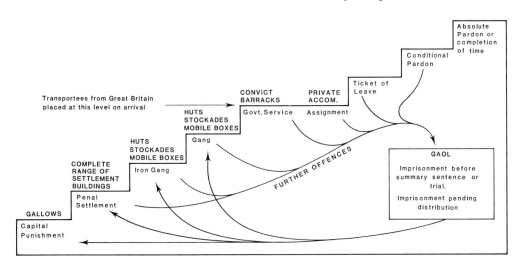

Figure 5.1   The convict system during the late 1820s and the 1830s,
showing (in capitals) the facilities needed for each step. (After Kerr 1984.)

was so located and so designed as to make life as unpleasant as possible. Beyond that there was only the death sentence, and the gallows were always ready. Except from the extreme ends of the stairway, further offences led back to jail and to relocation on a more appropriate step in the system. Added to this were a variety of incidental punishments of which flogging and solitary confinement were probably the most common, but which could also include marooning on a convenient unoccupied island or other more bizarre punishments.

Such was the convict 'system' although many, both at that time and since, have claimed that, in practice, there was very little that was systematic about it. Nevertheless, a convenient way to examine the archaeological record of Australian convictism is to divide the evidence into that which throws light on the activities of those who were going up the stairway and that which informs us about those who were going down. The evidence can also, to some extent, be subdivided, with different material remains telling us about different steps in the stairway. The main problem is that those going up become increasingly difficult to identify unless there is specific documentary evidence. The higher they got, the more difficult it is to distinguish the archaeological data produced by their activities from that resulting from the activities of free men and women. This is not surprising because convicts on the way up were, in fact, in the process of becoming free. The difficulty for the archaeologist, however, is that it will be the darker sides of convictism that will be most readily available for study, its successes will have often disappeared.

Fortunately this is not always the case. One convict who was immediately grabbed for government service, and who achieved a ticket of leave and an absolute pardon in a relatively short time, was the gifted architect Francis Greenway whose buildings have already been mentioned in Chapter 3. Most of his work consisted of designing public buildings and for this reason there survives a considerable amount of evidence for his remarkable skills. It is with some justice that Greenway has been called 'Australia's first and perhaps greatest architect'.[2] His designs were of what is loosely called the Georgian style, an English expression of classical ideas involving rational and strict control of form, decoration and details. His background was in the architecture of the Bristol area of England, but his Australian buildings have distinctive and original qualities. One of the best known of these buildings is Hyde Park Barracks in Sydney, now easily accessible to the public as a museum. In this building an elegantly proportioned central structure of brick and stone was originally surrounded by an oblong courtyard defined by other buildings and screens. The barracks was intended to hold 400 convicts, but could accommodate 800. As a secure place to lock convicts for the night it was not very successful, but as architecture it was brilliant. Amongst the more remarkable of Greenway's other buildings that still survive are St James' Church, Sydney, St Matthew's Church, Windsor, and the Convict Hospital at Liverpool. These and further buildings establish Greenway quite definitely as a convict who made it to the very top of the stairway, a remarkable achievement for a man who, in 1812, had been sentenced to death for forgery. Admittedly, he was eventually to die in poverty and misery, but to a large degree this was brought about by his own behaviour rather than by his treatment in colonial society.

The archaeological record also contains evidence of other convicts who were successful in rising to the top of the system. One of the most interesting examples is that of the Ross Bridge, spanning the Macquarie River in eastern Tasmania, which has been studied by Maureen Byrne.[3] This beautifully designed and constructed stone bridge, completed in 1836, is one of the oldest surviving bridges in Australia (Figure 5.2). The credit for its erection, accomplished in just over a year after six years of corruption, inefficiency and

Figure 5.2 Ross Bridge, Tasmania, 1976. View from north, with mechanical excavator in use during resurfacing. (Photograph by Maureen Byrne, courtesy of Ian Jack.)

mismanagement by others, must go to two convict masons, James Colbeck and Daniel Herbert. The bridge consists of three equal arches supporting a symmetrical structure that has, at each corner, a curved flight of stone steps down to the river bank. Built of a local sandstone that varies from white to yellow, the bridge is approximately 38 metres long and its carriageway about 8 metres wide. Its most remarkable feature, however, consists of 186 intricate carvings on the outer faces of the stones that make up the arches, 31 over each arch. Many of these carvings are not directly representational although stylized wool bales and wheat sheaves can be recognized. Others depict an amazing assortment of animal and human figures including a crowned beast that grips a lamb in its claws, a Celtic horned god, a Tasmanian Aborigine and a number of individuals who can be identified. Among these are a local grazier, a schoolmaster, the sixteenth-century John Calvin, a Danish adventurer and his wife, the Governor George Arthur caricatured in his top hat, Daniel Herbert's wife and even Daniel Herbert himself. Thus, although the imposing inscriptions on the bridge make no mention of the two masons who produced this masterpiece, one of them at least made sure that he was not forgotten. This fact, plus the caricature of the Governor, would suggest that these craftsmen knew just how indispensable their services were. Indeed, their payment for completion of the bridge was their emancipation, which was promised as an incentive before they started and granted after they had finished. They, like Greenway, had made it to the top of the convict stairway.

There were, of course, many other less-gifted convicts who still managed to graduate from government service, or from assignment, to a ticket of leave and perhaps even a conditional pardon. Again, some of the stages of their progress have left material evidence that is available for study. On the pastoral stations of the Braidwood district of southeastern New South Wales, for instance, the assigned convicts lived in small barrack buildings consisting of a large room with a fireplace and a sleeping loft above. Dennis Jeans has described an example of one of these that was in use on Ballalaba Station in the 1830s; this survives as a solid building constructed of coursed granite rubble and the iron bars are still in position on the windows. For safety and privacy it was located nearly 2 kilometres from the station homestead, but at Mount Elrington, another station in the Braidwood district, the convict barracks actually forms a wing of the house itself. Some indication of the importance of convicts in the early years of settlement in this district may be gained from the fact that, in 1841, the male population was 814, of whom 305 were convicts, with most of them living on the stations. This necessitated a district headquarters for convict administration, of which a storehouse survives as a fine granite-built ruin on Strathallan Station (Figure 5.3). With it is the remains of a row of punishment cells, for this place acted as a headquarters for convict road gangs working in the vicinity as well as, no doubt, keeping an eye on local assigned convicts.[4]

Some convicts were not assigned to private landholders but remained in government service. This was particularly common before the 1820s. Whereas assigned convicts were provided with accommodation by their employers, government convicts had to be housed by the government. This was done either in specially constructed barracks, of which Hyde Park Barracks in Sydney is a notable example, or in do-it-yourself huts like the one excavated at Parramatta (see Chapter 3). This hut is direct evidence of a settlement of convicts, in government service, who were Australia's first successful agriculturalists. A similar agricultural settlement existed from 1801 to 1811 at Castle Hill, northwest of Sydney, and, although its surface archaeological traces are limited, it probably has considerable excavation potential.[5] Convicts retained in government service seem often to have included people with special skills. It seems likely, for instance, that the remarkable brick barrel-drain in Parramatta, parts of which have been excavated by Ted Higginbotham, was constructed by convicts during the 1820s — one of the three types of sandstock brick used in its construction is marked with a broad arrow indicating that it was a public work. As there

Figure 5.3   Granite-built storehouse of the district headquarters for convict administration, Strathallan Station, Braidwood district, New South Wales. (Photograph by Dennis Jeans.)

54

Figure 5.4 Brick barrel-drain at Parramatta, probably built by convicts during the 1820s. Diameter about 1200mm. (Photograph by Edward Higginbotham.)

was a convict barracks in Parramatta it was presumably a labour force from there that did the work. Whoever did it certainly knew how to lay bricks (Figure 5.4).[6]

Convicts who did not behave themselves went down the stairway, sometimes to the very bottom. The first two steps down, being put in a labour gang or in an iron gang, have left archaeological evidence that is similar. These gangs (Figure 5.5) were employed on public works, often deep in the bush, and this meant that they had to be housed in temporary, guarded camps that came to be known as 'stockades' — so called because they were at first surrounded by a high staked fence. Accommodation in these camps sometimes consisted of tents or of rough huts erected by the convicts themselves; sometimes it consisted of small sheds on wheels in which twenty men slept in a space measuring 4.3 by 2.2 metres and 1.8 metres high; sometimes it was even in the form of prefabricated and demountable buildings which could be moved elsewhere when the immediate job was finished. Whatever the form of the stockades, they were essentially of a temporary nature and therefore difficult to identify in the archaeological record. One of these has been studied by Grace Karskens, who has conducted a detailed survey of the surface remains of the convict road station at Wisemans Ferry, on the Hawkesbury River, northwest of Sydney. Dating from the late 1820s and early 1830s, the remains at this site consist of only a few tumbled groups of stones, seeming to indicate two separate encampments, with Group 1 representing an earlier, more roughly built assortment of structures, and Group 2 representing a slightly later attempt to improve both the accommodation and the security (Figure 5.6).[7]

The actual work that was accomplished by these convict gangs was of a more permanent character and in some cases it has survived for us to study and to admire. Thus, although the remains of the convict road station at Wisemans Ferry are not very impressive, the massive stone retaining walls that were built along parts of the Great North Road by the men who

Figure 5.5   Convict gang in Sydney, some in irons, most not. This drawing was originally published in A. Earle, 1830. *Views in New South Wales and Van Diemen's Land*, London. (By courtesy of the Mitchell Library, Sydney.)

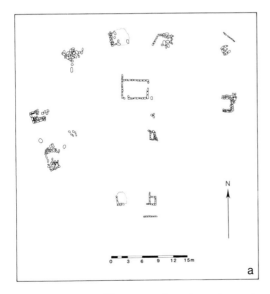

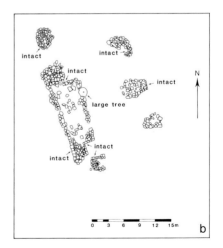

Figure 5.6   Site of convict road station at Wisemans Ferry, New South Wales. (a) Plan of Group 1 earlier structures. (b) Plan of Group 2 later structures. (Courtesy of Grace Karskens.)

lived in camps such as this are very impressive indeed. Some examples of the best workmanship can be seen on Devine's Hill, north of Wisemans Ferry, where retaining walls of beautiful ashlar masonry, with some of the individual stones up to a metre square, rise to a height of over 9 metres. It seems that amongst the convict gangs who worked on this road there were those capable of work of the highest quality. Others, however, did poorer work, and some did very poor work indeed. As Grace Karskens has pointed out, the varying quality of the workmanship has much to tell us about the skills and the attitudes, not only of the surveyors and the overseers, but also of the convicts themselves.[8] These were gangs of men, many of them in chains, who punched a new road through difficult country all the way from Sydney to the Hunter Valley. It is difficult not to be impressed by this achievement, which took ten years to accomplish and was done with forced labour. The Great North Road, like the Great West Road over the Blue Mountains, was a remarkable convict contribution.

Labour gangs and iron gangs did more than just build roads. In the early 1840s, they quarried away the whole of the top of Pinchgut Island in Sydney Harbour and prepared the site on which Fort Denison was subsequently constructed. This fort, complete with martello tower, survives as an intriguing example of mid-nineteenth-century harbour fortification. Convict gangs also worked on Goat Island in Sydney Harbour constructing a powder magazine, a barracks for its guard and a wharf. This was during the 1830s, and substantial parts of the results of their labours are still standing. After the completion of that work the same convict workforce was transferred to Cockatoo Island, also in Sydney Harbour, where they were employed to construct a gaol, much of which survives.[9] These are but a few of the more notable examples of important public works that were accomplished by convicts as a form of punishment. Indeed, Goat Island has one piece of archaeological evidence that serves as a vivid reminder of some of the more objectionable aspects of that punishment. This is a man-sized bench cut into a rock on the south side of the island. Oral tradition describes this as the sleeping place of a convict called Charles Anderson, who is known from historical sources to have slept in such a hollow when he was chained to a rock on this island as a punishment. When we look at some of the things that were accomplished by convict labour gangs and iron gangs, it is well to remember the price that was paid in human suffering.

It was the penal settlements, however, that achieved the reputation of specializing in human suffering, and it was to these that convicts were sent if service in an iron gang failed to moderate their behaviour. At one time or another there were penal settlements at Port Macquarie and Cockatoo Island in New South Wales, at Moreton Bay, in what is now Queensland, at Maria Island off the southeast coast of Van Diemen's Land (now Tasmania), and at Sarah Island in Macquarie Harbour, also in Tasmania. Situated on the bleak western coast of Tasmania, it was Sarah Island that was the most dreaded. With incessant rain, and winds so strong that the settlement had to be protected by specially constructed fences up to 9 metres in height, it was so inaccessible and in such difficult country that there was nowhere for the convicts to escape to. Eventually it was closed down by the government because of the inconvenience of its extraordinary remoteness. In contrast, both Port Macquarie and Moreton Bay gradually became insufficiently remote with the spread of settlement so that they were too easy to escape from.

All these penal settlements and some others have long interested historians, but archaeologists have concentrated their attention on the two best-known examples which have not yet been mentioned. These are Norfolk Island, far to the east of the New South

Wales coast and actually closer to New Zealand than to Australia, and Port Arthur, on the Tasman Peninsula in the southeast of Tasmania. In both of these places substantial buildings were erected and, as a consequence of this and of their relative remoteness, extensive physical remains have survived to the present time. These places constitute, without any doubt, two of Australia's most important historic sites.

The earlier of these two settlements was Norfolk Island which was originally occupied in the same year as Sydney Cove and which, from an early date, was used as a place to which were sent convicts serving life sentences and those convicts who were found to be intractable. For reasons of economy the island was abandoned in 1814, but was reoccupied in 1825 with the purpose of creating a place of severe punishment. From then until 1856, the entire island formed a penal colony that was justifiably notorious and at one time numbered 1500 people. The main settlement was at Kingston, on the south side of the island, where a considerable number of stone buildings, stone ruins and sites survive. These include Government House and its associated buildings, a row of buildings that provided accommodation for officials, a commissariat store, two military barracks, a prisoners' barracks, a hospital, a lumberyard and a crankmill where prisoners ground the settlement's grain by sheer muscle-power. Particularly interesting, from the point of view of the development of prison design during the nineteenth century, is the radial layout of the foundations of the New Jail (Figure 5.7). This took some years to build and suffered several modifications of

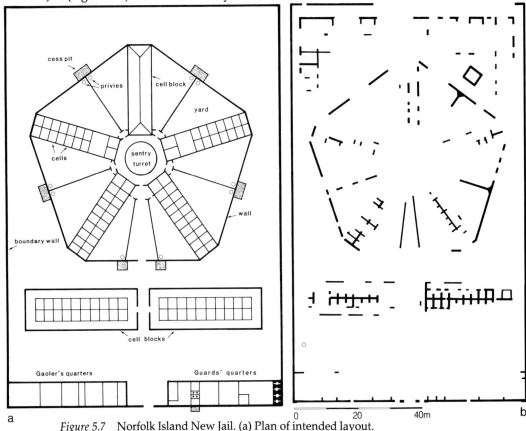

Figure 5.7 Norfolk Island New Jail. (a) Plan of intended layout.
(After Kerr 1984.) (b) Plan of archaeological traces. (After Wilson and Davies 1983.)

plan, being finished only shortly before the entire penal settlement was closed. Its traces provide an archaeological reminder that official incompetence is nothing new. Other features of archaeological interest in the Kingston area include a group of underground grain silos, the site of a windmill, the remains of several limekilns, the ruin of a saltworks, a cemetery, a watermill, several bridges, a series of drainage channels and a number of quarries. In other parts of the island there are also archaeological features at Longridge and at Cascade, as well as the remains of small cottages nearer to Kingston itself. The archaeological potential of Norfolk Island is obviously substantial, and includes far more structures and features than have been mentioned here. There is one more site that cannot be forgotten, because somehow it epitomizes the whole sorry history of this penal settlement. This is the so-called 'Murderers' Mound' in Kingston, where twelve of the convicts who were executed after an uprising in July 1846 were buried in unconsecrated ground. They were buried in a disused sawpit and covered with a mound of earth — in an age when reverence for the dead was paramount, their punishment extended even to the grave.[10]

Port Arthur, Tasmania, originated as a timber-getting establishment in 1830, but it was soon developed into a large and important penal settlement that eventually replaced both Macquarie Harbour and Maria Island in Tasmania. It was seen not only as a place of punishment, but also as a place of economic usefulness. Thus it is important to consider it in the context of the whole of the Tasman Peninsula, particularly during the 1840s when a number of convict out-stations on the peninsula were developed as probationary settlements (Figure 5.8). Indeed, the entire peninsula was really one gigantic prison, with a cordon of ferocious dogs and lights, and a constable and military guard making sure that no convicts escaped across the narrow neck of land that connected the peninsula to the rest of Tasmania. Eagle Hawk Neck, as this heavily guarded piece of ground was called, has rightly passed into the historical mythology of Australian convictism. In this case, however, the mythology can hardly exaggerate the reality.

Central to the convict stations of the Tasman Peninsula was the Port Arthur settlement itself. This was laid out with a complete range of settlement buildings of a permanent character. Thus there was accommodation for the convicts, a military barracks, a wharf, a hospital, store buildings, houses for officials, a residence for the commandant and a church. There were also places of work to keep the convicts busy including a bakehouse, a carpenter's shop, a shoemaker's shop, a blacksmith's shop and a shipyard. In addition, huge numbers of bricks were manufactured, lime was burnt, stone was quarried, timber was sawn and gardens and farms were cultivated. As time went on, the ingenuity of the authorities became even more impressive. In the early 1840s, a huge four-storeyed brick building was constructed as a granary and flour mill. This featured a treadmill that was driven by convicts walking on a moving staircase. Although a common enough feature of Australian convict establishments, the Port Arthur treadmill was an outsize version that required no less than twelve men at a time and was supplemented by a waterwheel. After 1857 the building was converted into a penitentiary, and has survived till the present time as one of Port Arthur's most notable ruins. Perhaps the most impressive of the many convict activities on the Tasman Peninsula, however, was the development of extensive underground coal mines on the north coast of the peninsula. These functioned during the 1830s and 1840s and seem to have been the main reason for another remarkable achievement: the construction of one of Australia's first railways. This ran for 7.2 kilometres from north to south across the peninsula and carried small 0.5-tonne carts that were pushed along the

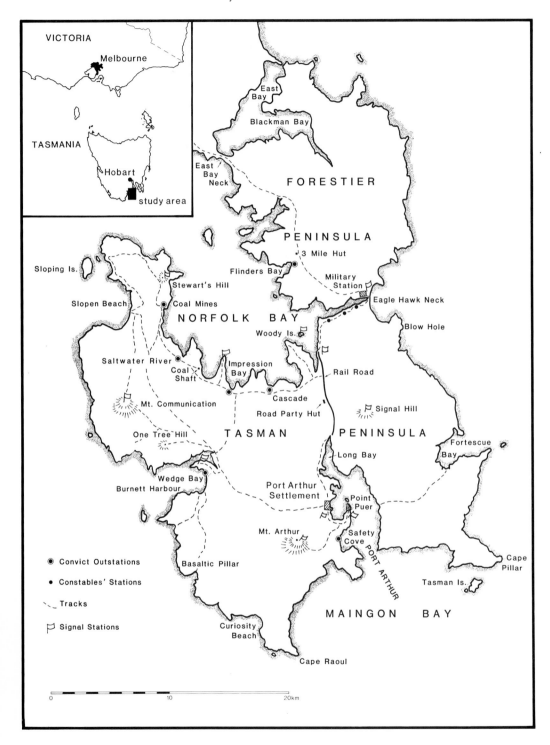

Figure 5.8 The Tasman and Forestier Peninsulas in the 1840s. (After Kerr 1984.)

wooden rails by convicts. Constructed in 1836, it was still working in the 1850s and, indeed, was still in existence when Port Arthur was finally abandoned as a penal settlement in 1877. Port Arthur and its associated out-stations seemed to have everything. It even had a special establishment for boys, suitably removed from the main settlement, and located at the appropriately named Point Puer.[11]

The very varied convict activities at Port Arthur and in other parts of the Tasman Peninsula have left a rich archaeological record. There are extensive building remains at Port Arthur itself and other structures at Cascade Probation Station, at Coal Mines Station and elsewhere. So far archaeological studies have concentrated on Port Arthur, where a number of investigations have been carried out. Martin Davies and Brian Egloff, for instance, have been able to show, by careful structural analysis, how the Commandants' House changed and grew through time to meet the different demands that were made on it (Figure 5.9). Some excavations have also been undertaken, such as those by Maureen Byrne, on the site of the earliest prisoners' barracks. A study of the clay smoking pipes from this site, by Alexandra Dane and Richard Morrison, has revealed that ninety-five per cent of the identifiable examples were manufactured in Scotland, almost all in Glasgow. Comparison of the dates of occupation indicated by these pipes with the historically known dates of occupation shows a reasonably close agreement, and throws light on the reliability of such archaeological dating methods on historical archaeological sites that lack documentation. Other excavations include those at Port Arthur's Dockyard Cottage, 'Lithend', where Angela McGowan has discovered that the building was constructed over the remains of a blacksmith's shop, dating from before 1848, and that, prior to this structure, there was a sawpit in the area.[12] Port Arthur lasted longer than any other penal settlement in Australia and it is likely that the full potential of archaeological research at this site has not yet been demonstrated.

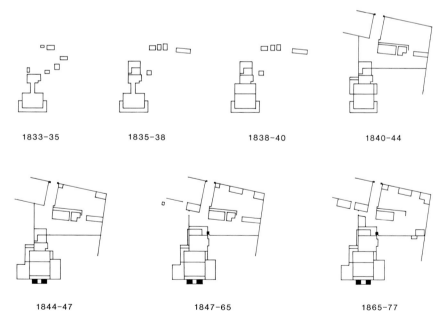

| 1833–35 | 1835–38 | 1838–40 | 1840–44 |
| 1844–47 | 1847–65 | 1865–77 | |

Figure 5.9 Simplified plans showing the changes through time to the Commandants' House at Port Arthur. (After Davies and Egloff 1986.)

Convicts made very important contributions to the colonial settlement of Australia and those contributions have, in many cases, left patterns in the archaeological record that can increase our understanding of the convict role. Those patterns reflect the graded character of the penal system. At the top end, the surviving buildings of Francis Greenway represent success and fame. At the bottom end, the 'Murderers' Mound' on Norfolk Island represents failure and disgrace. In between these extremes, the archaeological evidence tells us something of the wide range of activities in which convicts of different grades were engaged and tells us something of the different ways in which society treated them. Archaeology provides a necessary reminder of the debt that Australia owes to these men and women who, both good and bad, played a vital role in the origins of this nation. Anyone who doubts that should ponder the history of Western Australia where, in 1849, after twenty-one years of struggle, the new colony made a special request that convicts be sent there. Between 1850 and 1868, nearly ten thousand of them arrived, and Western Australia never looked back.[13]

Notes

[1] J.S. Kerr, 1984. *Design for convicts: An account of design for convict establishments in the Australian Colonies during the transportation era*, Library of Australian History, Sydney.

[2] M. Dupain, 1980. *Francis Greenway: A celebration*, Cassell, North Ryde.

[3] M. Byrne, 1976. *Ross Bridge, Tasmania*, Australian Society for Historical Archaeology, Studies in Historical Archaeology No.3, Sydney.

[4] D.N. Jeans, 1984. Braidwood, New South Wales. In D.N. Jeans (ed.), *Australian historical landscapes*, Allen & Unwin, North Sydney, pp. 62-73.

[5] J. Birmingham (ed.), 1984. *Castle Hill: Archaeological report*, Heritage Council of New South Wales, Sydney.

[6] E. Higginbotham, 1983. The excavation of a brick barrel-drain at Parramatta, N.S.W. *Australian Journal of Historical Archaeology* 1, pp.35-9, and E. Higginbotham, 1981. The excavation of a brick barrel drain at Parramatta, N.S.W. Unpublished report for Heritage Council of New South Wales, Sydney.

[7] G. Karskens, 1984. The convict road station site at Wisemans Ferry: an historical and archaeological investigation. *Australian Journal of Historical Archaeology* 2, pp.17-26.

[8] G. Karskens, 1986. Defiance, deference and diligence: three views of convicts in New South Wales road gangs. *Australian Journal of Historical Archaeology* 4, pp.17-28.

[9] J.S. Kerr, 1986. *Fort Denison*, National Trust (N.S.W.), Sydney; J.S. Kerr, 1985. *Goat Island*, Maritime Services Board of N.S.W., Sydney; J.S. Kerr, 1984. *Cockatoo Island*, National Trust (N.S.W.), Sydney.

[10] J. Birmingham, 1984. Norfolk Island, New South Wales. In D.N. Jeans (ed.), *Australian historical landscapes*, Allen & Unwin, North Sydney, pp.22-33; and G. Wilson and M. Davies, 1983. *Norfolk Island: The archaeological survey of Kingston and Arthur's Vale* (2 vols), Australian Government Publishing Service, Canberra.

[11] R.I. Jack, 1984. Tasman Peninsula, Tasmania. In D.N. Jeans (ed.), *Australian historical landscapes*, Allen & Unwin, North Sydney, pp.48-61; J. Birmingham, I. Jack and D. Jeans, 1979. *Australian pioneer technology: sites and relics*, Heinemann, Richmond, Victoria; J. Birmingham, I. Jack and D. Jeans, 1983. *Industrial archaeology in Australia: rural industry*, Heinemann, Richmond, Victoria. Also J.S. Kerr, 1984.

[12] M. Davies and B.J. Egloff, 1986. The Commandants' Residence at Port Arthur: An archaeological perspective. In G.K. Ward (ed.), *Archaeology at ANZAAS Canberra*, Canberra Archaeological Society, Canberra, pp.46-55; A. Dane and R. Morrison, 1979. *Clay pipes from Port Arthur 1830-1877*, Technical Bulletin No.2, Department of Prehistory, Research School of Pacific Studies, Australian National University, Canberra; A. McGowan, 1985. *Excavations at Lithend, Port Arthur Historic Site*, National Parks and Wildlife Service, Tasmania, Occasional Paper No.11, Sandy Bay.

[13] J.M.R. Cameron, 1981. *Ambition's fire: The agricultural colonization of pre-convict Western Australia*, University of Western Australia Press, Nedlands.

Chapter 6

'I built a little homestead'

EXTRACTING HISTORY FROM HOUSES

The first task of European settlers arriving in Australia or of colonial Australians moving into a part of the continent that was new to them was to build somewhere to live. Initially the shelter might be rough and temporary, to be replaced by something better when circumstances permitted. Nevertheless, however small, of whatever materials, and irrespective of the quality of its construction it was still a home, usually for a group of people, often for a family group. As time went on, succeeding generations also built houses or added to those of their forbears. Almost every family wanted its own separate house, and almost every individual wanted a measure of privacy within that house. By the middle of the twentieth century, as the architect Robin Boyd pointed out in his classic book *Australia's home*, a population of just over eight million had built nearly two million houses.[1] With the population now twice that figure the number of houses is commensurately greater. It is possible that houses form the most numerous category of material evidence for Australia's history. They are also representative of all its periods: the oldest surviving colonial building in Australia (Elizabeth Farm, Parramatta, 1793-4) is a house and, even as you read this, houses are still being built.

'Buildings', wrote the architectural historian J.M. Freeland, 'carry more history than a library of books — and it is not second-hand.'[2] Houses are particularly informative documents and especially valuable for the light they shed on patterns of human behaviour. More so in the past than in the present, houses have been inextricably associated with a greater range of human activities than any other type of building. People have slept in them, have prepared and eaten their food in them, have taken their recreation and entertained their friends in them. They have been born in them, spent much of their childhood in them, have made love in them, have lain ill in them, have died in them. Houses have been the scene of remarkable family solidarity and continuity and they have equally been the places where families have disintegrated and people have sometimes resorted to violence. In short, houses have been and remain containers of human life, sometimes over very long periods. If we can but learn to read the evidence there is clearly a great deal that houses have to tell us and there are a great many of them around for us to study.

Archaeologists in many parts of the world have long been interested in the houses of the remote past and have frequently excavated the last traces of a house plan in order to learn about the people who lived there. Indeed, excavation is an appropriate means of investigating some of the earliest houses of colonial Australia which have left little or no surface remains. Very large numbers of older houses are still standing, however, and many of them are still in use. The archaeologist can study these without excavation and, by so doing, can gain information that will be of great value when interpreting excavated evidence from the sites of houses long vanished. There is now a growing interest in what is loosely called the archaeology of standing structures. Of such structures, houses clearly form a very important part. Some people have been surprised that archaeologists should be interested in buildings that not only still have their roofs on but still have people living in them. It is the business of the archaeologist, however, to extract information from things that were made by human beings in the past. Surely it would be foolish to limit such studies merely to the remnants that have survived beneath the ground while ignoring complete structures that are still standing? Houses are artefacts, archaeologists study artefacts — why confine oneself to broken or buried examples when there are complete ones around?

From the archaeologist's point of view, one of the most interesting things about Australian houses is the variety of building materials and constructional techniques that have been used in the past.[3] The European colonizers of Australia, mainly, but by no means exclusively from the British Isles, were able to draw on the varied building traditions of their homelands in order to handle a wide range of materials. At the same time they had to adapt to the particular conditions of the part of Australia in which they found themselves and adopt the materials and techniques that were most suited to their locality and to their circumstances. In so doing they sometimes built in ways that would have been unusual in their countries of origin and sometimes had to find totally new methods of building.

Stone was the material to which most prestige was attached. It was the favoured material for public buildings and was used in many areas in the houses of the more wealthy. However, it was also used in far humbler dwellings, in a more rough-and-ready fashion, particularly in regions where it was readily available without laborious and expensive quarrying. The extent to which houses were built of stone obviously depended very much on the geology of the area concerned and on the ready availability of alternative materials. Sydney was fortunate in possessing a sandstone of high quality that was relatively easy to quarry and to dress. Fremantle, in Western Australia, was similarly lucky with its easily worked limestone. In South Australia, Victoria and Tasmania there were also places that were particularly well endowed with building stone. In Queensland, however, the ready availability of timber meant that stone was relatively rarely used for domestic building. In contrast, people in some of the drier areas of the continent, which lacked timber suitable for building, had to make use of almost any stone that was available. Thus, in the far west of New South Wales, building in stone was more common than in the eastern parts of the state where the rainfall was much higher (Figure 6.1).

The walls of houses could be built of stone in a number of different ways depending on the characteristics of the particular material and also on the skill of the builder and on the finances of the intended occupier. There were three main types of masonry (Figure 6.2), each of which, in practice, had their own variants. At the top end of the scale there was 'ashlar' work, where pieces of stone were each dressed into a standard rectangular shape and size and laid in horizontal courses, usually with a lime mortar which formed narrow, uniform joints. For this sort of masonry one needed an easily worked stone, such as the Sydney sandstone, and one needed skilled masons and builders. Next was 'coursed random rubble', where roughly rectangular stones of a variety of sizes were laid in such a way that collectively they comprised regular horizontal courses. The joints between the individual stones and between the courses were wider and less uniform than was the case with ashlar, and the bonding material might be a lime mortar or might merely be clay. The poorest quality of masonry was 'random rubble', where stones of different sizes and shapes were bonded together with either a lime or clay mortar, but without any regular coursing being apparent. Both coursed random rubble and random rubble techniques made it possible to build with hard or otherwise intractable stones, such as granite and basalt, and less knowledge of the mason's craft was required, although to do them well one needed a skilled builder. Indeed, to make even the roughest stone walls stand up needs a surprising amount of skill, as anyone who has ever attempted the task will agree.

Stone was also used in housing construction for purposes other than walling. Slates for roofing came both from Wales or the United States, and from local sources in South Australia, Tasmania, Victoria and New South Wales. Flagstones were sometimes used for flooring, particularly in entrance halls or in kitchens. Stone was especially valuable, however, for the construction of chimneys for houses of wood or of other highly combustible materials. Failing this, some wooden chimneys were lined with stones and clay in order to reduce the danger of fire. Scattered across the paddocks of many parts of Australia are small heaps of chimney stones that are all that remain of early settlers' houses. Occasionally, a particularly well-built stone chimney, or one of rather later date, still stands as a solitary reminder of a vanished house.

Almost as durable as many stones, and rather easier to build with, were bricks. These have been used for housing construction throughout Australia's history. The earliest bricks were handmade and often rather poorly fired, but as time went on machine-made bricks became available and firing methods were improved. The use of bricks for housebuilding

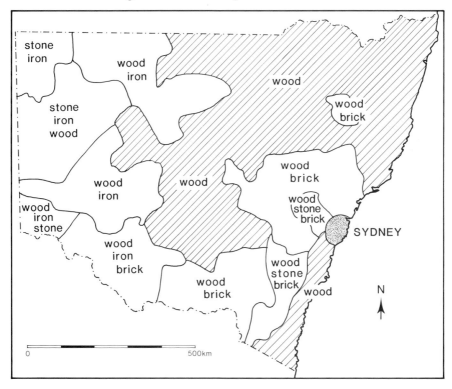

Figure 6.1 Building materials of house walls in rural New South Wales in 1901. (After D.N. Jeans and P. Spearritt, 1980. *The open air museum: The cultural landscape of New South Wales*, Allen & Unwin, North Sydney.)

STONE COURSING   BRICK BONDS

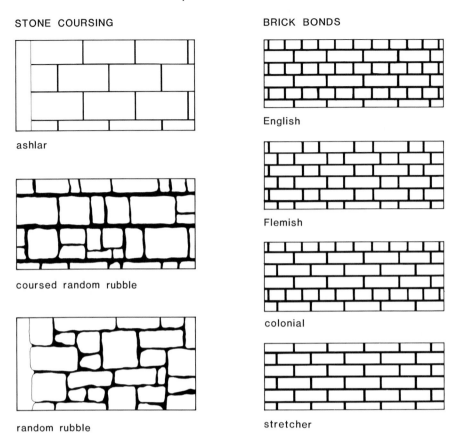

ashlar

English

coursed random rubble

Flemish

colonial

random rubble

stretcher

Figure 6.2 Principal building techniques in stone and brick. (After
Stapleton and others, 1980.)

depended, as with stone, on the geology of the area concerned, for there had to be clays or
shales that were readily available. In the case of bricks, however, there also had to be large
supplies of a suitable fuel, either firewood or coal. The raw material, the fuel and the
finished bricks were all heavy and expensive to transport, so that brick production and
building in brick tended to be restricted to suitable localities until fairly recent times (Figure
6.1).

If bricks were available in an area, and if the housebuilder could afford to use them, then
the major question was how to tie the bricks together to produce walls of adequate strength.
There are four main brick 'bonds' that have been commonly employed in Australian
housebuilding (Figure 6.2). Ordinary bricks are made with their length equal to twice their
width, so that two bricks laid side by side across a wall are equal to one brick laid longways,
therefore creating a bond. Bricklayers in colonial Australia used bonds that had been
employed successfully for several centuries in Britain. 'English bond', for instance, consisted of alternate courses of 'stretchers' (bricks side-on) and 'headers' (bricks end-on),
while 'Flemish bond' consisted of alternating stretchers and headers in each course.
Because of the necessity to stagger the vertical joints in brickwork (as also in stonework),
Flemish bond produced an attractive decorative pattern if it was laid properly. Both English

and Flemish bonds produced strong walls, but the task of bricklaying was made easier if headers were only used in every fourth or fifth course. This produced what was known as 'Colonial bond', which (in spite of its name) had also been used in Britain for some time. It also produced a weaker wall. The fourth and final type of bond, 'stretcher bond', has only become common in relatively recent times. Many Australians now live in brick veneer houses which consist of a skin of stretcher-bond brickwork covering a wooden framework, but this is a twentieth-century technique. At a somewhat earlier date, in the latter part of the nineteenth century, stretcher bond was also necessitated by the building of cavity walls which consisted of two separate skins of brickwork held together with cast-iron ties. This innovation was, along with the development of damp-proof courses, designed to prevent dampness either penetrating a brick wall or rising from the ground on which it stood. Moisture was a long-standing problem with brick walls and, prior to these developments, many such walls were coated with lime-wash or plastered with stucco in an attempt to control it.

As with stone, bricks were also used for purposes other than walls. They were sometimes employed for paving floors or for constructing underground water tanks. They were essential for making a good bread oven, and hearth and chimney were often constructed of bricks when all the rest of the house was of wood or some other less durable material. The roofing equivalent of the brick is the terracotta tile, and these were used in huge numbers on Australian houses from the late nineteenth century onwards. Originally they were imported from France, becoming known as Marseilles tiles, but from the time of World War I they were manufactured in Australia.

Whether the walls of a house were of stone or of brick, the building material had to be bonded together with mortar. Until quite late in the nineteenth century the best available mortar consisted of a soft mixture of sand, lime and water. Only in more recent times have cement mortars become usual. The problem for many early settlers in Australia was that sources of limestone were limited and sometimes so far away that the price of lime was prohibitive. As the geology of the continent became better known more deposits of limestone were discovered, but the earliest settlers of Sydney, for instance, had to make do with poor mortars of clay or loam, or with mixtures of animal hair, sand and lime obtained by burning seashells, which, in many instances, were dug from prehistoric Aboriginal shell middens. Even in later times, settlers in districts remote from sources of lime or settlers who simply could not or would not pay for lime, had to rely on clay or other earthy mortars. Thus, Captain William Richards, building an imposing stone house in the wilds of the New England Tablelands of New South Wales during the late 1840s, used only clay for the mortar of its walls.[4] The general tendency towards single-storey construction in Australian houses (in contrast to the two or more storeys common in Britain) resulted not only from the greater availability of space but also from the former lack of mortars strong enough to carry walls above a certain height. Similarly, the prevalence of the hipped roof on earlier Australian houses may have resulted, in part, from the necessity to avoid building high gable walls.

Houses of stone or brick were fine for those who could afford them or who lived in a suitable area, but the most commonly used building material in colonial Australia was wood, and as most settlement took place in regions where forest resources were plentiful they were exploited to the full. Many of the early settlers were not unfamiliar with methods of building in wood, but most Australian timbers proved too hard and intractable to do much shaping with the tools available. For this reason, one of the most common ways of building in timber was to construct a framework of logs that supported walls of split slabs (Figure 6.3) topped by a roof structure of saplings. The roof would then be covered with large sheets of bark removed from trees using methods learnt from Aborigines. A settler in a remote spot could build such a dwelling using only axe, mallet, wedges, saw and a few iron spikes, and perhaps with the assistance only of his wife and children. The slabs were usually set vertically, but horizontal slabs were also used and, as time went on, the slabs might be pit-sawn, or even power-sawn, rather than split. Some houses were even constructed of logs in the American fashion, but the relative rarity of Australian trees with straight trunks of uniform thickness made this rather unusual. The most typical bush dwelling of much of nineteenth-century Australia was the slab cottage with bark roof. It was quite likely a homestead of this sort that Henry Lawson had in mind when he wrote his poem *Reedy River*. Indeed, one of the most quaint artefacts to survive from nineteenth-century Australia is a contemporary model of such a dwelling that was built at McDonald's Creek, near Mudgee in New South Wales, sometime prior to 1857 (Figure 6.4).

A somewhat more sophisticated way of building in wood consisted of a sawn timber framework clad in weatherboarding (Figure 6.3) and with a roof of wooden shingles. Very large numbers of houses were built in this way after the development of power-sawing from the 1830s onwards. That innovation, plus the increasing availability of cheap machine-made nails, made it possible to construct relatively light frameworks which could be clad outside and inside with boarding. Prior to power-sawing, it had been both laborious and expensive to pit-saw the enormous quantity of lumber that was necessary for this type of building. Furthermore, before machine-made nails became common, every nail had had to be made by hand at the forge, so that the time-consuming method of mortise-and-tenon joints secured with wooden pegs was often used instead of nails. Such relatively heavy

Figure 6.3 Principal building techniques in wood. *Left:* split slabs and shingle roofing. *Right:* sawn framework and weatherboarding. (After D. N. Jeans and P. Spearritt 1980. *The open air museum*, Allen & Unwin, North Sydney.)

Figure 6.4   Model of slab cottage with bark roof, built by James
Rushby at McDonald's Creek, near Mudgee, New South Wales. The
model was made by his daughter, Charlotte, prior to 1857. (By
courtesy of Women's Committee, National Trust (N.S.W.), and of
the Trustees, Museum of Applied Arts and Sciences, Sydney.)

framework was sometimes filled with brickwork, a technique known as 'brick-nogging',
and plastered on the inside. From the 1850s onwards, however, the by then lighter
frameworks could be clad with sheets of corrugated galvanized iron, a material that became
very popular for roofing but was also used for walls. In Queensland, the framework of the
walls was left bare on the outside and lined with corrugated sheets on the inside to produce
one of the most characteristic features of a specialized tropical dwelling, one that has
become known to architects as 'the Queensland house'.[5]

Wood was also used in a variety of other ways in traditional Australian housebuilding.
With the aid of a light sapling framework it was possible to construct a dwelling of which the
walls, as well as the roof, consisted merely of sheets of bark. More remarkably, perhaps,
some of the early German settlers of South Australia employed sophisticated timber-
framing techniques that are reminiscent of late medieval building methods in Western
Europe. They also sometimes constructed dwellings that had a supporting wooden framework of earthfast posts that were buried within non-load-bearing stone walls.[6] There was
an amazing number of ways in which wood could be used in housebuilding and, of course,
even dwellings with stone or brick walls needed a considerable amount of timber for their

roof structures, windows, doors and other fittings. Timber has remained an important component in house construction and, since late in the nineteenth century, substantial quantities, particularly of softwoods, have been imported from overseas.

There was one further way of using wood in housebuilding that has not been mentioned, and this was wattle-and-daub. Comprising one of the five different ways of building with earth that were employed in colonial Australia, it is best considered with those techniques that are so often confused by modern writers. Wattle-and-daub could be done in several ways, but basically it consisted of mud plaster over a framework of thin branches that was used as an infill for timber-framed buildings (Figure 6.5). A very different method of earth construction was that of pisé, in which loam mud was rammed into a wooden formwork

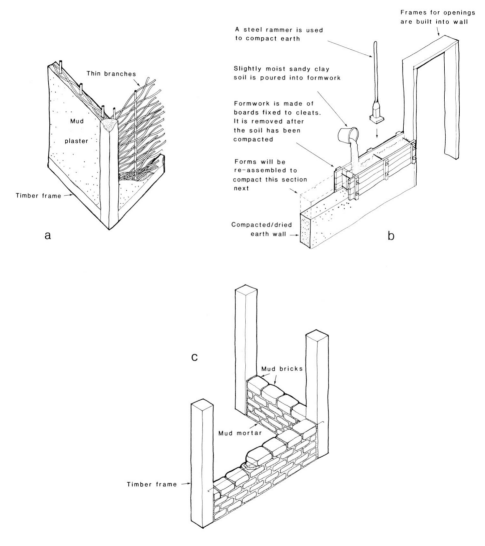

Figure 6.5 Principal building techniques in earth. (a) Wattle-and-daub. (After Young 1986.) (b) Pisé. (After Irving 1985.) (c) Adobe. (After Irving 1985.)

that was moved along the wall, bit by bit, and upwards, layer by layer, as the material dried and hardened (Figure 6.5). Like all methods of building in earth, pisé required certain types of soils and was more suited to drier environments. Nevertheless, cultural factors were also important in the selection of building techniques and it is interesting to observe that pisé houses occurred in the late-nineteenth-century Italian settlement of New Italy, near the Richmond River in sub-tropical northern New South Wales. Pisé was fairly widely used for housebuilding in Australia and, if it could be suitably protected against moisture, it lasted a long time (Figure 6.6). The oldest-known pisé building is a two-storey house, Wanstead Park, near Campbell Town in Tasmania, that was built in 1827. A third method of building that used earth as a raw material was adobe, in which clay was puddled with chopped straw, formed into large bricks in moulds, and left to dry. These sun-dried bricks could then be laid in courses using a mud mortar (Figure 6.5). Adobe houses were not as common in Australia as those of pisé, but they occurred in many areas, being known in South Australia, Victoria, New South Wales and Queensland. The last two methods of building with earth seem to have been even less common in Australia. These consisted of sod walling, in which lumps of turf were employed as a building material, and cob, in which walls were built of clay piled up in layers without any formwork and then trimmed smooth. None of these methods of earth construction were ever as important for Australian housebuilding as the techniques employing stone, bricks, wood or sheet iron, but earth was free, and its use as a building material not so very difficult to learn. As soon as they lost their roofs, however, houses with earth walls rapidly decayed, so that the amount of archaeological evidence that we have for them is almost certainly underrepresentative. This is a great pity because

Figure 6.6   Pisé building (perhaps a dairy) built in the 1860s at Arding, near Armidale, New South Wales. The photograph shows its condition in 1987. (Photograph by Luke Godwin.)

Australian earth construction reflected a wide range of cultural influences including English, Irish, German, Italian and even Mexican.

Both the materials and the constructional techniques generally used in Australian housebuilding continually remind us of the homelands of many early settlers. They also remind us of the amazing capacity to adapt, to improvise, to 'make do', that became almost an Australian national characteristic. The split slab walls and the bark roofs were indigenous developments, rather than imported techniques. So were some of the more unusual strategies that were resorted to by some settlers in their desperation to create a home. Many lived for long periods of time in tents, others lived in hollow trees or hollow logs,[7] and still others dug themselves subterranean houses. A later innovation was to construct a dwelling from discarded cement sacks soaked in water and allowed to set. Ingenuity was almost limitless and it is hardly surprising that people came to shrug their shoulders and say 'She'll be right'; they often had no choice.

Another aspect of Australian houses that interests the archaeologist is the design and style of the buildings that were constructed. Here again we find evidence of a complex mixture of overseas influences and indigenous ideas. Architectural historians have spent a lot of time studying the changes in the form and appearance of Australian houses that have taken place over the last two hundred years. Architect Robin Boyd was able to recognize five principal plan types, although he pointed out that there was an infinite number of minor variations (Figure 6.7).[8] The principal types consisted of: 'The Primitive Cottage', of only two rooms; 'The Bungalow', of four or six rooms with a central passage; 'The Asymmetrical Front', in which one of the front rooms of the bungalow plan was thrust forward; 'The L-shape', an inverted L-shaped plan of multiple rooms with its main entrance in the internal corner; and 'The Triple-front', in which a multiple-room bungalow plan had a central portion which protruded. The basic inspiration for these plans seems to have been from British dwellings, but Australian conditions brought about two important innovations that appeared at an early date in the design of settlers' houses. The first was the tendency to construct single-storey houses that has already been mentioned. Usually, it was only the house of the wealthy person that had more than one storey. The second innovation was the addition of the verandah to several of the plans. This idea seems to have arrived in Australia via military establishments in British India. In all except more southerly areas the verandah was virtually a climatic necessity for Australian houses. It also extended the living area of houses which were often quite small in size.

Boyd's five principal plans are arranged very approximately in chronological order, but rural conservatism and other complicating factors prevent them from having much value for dating purposes. More useful, in this respect, are the changes in style which occurred as time went on. These did, at times, involve alterations in plan, but more commonly they resulted in differences in the external appearance of both the structure as a whole and of its component parts. A stimulating game that we can all play is to look at the houses of the area in which we live and attempt to guess the construction date of each one. Unless we happen to live in a very recently developed suburb we will soon realize that houses built at different times usually look different. It is by analysing those differences that architectural historians have been able to suggest a stylistic sequence for Australian houses. One of the most useful versions of this was proposed by Robin Boyd, and it is his ideas that are followed here (Figure 6.8).

The first style was that of 'Georgian Primitive', in which houses were built as simplified imitations of fashionable dwellings in Britain. The emphasis was on symmetry, the roof was

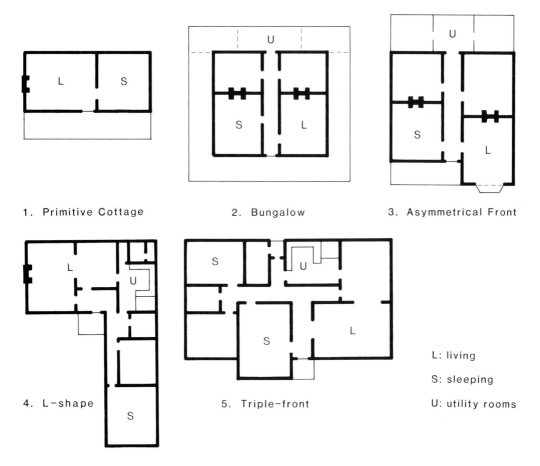

1. Primitive Cottage   2. Bungalow   3. Asymmetrical Front

4. L-shape   5. Triple-front

L: living

S: sleeping

U: utility rooms

Figure 6.7   Principal plan types of Australian houses. (After Boyd 1952.)

high-pitched, usually hipped, and lacked eaves. Quite soon after first settlement this style was modified into 'Colonial Georgian'. This was achieved by the addition of a verandah supported by light, round, wooden columns. After 1840, the most significant style became 'Gothic Revival', characterized by an asymmetrical front, high gables, carved bargeboards, stucco and a wooden porch. In the period from the early 1850s to the early 1880s the 'Italianate' style became typical, with a more heavily ornamented stucco facade incorporating an iron porch with cast-iron lace and a tiled floor. In this style the roof was again hipped. The late 1880s and early 1890s saw the 'Boom Style' burst on the scene, with its extraordinarily heavy ornamentation of the facade. The roof was now hidden behind a stucco parapet or balustrade, and coloured-brick patterning was common along with a cast-iron verandah and coloured glass around the front door. From the late 1890s till World War I, the characteristic style was 'Queen Anne', perhaps better known as the 'Federation Style'. Its chief feature was a red terracotta-tile roof of complex structure, with false gables and decorated ridges. The cast-iron on verandahs was replaced by wooden posts and fretwork. Both the latter and the leadlighted windows featured Art Nouveau motifs which betrayed the European origins of some aspects of this style, just as other features indicated a

73

Figure 6.8(a) Stylistic sequence of Australian houses. *Left*: Georgian Primitive. *Right*: Colonial Georgian. (After Boyd 1952.)

Figure 6.8(b) Stylistic sequence of Australian houses. *Above*: Gothic Revival. *Below*: Italianate. (After Boyd 1952.)

Figure 6.8(c) Stylistic sequence of Australian houses. *Left*: Boom Style. *Right*: Queen Anne or Federation Style. (After Boyd 1952.)

Figure 6.8(d) Stylistic sequence of Australian houses. *Above*: Californian Bungalow. *Below*: Spanish Mission. (After Boyd 1952.)

Figure 6.8(e) Stylistic sequence of Australian houses. *Above*: Waterfall Front. *Below*: Post World War II Austerity. (After Boyd 1952.)

certain amount of American influence. American ideas became more apparent, however, in the next two styles. The first of these was the 'Californian Bungalow' of the 1920s. This was characterized by the chimney becoming part of the facade, by lower gables of which the ends were shingled, by cement-tile roof, clinker-brick chimney and rough-cast walls. Particularly distinctive features were the massive, often tapering pylons which supported the flat roof of the porch. The second of these styles that was American-inspired was the 'Spanish Mission' style, which appeared in Australia in the late 1920s, and became popular in the 1930s. This was marked by smeared yellow stucco, twisted pre-cast concrete columns (often supporting triple arches at the porch), Cordova tiles decorating chimneys and feature walls, boxed eaves, wrought-iron window grille, ornate lantern and a porch with parapet and tiled floor. In contrast, the 'Waterfall Front' style of World War II was very different in appearance. The more pretentious houses, at least, were given rounded corners so that they had a streamlined look. Even the steel windows were curved round the corners, and the glazing bars and the areas of dark brick and cream stucco were arranged in such a way as to emphasize horizontality. The effect was completed by boxed flush eaves and flush front door with a circular window in it. The last of Boyd's styles that need concern us here is that of 'Post World War II Austerity', round about 1950. The most important determinants of this style were shortage of materials and a concern to keep costs as low as possible. All pretensions were abandoned: there were plain windows of wood or steel, the simplest possible porch, red brick walls and a cement-tile roof.

It should now be apparent that two centuries of Australian housebuilding have given us a complex sequence of styles that not only help to date individual buildings, but also demonstrate how overseas ideas were continually adopted, modified and replaced. In practice, however, the situation is very much more complicated than the sequence would suggest. Houses are rarely artefacts frozen in time. As the years go by they are extended, or parts of them are demolished, internal walls are removed or new ones built, windows are replaced, doors are changed, and many smaller fittings wear out and have to be renewed. Thus it is, as archaeologist Peter Coutts once claimed, that 'old buildings tell tales'.[9] That being the case, it is possible to conduct an archaeological analysis of an old house in order to extract from its structure a detailed history that will almost certainly contain more information than any surviving documentary record. The work of Martin Davies and Brian Egloff on the Commandants' House at Port Arthur, which was mentioned at the end of Chapter 5, is a good example of such an analysis (see Figure 5.9).[10] These two archaeologists have adapted the stratigraphic sequence matrix evolved by Edward Harris[11] so that it can be used for the analysis of a building sequence. The result is highly complex (Figure 6.9), but it should serve to remind us that many houses have very complicated structural histories. It is not enough merely to say that a particular house is of such-and-such a style.

Archaeologists are interested in more than just the materials, constructional techniques, design, style and structural history of a house. Houses are places where people live, they are structures that reflect human behaviour. By examining the functions of the various parts of an old house we can begin to understand more about the day-to-day life of the people who lived there. The simplest two-roomed dwellings, for instance, consisted of a bedroom and a living room. At one end of the living room there was a chimney and a fireplace where all the cooking would have been done. The occupants of the house would have used the living room for a wide range of daytime activities including food preparation, eating, resting after work, entertaining friends and so on. The bedroom would have provided space for a number of people to sleep, very likely people of different ages and sex if the occupants were of the one family. Such a house contained no laundry, no kitchen, no bathroom and no toilet. In such a house privacy was virtually unknown, because it was very nearly impossible to achieve. Individuals who grew up in a house of this sort could hardly fail to have their social attitudes influenced by that experience.

As time passed by, the more successful settlers enlarged their two-roomed homes or even replaced them with far more spacious dwellings. Irrespective of their size, however, many houses of the first half of the nineteenth century lacked what we would now regard as basic facilities. A perusal of contemporary plans shows that they ideally consisted of parlour, drawing room, dining room, bedrooms, dressing rooms and access hall or passage. The kitchen was often a separate building behind the house, kept apart from the house not only because of the cooking smells and the heat from the open fire but also because of the fire-risk. By the time food arrived in the dining room it was quite often tepid having been carried for a long distance, sometimes through the open air. Clothes had to be washed by hand, either in the kitchen or in a separate wash-house. The occupants of the house had to wash themselves in a metal bath, each in their own bedroom, and using water that had been heated in the kitchen and laboriously carried to the bedroom in buckets. The toilet was located in a small building some distance from the house and was provided with a cesspit, or emptied regularly by a night-soil service. The smelly condition of such a convenience made it most undesirable to have it situated either in the house or too near to it. This meant that a visit to the toilet at night could be most inconvenient: stumbling along with a lamp, in one's night-clothes, when it might be cold and raining. It was for this reason that every bedroom

'Of the hut I builded'

1960–1980
1920–1960
1900–1920
1880–1900
1870–1880
1865–1870
1854–1865
1847–1848
1844–1845
1839–1844
1838
1837
1834
1833
1830–1831
Pre–1830

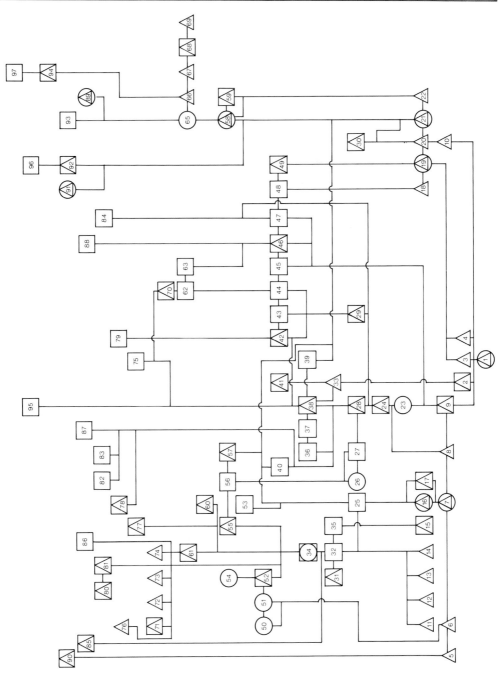

opposite: *Figure 6.9* Structural sequence matrix for the Commandants' House, Port Arthur. Examples of building units considered to be site phases: 1: preconstruction. 2-3: early structure. 4: garden. 5: fowl house. 6: piggery. 7: kitchen I. 8: covered way. 9: timber structure. 10: fence. 11: stable I. 12: privy. 13: shed. 14: store. 15: piers. 16: pavement. 17: kitchen II. 18: paths. 19: ornamental garden. 20: fence. 21: east paths. 22: jetty I. 23: retaining wall. 24: brick addition. 25: second storey on kitchen II. 26: barrel-drain. (Remaining phases omitted.) (After Davies and Egloff 1986.)

△ phase identified from historical document.

▢ phase identified from standing fabric.

◯ phase identified from sub-surface fabric.

was provided with a chamberpot, and, at some time each day, someone would have had the unpleasant task of emptying them and washing them out. When looking at the imposing facade of many a surviving early-nineteenth-century building, it is well to remember those smelly utensils. Thus Sir John Jamison's mansion completed in 1825 at Regentville, near Penrith in New South Wales, had an entrance hall, two drawing rooms, a dining room, a breakfast room, a study, a library and nine bedrooms, but all other facilities were in separate buildings to the rear, except for the wash-house and laundry which were attached to the back of the house.[12]

In the second half of the nineteenth century, and in the early part of this century, houses gradually incorporated all the services that we now take for granted. The kitchen came into the house, the bathroom developed and became a part of the main structure. Piped water, and more efficient means of heating it, assisted in these changes, and led also to the inclusion of a laundry within the house itself. Eventually even the toilet was brought indoors, made possible by the improvement of the water closet and the development of sewerage and septic tank systems. To this day, however, there are still some Australians who think that it is rather unpleasant to have a toilet inside a house; in their view the proper place for it is outside and some distance away.

There are many ways in which old houses can inform us about the manner of life of their former occupants. It is impractical to consider them all, but one further aspect is so very important that it must be given some attention. This concerns the way in which houses are fairly sensitive indicators of the socioeconomic status of their occupants. The sort of house a person lives in and its size and location can tell us quite a lot about that individual's financial position and social pretensions. This seems to have been as true in the past as it is in the present and so it is hardly surprising that archaeologists have long regarded the dwellings of former generations as an extremely important source of information of this sort. To some degree, however, historical archaeologists have a problem when they examine surviving colonial Australian houses with such matters in mind. As has already been pointed out, houses that are being lived in are continually changing. As they age, and perhaps deteriorate, they may also move sharply down the socioeconomic ladder, so that a house originally constructed as a status symbol by a wealthy and powerful owner may, in time, degenerate to slum apartments. Given such a situation it can be difficult for the archaeologist to extract information about the earliest occupants from a structure that has suffered so much modification with the passage of time. For this reason the excavation of the sites of

Figure 6.10   Excavations in progress in 1985 on the main block of Sir John Jamison's mansion at Regentville, near Penrith, New South Wales. (Photograph by Andrew Wilson.)

houses which did not survive beyond their general period of origin can be very helpful. Two strongly contrasting examples will serve to illustrate the point.

The first is the imposing mansion built by Sir John Jamison in 1825, which has already been mentioned. Jamison lived in this house until his death in 1844, after which it was used first as a lunatic asylum and then as a hotel, before being burnt down in 1869. A painstaking archaeological survey of the site by Andrew Wilson, and limited excavations by the author and Judy Birmingham (Figure 6.10) have provided a reasonably detailed plan of this stately residence (Figure 6.11). Here is the dwelling of a man who was one of the richest people in New South Wales. The main block, constructed of sandstone, was two storeys high, with a verandah and first-floor balcony around three sides. It contained a total of sixteen rooms, with cellars beneath it and more rooms in its two wing buildings. In front was a private carriageway, behind it was a large walled yard containing stables, kitchens and other services. The site was chosen carefully so that, from the front verandah or balcony, the occupants could enjoy a superb view across the valley of the Nepean River towards the Blue Mountains beyond. This was a building that proclaimed both wealth and status. Even people at the time acknowledged that it was one of the finest houses in New South Wales.

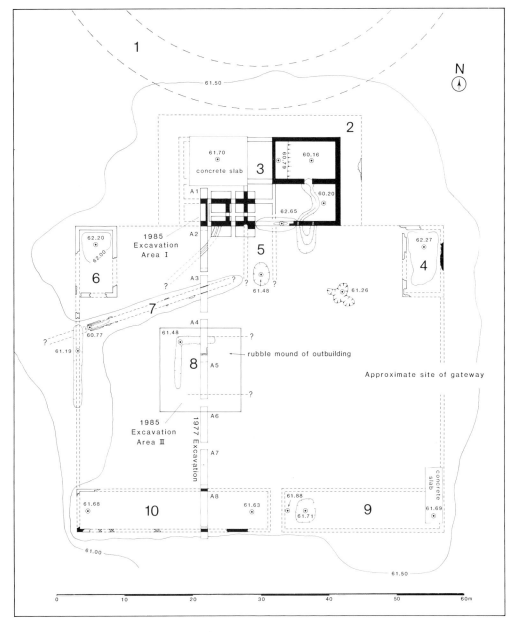

Figure 6.11 Archaeological plan of the site of the Regentville mansion, showing 1985 excavations. Standing or excavated structures are shown in black, walls that are partly visible though buried are shown in outline, conjectured features are indicated by broken lines. Heights are in metres. Numbers are as follows: 1: carriageway. 2: verandah. 3: main block of house (cellars beneath eastern end). 4: billiard room. 5: site of wash-house and laundry. 6: coach house. 7: drain. 8: site of outbuilding containing kitchens etc. (further excavated in 1987). 9 & 10: stables. (Plan by Andrew Wilson, redrawn by Douglas Hobbs.)

81

Contrast that with the tiny one-roomed dwelling that Patrick O'Neil built at White Range on the Arltunga Goldfield in about 1903. This remote part of the Northern Territory, to the northeast of Alice Springs, was the scene of a short-lived and modest gold rush at that time. O'Neil, however, was no ordinary miner. He transported a billiard table to this unlikely spot and set it up in another rough building that was more than twice the size of his dwelling. He obviously hoped to make a profit by providing some entertainment for the bored miners in the vicinity. Although he had his wife with him, his house was of the simplest sort, barely 3.5 metres long with a chimney of undressed stones attached to one end (Figure 6.12). Its floor was of rough stone slabs, its walls and roof of corrugated iron attached to a light wooden framework. We know about Patrick O'Neil's hut because of the excavations of Kate Holmes[13] which have provided useful information about the short-lived settlement of which it was a part. Given the climate of the area, it must have been a harsh existence living in dwellings of this sort. O'Neil's house was about as basic as it could be and suggests not only severely limited finances, but also local shortage of materials and short-term expediency in a settlement that was probably never regarded as anything more than temporary.

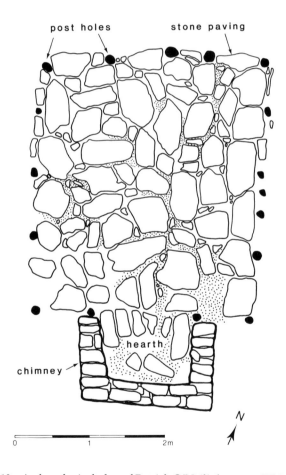

Figure 6.12   Archaeological plan of Patrick O'Neil's house at White Range on the Arltunga Goldfield, Northern Territory. (After Holmes 1983.)

Admittedly, a separate building possibly functioned as a kitchen, but living conditions in O'Neil's house must have been as far removed from those of the Regentville mansion as one could imagine.

Old houses, and even not-so-old houses, are vital documents of past life. There is an extraordinary wealth of information that can be extracted from them if one knows how to read the evidence. They tell us about the availability of raw materials, about the methods of their builders, about the designs and styles that characterized different periods, and they tell us also about the economic condition, the social status, the lifestyle and the aspirations of the people who lived in them. These are important matters that have a significance beyond what is immediately apparent. They allow us to study the process whereby European settlers, arriving in a strange environment, gradually modified their culture to suit the new conditions. The history of Australian colonial settlement is written into its houses. If we wish to understand how a disparate collection of English, Scots, Irish, Welsh, German, Italian, Greek and other peoples became Australians, then we should pay careful attention to what those houses have to tell us.

Notes

[1] R. Boyd, 1952. *Australia's home: Its origins, builders and occupiers*, Melbourne University Press, Carlton, p.4.

[2] J.M. Freeland, 1968. *Architecture in Australia: A history*, Cheshire, Melbourne. Preface.

[3] The discussion of building materials and constructional techniques is based on R. Irving (ed.), 1985. *The history and design of the Australian house*, Oxford University Press, Melbourne; I. Evans, 1985. *The Australian home* (first published 1983), Flannel Flower Press, Sydney; and M. Stapleton, C. Burton and I. Stapleton, 1980. *Identifying Australian houses*, Historic Houses Trust of New South Wales, Sydney.

[4] G. Connah, M. Rowland and J. Oppenheimer, 1978. *Captain Richards' house at Winterbourne: A study in historical archaeology*, Department of Prehistory and Archaeology, University of New England.

[5] For example: P. Bell, 1984. *Timber and iron: houses in North Queensland mining settlements 1861-1920*, University of Queensland Press, St Lucia, Brisbane.

[6] G. Young, 1986. Colonial building techniques in South Australia. *Vernacular Architecture* 17, pp.1-20. Also D.W. Berry and S.H. Gilbert, 1981. *Pioneer building techniques in South Australia*, Gilbert-Partners, Adelaide.

[7] M. Walker, 1978. *Pioneer crafts of early Australia*, MacMillan, Melbourne, pp.20-1, 77.

[8] R. Boyd, 1952.

[9] P. Coutts, 1977. Old buildings tell tales. *World Archaeology* 9(2), pp.200-19.

[10] M. Davies and B.J. Egloff, 1986. The Commandants' Residence at Port Arthur: An archaeological perspective. In G.K. Ward (ed.), *Archaeology at ANZAAS Canberra*, Canberra Archaeological Society, Canberra, pp.46-55.

[11] E.C. Harris, 1979. *Principles of archaeological stratigraphy*, Academic Press, London.

[12] G. Connah, 1986. Historical reality: archaeological reality. Excavations at Regentville, Penrith, New South Wales, 1985. *Australian Journal of Historical Archaeology* 4, pp.29-42.

[13] K. Holmes, 1983. Excavations at Arltunga, Northern Territory, *Australian Journal of Historical Archaeology* 1, pp.78-87.

Chapter 7

'I cleared the land and fenced it'

READING THE RURAL LANDSCAPE

Archaeologists use the word 'artefact' to distinguish a product of human workmanship from an object which has been naturally produced. For most people, such artefacts are the things that they see on display in museums, usually arranged in such a way as to represent different periods of the past. As we have seen in previous chapters, however, there is a great variety of material evidence for our history that is scattered around in the everyday world in which we work and live. Indeed, as was argued in the first chapter, the very landscape around us is an artefact of past and present human occupation. This is very obvious in the case of towns and cities, but less obvious in rural areas, so that there is a widespread and long-standing conviction that the countryside is 'natural' and 'unspoilt' by human activity. Nothing could be further from the truth. The greater part of the Australian landscape looks the way it does *because* of human activity. It is the landscape that forms the most important artefact of the European colonization of this continent.

The central fact of Australian history is the occupation by immigrant agriculturalists of a land previously exploited only by hunter-gatherers. Except where climate, terrain or soil made it completely impossible, this occupation involved extensive modification of the vegetation cover and the imposition on the landscape of a variety of structures and buildings. The most urgent tasks of the European settlers were, first, to feed themselves and, second, to produce exportable commodities that could enable them to purchase overseas both necessities and luxuries that were not available locally. In the outcome this agricultural invasion was virtually complete by 1900, with only a few less useful areas remaining to be occupied. Historical geographer Dennis Jeans has commented on the 'phenomenal' speed at which agriculturally useful land was both discovered and taken up. As he has pointed out, the whole process took only about one hundred years, whereas in the United States of America it had taken three hundred years to settle an equivalent area of land, much of which was of better quality. Jeans has explained this as largely resulting from the fact that the European settlement of Australia took place during the so-called Industrial Revolution. Factories, both overseas and in Australia, produced implements and machines which enabled a small population to subdue a whole continent. As Jeans says: 'From ploughs to fencing wire and windpumps, the muscle of Australian farming lay in the factories.'[1] There is, however, another factor that helps to explain this rapidity of settlement. This is that climate and soil quality made the greater part of Australian agriculture extensive rather than intensive. The yield per hectare was generally low, both for cultivation and for pastoralism, and this was particularly the case in the earlier years of settlement. Thus there was a strong incentive for individual settlers to take up very large areas of land, and the main strategy for

84

increasing production was to enlarge those holdings even further. In such circumstances it is hardly surprising that the agricultural settlement of Australia took place so quickly.

It is the purpose of this chapter to examine some of the more important aspects of the archaeology of Australian agriculture. By 'agriculture' is meant both the cultivation of the soil and the rearing of animals, or 'pastoralism', as it is usually called. The principal problem for the archaeologist interested in this aspect of Australia's history will be that the agricultural exploitation of the landscape has not remained static but has constantly changed and continues to change. The successful farmer or pastoralist continually replaces obsolete buildings, worn-out machinery or broken-down fences. That being the case, it might be wondered what there is left for the archaeologist to study. Sometimes, indeed, there is very little, and our sources of information on a particular agricultural system of the past will be limited to documentary records and to oral tradition. In most cases, however, there survives what has already been called an 'archaeological landscape' consisting of features that do not relate to recent activities and that are remnants of a previous landscape which is in the process of disappearing. Such features can be particularly noticeable if there has been a marked change in land use, such as from cereal growing to sheep rearing. When that has happened, abandonment or adaptation has allowed evidence to survive that might otherwise have been swept away in the course of routine replacement. The most extensive material evidence is to be found in agriculturally marginal areas, such as the far west of New South Wales or parts of South Australia, from which agriculture has largely withdrawn following early attempts that led to disaster. For the historical archaeologist the sad fact is that the more successful an agricultural district has been, the less there will be left to study.

Nevertheless, the overall characteristics of many landscapes still provide evidence of the initial impact of agricultural settlement. In most districts it was necessary to clear much of the natural vegetation before crops could be grown or animals grazed. In the moister areas of Australia this meant felling large numbers of substantial trees, or at least ringbarking them so that they died. The problem then was what to do with the fallen timber or the dead trees, which, being mostly hardwood, could survive for many years. Some of the wood could be used for building a homestead and outbuildings, some of it could be used for making fences, some of it could be used for firewood. Even then there was still likely to be far too much wood lying about, as many a nineteenth-century photograph shows. A contemporary observer recalled that, in 1910, 'You could walk all over the grassed area without getting off fallen timber' on one property in the south of Victoria.[2] Eventually the land would be cleared of the unwanted timber, usually by repeated fires, but later settlers in Western Australia also used dynamite to shatter the logs. After all that labour, however, the initial settler still had the problem of the stumps that must be grubbed out, winched out, burnt out or somehow avoided, if the land was to be cultivated. Much of the now-productive agricultural land of Australia is incontrovertible evidence of the dogged toil of pioneer settlers.

One of the most remarkable of these landscape changes is in southeastern South Australia and western Victoria, where the clearance of mallee scrub and mallee-heath woodland presented special problems in the late nineteenth and early twentieth centuries.[3] Mallee consists of a dense scrub-like cover of small trees that grows in areas of low rainfall or impoverished soils and can be very difficult to clear. Even after it has been cut down, its mass of tuberous roots can still sucker and regrow. If clearance is to be completely successful, all the roots must be dug out and burnt. It was eventually discovered that the best way to deal with mallee was to crush it with a large iron roller, often made from an old boiler, pulled through the scrub by a horse or bullock team, a steam traction-engine or, in later times, by a tractor. Variants on this technique were to drag a heavy log through the scrub, or even a length of anchor chain. This effectively smashed down the stems of the mallee, but they still had to be piled together and burnt, and the roots still had to be grubbed out. Fortunately, some additional incentive to remove the roots was provided by the fact that they could be sold in the adjacent cities and towns as firewood or even used to construct fences or rough buildings. Originally, more than seventy per cent of the now-settled portions of South Australia were covered by mallee of one sort or another. Its removal from extensive areas of South Australia and western Victoria has provided huge expanses of cleared agricultural land (Figure 7.1). These landscapes created by humans are the archaeological evidence for the difficult process of mallee clearance, as also are examples of equipment that have survived in local museums such as the mallee roller in the Wimmera-Mallee Pioneers Museum at Jeparit, Victoria.[4]

Figure 7.1 Aerial photograph of cleared agricultural land at Blanche Town on the River Murray, South Australia. This area was originally covered with mallee vegetation, although rather different shrubland and woodland were found along the course of the river itself.
(Photograph by courtesy of the Department of Lands, South Australia.)

Such massive removal of tree or scrub cover was not without its damaging consequences. Clearance caused increased runoff when rain fell and on steep slopes this could result in gullying or sheet erosion. In areas of higher rainfall, both soil and fallen timber could be washed into the creeks causing substantial changes in drainage patterns in some cases. In northeastern New South Wales, for example, a gigantic accumulation of such material has clogged over 15 kilometres of the Gwydir River west of Moree and has become locally known as 'The Raft'.[5] In areas of lower rainfall, wind erosion could create problems that were just as serious. Large parts of the mallee, for instance, covered light sandy soils which, when cleared and cultivated, could be blown away in dust storms. Extensive parts of Australia now suffer from soil erosion or landscape degradation of one sort or another, and such areas are just as much the result of clearance by early settlers as are substantial portions of the agriculturally productive land.

The clearance of much of the natural vegetation was the most frequent form of initial land preparation that Australia's first agriculturalists had to undertake. In some areas, however, there were other tasks that also had to be attended to before land could realize its productive potential, and these too have left their mark upon the landscape. In parts of South Australia and Victoria, for example, there were extensive swamps that had to be drained which resulted in the excavation of numerous drains that brought about the tranformation of whole districts. Equally, there were other areas whose appearance changed as a result of the development of irrigation systems, particularly in the lower Murray Valley of South Australia, New South Wales and Victoria. In addition there were highland areas, such as the New England Tablelands of northern New South Wales, where enormous quantities of loose stones had to be removed from the ground surface, usually by hand. Depending on the area, these were sometimes used as building material, sometimes used for constructing field walls, and sometimes merely collected into low banks or mounds within the paddock.

Having prepared the ground, or sometimes even before preparing it, pioneer agriculturalists had to get a fast return in crops or livestock products and frequently had little time or energy to spend on improvements. When they did turn to such matters the construction of a homestead was usually the first priority, if indeed it had not been attended to already. Almost equally urgent, however, was the erection of some fencing which was required to protect growing crops and homestead gardens from livestock and to provide yards to facilitate the handling of flocks and herds. At first pastoralists had very few fences preferring to employ shepherds to watch the sheep by day, the animals being enclosed with portable wooden hurdles at night and the shepherd sleeping nearby in an equally portable 'watch box'. This was a good arrangement while cheap labour remained available, but this ceased to be the case during the gold rush of the 1850s so that fencing became increasingly common from then on. It was at about this date that the construction of fences was made easier by the appearance of factory-produced wire. In addition, as time went by, there were more and more reasons for building extensive fencing even on pastoral properties. Not only did fences prevent the settler's stock from straying, but they made sure that neighbouring or travelling stock, that might be suffering from infectious diseases, did not come into contact with his animals. Furthermore, from the 1860s onwards, many squatters fenced their runs as a means of discouraging selectors from encroaching on them. The selectors, in turn, were often required by law to enclose their land with a substantial fence and the demands of management also made it necessary to divide the total area into separate paddocks. Finally, in the 1880s and 1890s, the spread of rabbits provided yet another incentive for the construction of effective fencing, in this case 'rabbit-proofed' with galvanized-iron wire netting. Barbed wire also began to appear in the early 1880s. Thus, by the early twentieth century, the Australian agricultural landscape had acquired one of its most characteristic features — its division into a network of separate units by a seemingly endless system of fences.

Fences have been made in Australia in a great number of ways (Figure 7.2), more ways than most people would realize, and certainly in more ways than their modern examples would suggest.[6] The Australian rural landscape of the twentieth century is characterized by wire fencing held up by steel or wooden posts with multiple steel droppers, but for the early settlers wood was usually the most readily available material and it was used in a variety of ways. Post and rail fences were the most commonly constructed, consisting of split posts about 2.1 metres in length and split rails of about 2.7 metres. Some 90 centimetres of each post went into the ground and the number of rails varied from two to four, depending on the purpose of the fence. A fence to enclose cultivated land needed four rails to exclude pigs and other small stock, whereas sheep could be kept in with three rails, and only two rails were necessary to restrain cattle and horses. Stockyards for mustering cattle or horses needed rather more substantial fences, however, and these were usually higher with five or even six rails. Post and rail fences may still be seen in some parts of the Australian countryside and, to the modern eye, their most impressive feature is that the rails fit into holes that are cut right through the posts. The traditional way of doing this involved the skilled use of a mortising axe — a tool with a long, narrow head and a very short cutting edge. One great advantage of post and rail fences was that gates were not strictly necessary. The rails in a conveniently placed section could be left loose so that they could be slid to one side when access through the fence was needed. These sliprails, as they became known, were cheaper to make than gates and easier to repair.

There were many other forms of wooden fence, depending on the purpose being served and on the available time or money of the individual settler. Picket or paling fencing was common around homesteads and their gardens, with the vertical pickets sometimes neatly made and fastened with nails to a post and rail structure, but sometimes both pickets and rails consisting only of rough saplings nailed together. Sapling pickets could also be held together with wire, and split saplings could be woven horizontally between vertical posts to produce yet another kind of fence. Other techniques of wooden fencing included the palisade, or stub fence, in which close-set split slabs were stood with their bases buried in a trench. For those who wanted to build a quick fence or a particularly strong one, whole logs could be used to construct a 'chock-log' fence or a 'zig-zag' fence. For the poorer settler, desperate both to clear his land and to prevent his stock from straying, the easiest way to fence was to push the felled trees into a line and pile the loose branches on top of them, weaving some of the more pliable branches together so as to make as effective a barrier as possible. All these and other techniques were used to construct wooden fences in nineteenth-century Australia, with wire gradually being incorporated as time went on.

Wood and wire were not the only materials used in fencing. In some areas wood was not available, or was difficult to obtain. There were a number of possible solutions to this problem. Sometimes, for instance, banks of turf were constructed and used in combination with posts and rails or posts and wire. In parts of Tasmania, western Victoria and New South Wales, drystone-walling was built, sometimes again being used in conjunction with posts and wire. Perhaps the strangest of all fencing, however, was that erected in some of the cleared mallee country of South Australia and Victoria and which consisted of carefully

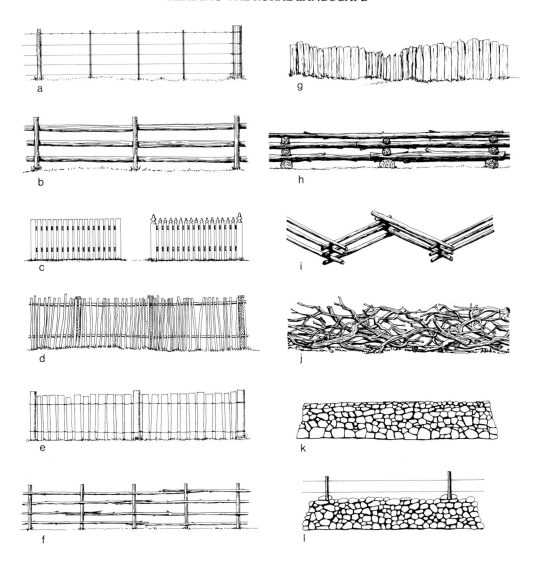

Figure 7.2 The principal types of rural fences in Australia. (a) wire with wooden posts and steel droppers. (b) post and rail. (c) nailed sawn picket, plain and fancy. (d) nailed sapling picket. (e) wired picket. (f) woven split saplings. (g) stub fence of split slabs. (h) 'chock-log' fence. (i) 'zig-zag' fence (elevated view). (j) brush fence. (k) drystone-walling. (l) drystone-walling with posts and wire. (After Kerr 1984; Walker 1978; and L.A. Gilbert and others 1984. *History around us: An enquiry approach to local history*, Methuen, North Ryde.)

stacked mallee roots. All these techniques of fencing showed a considerable ability to adapt to Australian conditions, more than the attempts to reproduce English hedgerows and to grow live fences. These attempts were spread from Queensland to Tasmania and made use of a diverse range of introduced species including hawthorn, gorse, broom, privet, lantana and prickly pear. In general, such fences were not successful, the climate was not always suitable for some of them and all of them required a great deal of skilled care that took time needed for other jobs. Perversely, several of the introduced species eventually found environments that were very much to their liking and they then ran wild like the introduced rabbits. Relatively few hedgerows have survived to the present day, although there are notable examples near Westbury in Tasmania (gorse), and at Dangarsleigh, near Armidale in New South Wales (hawthorn). At least these live fences have a chance of remaining with us, as do also the drystone-walls. As each year goes by, however, there will be fewer and fewer examples left of the other types of fence and archaeologists will eventually have to content themselves with the study of old fence-lines rather than of fences. This aspect of landscape archaeology will still remain possible, because many early lines are marked by replacement fences, and because a slight irregularity in the surface of a modern paddock can sometimes indicate the location of a vanished fence.

The pioneer settler in Australia cleared and fenced land in order to bring it into production. This could be done by growing crops, by raising livestock or by a combination of the two. In practice, both cultivation and pastoralism were often carried on at the same property, but their archaeological manifestations are sufficiently different to consider them separately. At the time of first settlement cultivation was the most urgent of the two activities simply because of the pressing need for food. This situation was to be repeated time and time again as European colonists gradually moved into all the agriculturally viable areas of the continent. To the poorer man, with a family to feed, it was vital to get a crop off his land as soon as possible. For this reason, we will examine cultivation first.

The long, complex, and at times tragic history of cultivating the Australian soil has left two main types of material evidence: first, traces of its impact on the land itself and, second, the machinery and implements that were used in the process of cultivation. Relatively few studies seem to have been made of the first type of evidence, but one particularly important example will give some impression of its potential. This is an investigation carried out by Twidale, Forrest and Shepherd into traces of ploughing, mostly dating from about 1870, which have survived in the Mount Lofty Ranges of South Australia.[7] These researchers were interested in the patterns of ridge and furrow, technically called 'lands', which can still be seen in some of the pastures of this area. The 'lands' are long, narrow strips of slightly raised ground, bordered on each long side by a shallow depression. Similar features are known in many parts of Britain where they result from a long-used ploughing procedure suited to the single-share plough. What is not certain is *why* this particular procedure was adopted, and it was to this question that Twidale and his associates principally addressed themselves. Their work is an excellent example of the ability of historical archaeology to suggest explanations for archaeology in general. In South Australia, in the 1960s, it was still possible to talk to men who had continued to plough in this way during the first half of the twentieth century.

'Lands' resulted from first throwing up a ridge across the paddock with the plough and then alternately ploughing along each side of it from opposite ends of the paddock. Because the mouldboard of the single-share plough consistently threw the soil in one direction, this had the effect of turning successive furrows against each side of the ridge so that, as ploughing continued, it grew wider and wider. At any point in this process, however, the ploughed strip was bounded by open furrows on each side. Clearly, the ploughman could have ploughed the whole paddock in this manner if he had wished, but the traditional British practice had not been to do this. Instead, after a varying number of furrows, the whole process was started again so that the paddock was eventually ploughed in the series of broad strips known as 'lands', separated by depressions two furrows wide.

Various explanations have been advanced in Britain to explain this ancient practice. It has been assumed that the same 'lands' persisted from year to year and that the most likely reason for ploughing in this way was that it assisted drainage, or that each 'land' represented a single day's work for a ploughman. Twidale and his colleagues have shown that, at least in South Australia, these explanations are unsatisfactory. Instead, they make two suggestions. The first one is that the practice was designed to save time and effort. Ploughing in the way that has been described meant that the plough had to be hauled along the unploughed 'headland' at each end of the field before it could cut the next furrow down the other side of the ridge. This was laborious and time-consuming and became more so as the 'land' became wider. A point would be reached when it was better to start a new 'land'. The second suggestion is that the early settler, usually dependent on the labour of himself and his family, needed to make sure of at least enough grain for home consumption. Rather than waiting till he had ploughed the whole paddock, by which time he might have missed the first rains that were so important for seed germination, it would have been wiser to plough and sow each 'land' before proceeding to the next. In this way he would have been certain to obtain some sort of a crop, however small. This explanation seems particularly likely in the South Australian environment, but even in Britain the small farmer must have been concerned to ensure bread for his hungry family. Given the necessity both to sow and reap by hand, it would have made sense to plough and seed the paddock strip by strip. Twidale and his associates were also able to show that, in South Australia at least, the location of the 'lands' changed from year to year, so that they were not perpetual features.

The South Australian 'lands' are also of interest for three other reasons. One is that they are remarkable archaeological evidence for the strength of tradition and the persistence of cultural practices. The man behind the plough imprinted onto the South Australian landscape a pattern that he had learnt in his homeland. The second is that the survival of the 'lands' has only occurred because of a marked change in land use. Until about 1870, the Mount Lofty Ranges and the Adelaide Plains were the most important wheat-producing area in Australia. After that date, wheat production developed in other parts of the continent, particularly Victoria, and in South Australia it moved north into more suitable country. Although the Adelaide Plains continued to be important for the production of wheat, in the Mount Lofty Ranges much of the ploughed land was turned into pasture and it is therefore possible to study the traces of the last ploughing that was done. The third additional reason for taking an interest in the South Australian 'lands' is the one that apparently drew attention to them in the first place. In many places the 'lands' run downhill and the double furrows have, in some cases, been sufficient to channel runoff and induce localized gully erosion. At first sight this would appear to be very bad farming practice when compared with the careful contour-ploughing that is now usual. Once again, however, the early settlers were limited by the equipment available to them. It was very difficult for a ploughman to control a horse or bullock-drawn single-share plough *across* a slope. Not only had man and beast, as it were, one leg longer than the other, but the plough would tend to swing downslope. Furthermore, when going in one direction the plough would be attempting to throw soil uphill, a task that was impossible until the advent of the tractor.

'Lands' have also been observed elsewhere such as near Armidale, in northern New South Wales (Figure 7.3), but in most places all vestiges of early cultivation practices have been erased from the landscape by the use of modern machinery. It is the ancestors of those machines that we must turn to for the other main type of material evidence for arable agriculture in the nineteenth and early twentieth centuries. Fortunately, a huge quantity of machines and implements has survived in museum collections up and down the country, although many of them lack adequate provenance or are of unknown manufacture. Much of this equipment came from the factories of Britain and the United States, but there was also a considerable quantity of it that was made in Australia.[8] Some of this was produced in local blacksmith's shops, some of it in numerous small factories that grew up as time went on, and some was made by manufacturers who worked on a very large scale. Examples of the latter were the McKay Harvester Co., first at Ballarat, then at Sunshine near Melbourne, and James Martin at Gawler, and D. & J. Shearer at Mannum, both in South Australia.

The most striking thing about the machines and implements that were used in Australian arable agriculture over the last two hundred years is that there were so many of them, and of so many different types. To begin with there was a huge range of hand tools including reaping hooks, scythes, slashers, billhooks, rakes, pitchforks, manure forks, spades, shovels, chipping hoes, grubbing hoes, breaking-up hoes, turnip hoes, burr hoes, mattocks, fencing bars and others. Archaeologists have as yet taken little interest in the almost infinite variations in such tools — variations that reflected both the geographic origins of the early settlers and the necessity to adapt to Australian conditions. Why, for instance, did

Figure 7.3 Aerial photograph taken July 1975 of 'lands' (bottom right) and associated homestead site (centre foreground) on bank of Saumarez Creek near Armidale, New South Wales.

Australian farmers adopt the long-handled shovel, which was certainly not the common form in England from where so many of them came? There has been rather more interest in the development of cultivation machinery, which again covered a very large range. This included single- and multiple-share mouldboard ploughs, a variety of disc-ploughs, skim-ploughs, scarifiers, harrows of different sorts, grain drills, strippers, winnowers, reapers, reaper-binders, stripper-harvesters, reaper-threshers and header-harvesters. To these might be added the mowers and hay rakes that were essential machines for cutting and collecting the hay needed for feeding livestock. All these machines were at first drawn only by horses (or sometimes by bullocks), but the steam engine, followed by the internal-combustion engine, gradually replaced animal traction. The great diversity of machinery, its relative sophistication at an early date, and the sheer number of machines that were imported or manufactured, tells us something about the development of Australian arable agriculture. This is that, as already mentioned, Australian agriculture tended to be extensive rather than intensive. Particularly in the early years the yield per hectare was generally low, and the main strategy for increasing crop production was to increase the cultivated area. In such circumstances there was very strong motivation to find machines to do the various jobs, especially as labour was often in short supply. As a result, Australia showed a remarkable level of inventiveness in agricultural technology that was, at times, ahead of much of the rest of the world. Thus, in 1928, the British Ministry of Agriculture and Fisheries sent two officials to Australia to study agricultural methods. In their report they wrote about 'the rapid development of agricultural machinery', and particularly about a combination cultivator and seed and fertilizer drill which had so impressed them that they recommended that examples be imported into Britain for trial and demonstration.

There is an abundance of material evidence for the exceptional ingenuity shown by the makers of Australian agricultural machinery, but two famous examples will suffice as illustration. The earliest of these is the grain-harvesting machine known as 'The Stripper' that was invented in South Australia in 1843. Its fundamental principle seems to have been discovered by John Wrathall Bull, but the first successful machine was made by John Ridley. The machine consisted of a horizontal projecting comb and revolving wooden beaters driven by the wheels on which it ran. The comb gathered the wheat heads and the beaters knocked the grain out of them into a container that formed the body of the machine. The earliest model was pushed into the crop by a pair of horses but, in later versions, the horses were harnessed to one side of it so that they could pull it through the standing crop whilst themselves walking on the edge of the area already harvested. The grain harvested by the stripper still had to be separated from the chaff and this was normally done with a winnowing machine that stood in the corner of the paddock, conveniently placed for the regular emptying of the harvester. The stripper was an instant success, and 10,000 of these machines were sold between 1843 and 1883. Although far more sophisticated machines evolved as time went on, strippers were still in use in some places as late as the 1940s. To appreciate fully its significance, it must be seen in the context of the manual methods that it replaced. At its first trial in 1843, it harvested 28 hectares of wheat in seven days. It took two men to operate it, one guiding the horses and the other the machine. This was at a time when all harvesting was done with the reaping hook or with the scythe, the latter being sometimes fitted with a 'cradle'. This cradle saved labour by laying the crop in swathes which were then picked up and tied into sheaves, even then an experienced worker could cut only about 0.4 hectares each day using this method. Furthermore, the sheaves still had to be threshed to extract the grain. In 1843, South Australia had 9300 hectares sown with grain and was faced with a crisis when it was realized that there was not enough labour available to harvest it. Soldiers were called in to help with the harvest, civilian volunteers also helped, and the Governor of South Australia appealed to New South Wales for more troops to assist, and was sent 150 men. In circumstances such as these, the Bull and Ridley stripper was little short of a godsend. The future of the infant colony of South Australia was assured.

The second example of Australian ingenuity with agricultural machinery is the stump-jump plough invented in South Australia in 1876 (Figure 7.4). Various people claimed to have thought of this first, but the person to whom credit seemed to be due was Robert Bowyer Smith. Given the tree stumps and roots and stones that Australian ploughmen had to deal with on freshly cleared land, the stump-jump plough was a brilliant adaptation to the environment. It is not surprising that the idea came from a state that was in the early stages of struggling to clear the mallee. Early settlers had had their problems with ploughs: the English long-mouldboard plough proved unsuitable in many areas of Australia, and locally made wooden or iron ploughs had either cast-iron shares that could break, or wrought-iron ones that could bend. It was not until the end of the 1880s that steel shares became available. The great advantage of the stump-jump plough was that the share and mouldboard were hinged. When they hit a stump or a rock in the soil they were pushed up and rode over it, being returned to their position by a weight fixed to a lever once the obstruction was passed. The earliest stump-jump ploughs were of one to three shares, but as time went on the principle was applied to ploughs with as many as nine shares. It was also applied to the American disc-ploughs when they first appeared in Australia at the end of the nineteenth century. In addition, springs were eventually added to improve the efficiency of the return. The stump-jump principle was very successful and was gradually adopted for many other tillage, seeding and fertilizer implements. The plough itself was used in many parts of Australia and was even adopted in the United States. In its homeland of South Australia, the best tribute to this implement is the broad productive wheatland that now occupies what was once scrub country.

Arable agriculture, particularly grain farming, was extremely important for the development of modern Australia. It not only supplied much-needed food but in time it came also to provide exportable commodities. Nevertheless, it was pastoralism that contributed most in this latter respect. In the popular mind, Australia rode to wealth on the sheep's back, but cattle, both for meat and milk, played a bigger role than is often realized. Prior to the development of canning, and then of refrigerated transport, wool and tallow were the only practicable exports of animal products and, indeed, wool was to remain a major export down to modern times. This fact, plus the early profitability of wool, has given the sheep a certain romantic aura in the Australian national consciousness. There is no doubt that, for Australia, the golden fleece was indeed golden.

The Australian pastoral industry has left two main sorts of material evidence: first, traces of its effect on the landscape, and second, buildings and other structures, together with their associated equipment, that played a crucial part in the industry. The first sort of evidence consists both of overall environmental impact and of individual features. Without any question, the grazing of huge numbers of sheep and cattle has changed the appearance of most of Australia. Not only has much of the native vegetation been removed to encourage the growth of grass, but in many places the nutritional value of grazing land has been improved by the introduction of exotic grass species. In other places the effect of domestic animals has been little short of disastrous. Thus, for example, the western districts of New

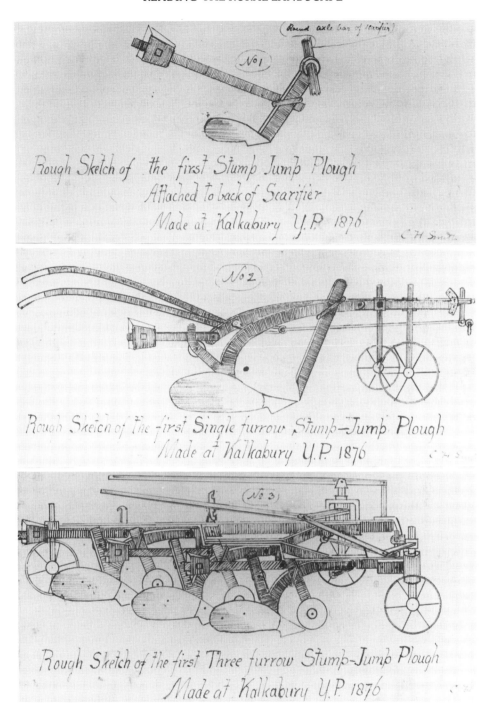

Figure 7.4 Photographs of original drawings, by the inventor's brother (Clarence Herbert Smith), showing the first stump-jump ploughs that were made. (By courtesy of the Mortlock Library of South Australiana, Adelaide.)

South Wales, assailed during the late nineteenth century by overgrazing, drought and rabbits, suffered damage to its vegetation from which it has never recovered.[9] The other major change to the overall environment was the growth of an extensive network of stock routes by which flocks and herds were moved into all suitable parts of the continent and along which they were moved to market. Although many of them are now disused with the advent of road and rail transport, these routes can still be traced both on the ground and on maps, and the drover on his horse can still be found moving stock along some of the remoter routes. In the changes to vegetation and in the growth of these stock routes can be discerned a pattern of considerable interest to archaeologists studying the impact of animal domestication on other parts of the world at earlier dates. As well as these overall landscape changes, however, there were also many individual features that were added to the scene. Stock need water, in particular, cattle need substantial quantities of water. One of the major constraints on stock-rearing in Australia was the shortage of surface water in many areas, particularly at certain seasons of the year. To overcome this problem innumerable dams were dug, at first by hand or with horse-drawn scoops, later with machinery. These are now an important element of many pastoral landscapes. In addition, countless wells were dug and often equipped with windmill-driven pumps that, in many cases, remain the only structures made by humans in an otherwise empty landscape. From the end of the nineteenth century onwards, artesian and sub-artesian bores were also drilled and, particularly in the northern and western parts of the continent, often provided the only reliable sources of water for stock. Their greatest impact on the environment is the complete stripping of vegetation that has often occurred around each one caused by the repeated concentration of stock at the watering point.[10]

It is the buildings and other structures that are often grouped near the homestead of the sheep or cattle station, or dairying farm, that provide the greatest concentration of material evidence for the growth of the pastoral industry. Best-studied of these, and perhaps most deserving of study, are woolsheds; specialized buildings that evolved quite independently in Australia.[11] The woolshed was specifically designed for the shearing of sheep, a task that could only occupy a short period of the year and for which the sheep had to be dry. The woolshed therefore came to consist of three main parts: large pens where the maximum number of sheep could be kept under cover until they were shorn; the 'board', where the shearing actually took place; and the 'wool room', where the shorn wool was classed, sorted, pressed into bales and stored prior to being transported to market. Shearers were paid according to the number of sheep that each shore, and obviously the grazier wanted the job done as quickly as possible. Also, in some of the bigger sheds, the total number of sheep that had to be handled was phenomenal. In 1899, at Bowen Downs in Queensland, 364,742 sheep were shorn. A little later, at Brookong, near Lockhart in New South Wales, 7000 to 10,000 sheep were being shorn each day. In such circumstances it was clearly in everybody's interest that the woolshed be designed in the most efficient way. Thus, smaller 'catching pens' were provided adjacent to the 'board', and these were kept filled with sheep from the larger 'sweating pens' so that each shearer could conveniently grab a fresh sheep when he had finished with the previous one. Also, each shearer's 'stand' was adjacent to his own 'counting pen' into which he could push the sheep when he had shorn it. Many sheds were equipped with chutes down which the animal was unceremoniously slid into counting pens outside the shed. Most of these arrangements came to be standard and can still be found in use. There was a constant search for the most efficiently planned woolshed and numerous different plans were tried. It is a search which still continues, but many of the

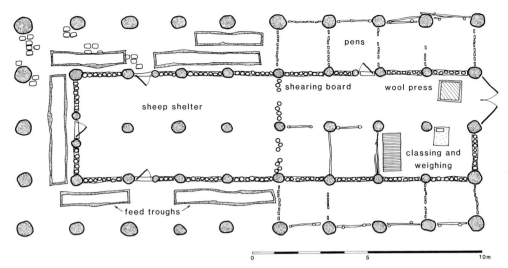

Figure 7.5   Plan of woolshed at Clayton Farm, near Bordertown, South Australia. (After Sowden 1972.)

sheds now in use are quite old and can tell us a good deal about the evolution of this type of building. For example, the woolshed at Clayton Farm, near Bordertown in South Australia, is an early pioneer structure with massive supporting posts consisting of whole tree trunks, walls of vertically fixed split slabs, a thatched roof and an earth floor (Figure 7.5). With space for only four or five stands on the board, this early (but apparently undated) shed is a far cry from the massive sheds of the late nineteenth century — two of the largest are claimed to have had 101 shearing stands. Both those sheds have since been demolished but Tubbo Station, near Narrandera in the Riverina district of New South Wales, has an example of one of these late-nineteenth-century large sheds (Figure 7.6). Clayton Farm woolshed stands at one end of the evolutionary series of layouts and Tubbo Station woolshed at the other end. There were, however, numerous experiments in between, one of which is the remarkable octagonal shed that still survives at Gostwyck, near Uralla in New South Wales. This shed was built in 1851 so that twenty-four blade shearers could work in a circle. An oblong extension was later added on one side and the shearing board re-sited there in a more conventional arrangement (Figure 7.7).

The casual observer of woolsheds might be forgiven for thinking that they are all wood-framed buildings clad in either weatherboards or corrugated galvanized iron, but there are several other materials that have been used in their construction. At East Loddon, near Serpentine in Victoria, a massive woolshed was built of bricks in 1869. The building, together with the paving of its yards, took 460,000 bricks. Similarly, the 1821 woolshed at Panshanger, near Longford in Tasmania, was built of bricks. Some woolsheds were even more imposingly constructed of stone. For example, the shed at Lovely Banks, near Jericho in Tasmania, was built of sandstone in 1842; a number of Victorian woolsheds were built of bluestone, such as the Eurambeen shed, near Beaufort, which dates from 1845; and both ironstone and limestone were used in South Australia. A final point about woolshed construction is that not all of them were originally designed for that purpose. For instance, the woolshed at Mountford, near Longford in Tasmania, was built around 1850 as a flour mill but never used as such. Other examples can be found of a former stables being converted into a woolshed, part of a meatworks which was shifted to a new site, and even

97

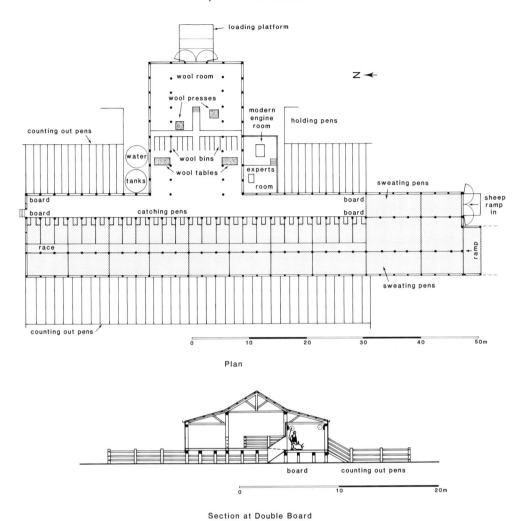

Figure 7.6 Plan and section of woolshed at Tubbo Station, near Narrandera, New South Wales. A southerly extension dating from the 1940s has been omitted. Pen areas with slatted floors are stippled. (After Freeman 1980.)

an exhibition hall that had to make the long journey from Melbourne to Longreach in Queensland. This was hardly the longest journey accomplished by a woolshed, however, because at Isis Downs, near Blackall in Queensland, is a curious semi-circular shed of steel and corrugated iron that was manufactured in 1908 by Dorman Long, in Middlesbrough, England!

Within the woolsheds there are often pieces of equipment that are informative about the history of the wool industry. Woolpresses, for instance, which are so necessary to reduce the bulk of the wool for transportation purposes, have sometimes remained in use for long periods. The earliest of these contrivances were screw presses, but from the 1860s onwards the more efficient rack press became common, only to be replaced by the modern hydraulic

Figure 7.7   Aerial photograph taken September 1980 of Gostwyck
woolshed, near Uralla, New South Wales. An unusual octagonal
structure built of wood in 1851, the other buildings and the yards are of
later date.

press in the 1960s. Rack presses can still be found in some woolsheds, particularly the
'Ferrier's' press made by Humble and Nicholson of Geelong, Victoria. Old woolpresses,
with their origins so often indicated by fancy sign-writing, are a subject in themselves. So is
the shearing machinery that gradually replaced the hand shears from late in the nineteenth
century. Shearing handpieces, in particular, display a complex typology resulting from
continual technical improvements as time has gone on. Although older handpieces have
usually disappeared from the sheds themselves, the same shafting and driving gear has
often remained in use for a long time. In addition, in spite of being superseded by electric
power, earlier power sources in the form of steam, oil or petrol engines have sometimes
survived.

The wool industry required other structures and facilities besides woolsheds and their
equipment. Outside the shed would be special living quarters for the shearers, and it was
useful to have some form of hoist to assist in loading the horse or bullock-drawn waggons.
Nearby there were often a number of fenced sheep yards arranged in such a way as to make
it easier to handle sheep during shearing or at other times. Somewhere in this area there
would also be a dipping bath to assist with the control of external parasites. Some sheep
stations even possessed special 'sheep bridges' built across creeks that were likely to impede
the movement of flocks when they were being mustered for shearing or other purposes.
More common, however, were facilities either for washing the sheep before shearing or for
scouring the wool after shearing. The aim of both of these processes was to remove dirt and

grease which could constitute fifty per cent of the weight of a fleece. Given the limitations of available transportation in much of nineteenth-century and early-twentieth-century Australia it is not surprising that the cleansing of wool should have been accorded considerable attention.

Few of these various features have survived till the present. Changing technology and gradual deterioration have usually led to their removal or to their replacement. For instance, the only obvious evidence of the former practice of washing sheep is often the existence of a place-name such as 'Washpool Creek'. Woolscouring, however, which was generally the later of the two processes, has left rather more evidence, and in one noted case this has been studied by an historical archaeologist. The woolscour at Mount Wood Station, near Tibooburra in the extreme northwestern corner of New South Wales, seems to have been operated from the late 1890s to the 1920s, and its site is now part of the Sturt National Park.[12] The extreme remoteness of this semi-arid area at the beginning of this century made the transportation of wool to market particularly difficult; indeed, it was necessary to use camels for this task. In such circumstances the scouring of wool, which could reduce its weight by so much, was obviously very desirable. The problem was that the area was so dry that sufficient quantities of water to scour wool were not readily available. In addition, the relatively large amount of building materials needed for the construction of a woolscour were not easy to obtain in this remote spot. The excavation of the Mount Wood woolscour site by Michael Pearson was able to show how these constraints were sufficiently overcome to permit the operation of a scour in this unlikely place. It was apparent that the scour had been designed in such a way that the water was recycled back to the dam from which it had been pumped in the first place (Figure 7.8). A pump driven by a steam engine supplied water to raised water tanks, from there it was fed through special nozzles into perforated zinc 'William boxes' which contained the wool and were suspended in a concrete rinsing tank. From there, the water ran back to the dam through an open channel. Similarly, although this is less certain, the pump delivered water to the boiler or water-heater that fed the two hot scour tanks in which the wool was washed before being transferred to the rinsing tank by means of rocking drainers. The water from the hot scour tanks was also channelled back to the dam. Even the steam-driven 'hydro-extractor', a sort of early spin-drier that removed the greater part of the water from the wet fleeces after they had been rinsed, was not allowed to waste any water. Its exhaust steam was fed into a condenser, from which water would have been recovered for re-use, and the water spun out of the wet wool seems likely to have been fed back into the dam by a separate pipeline. Given that there seems to have been a minimum flow of 25,920 litres per hour through the rinsing tank alone, it is apparent that every means of saving water must have been important, and that it must have been difficult to keep the water in the dam clean enough for it to be used over and over again. Some of the dirt from the fleeces, however, accumulated at the bottom of the rinsing tank and in its drainage channel. The resulting deposits of bright red and white sands have been interpreted as indicating the grazing of sheep on both sandhill country (red) and clay-pan country (white): an interesting example of the sort of information derivable from archaeological evidence. Figure 7.8 shows both the flow of wool through the Mount Wood woolscour and the flow of water. The other problem at this woolscour, that of availability of building materials, seems to have been overcome, as it so often was in rural Australia, by combining absolutely essential and purchased manufactured components with ingenious bush workmanship and 'make-do'. The hot scour tanks consisted of inverted ships' tanks with their bases cut off. The rocking drainers were

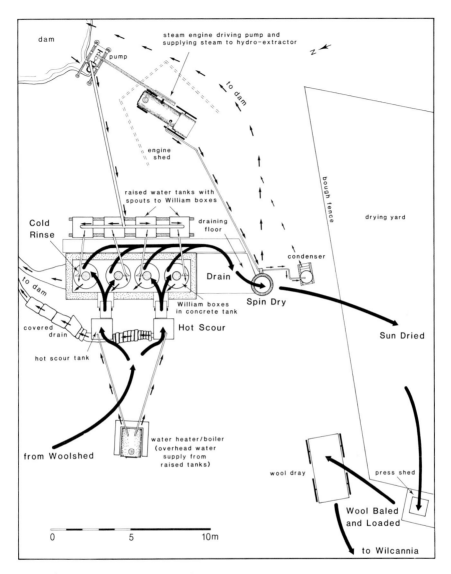

Figure 7.8 Reconstruction of the Mount Wood woolscour, Tibooburra, New South Wales, to show the flow of wool through the scour (large arrows) and the recycling of water to the dam (small arrows). (After Pearson 1984.)

home-made from pieces of sheet iron with holes punched through them. Similarly, the wooden framework to support the William boxes in the rinsing tank, and the clay working surface around the scour, resulted from local initiative.

In addition to those associated with wool production, there are many other buildings and structures that provide us with information about the growth of the Australian pastoral industry. Special buildings were sometimes constructed for boiling-down the carcasses of sheep and cattle to produce tallow, and these were particularly important in periods of economic depression. Some of these buildings survive, and the sites of many others must exist. Another specialized structure was the custom-built killing shed so designed to make the slaughtering of steers an easier and safer task. A fine late-nineteenth-century example exists at Saumarez Station, near Armidale in New South Wales, complete with concrete floor, blood channel, killing platform, block and tackle, winch and heavy wooden doors. Far more common as farm structures are the yards and loading ramps so necessary for the handling of beef cattle, although constant renewal and replacement has left us little evidence of the earlier forms. There are also numerous barns, stables and dairies covering a wide range of dates.[13] Some attention must be given to the various structures associated with dairy farming. Of these, dairies (the places where milk was stored, not where cows were milked) were perhaps the most important and amongst the most likely to have survived. Given the necessity, until the 1880s, to let milk stand for some time so that the cream could be skimmed off by hand for butter-making, dairies had to provide cool, clean environments to enable this take place. In the days before refrigeration this could prove difficult to achieve during the Australian summer and therefore the design of dairy buildings needed special care. Some dairies were partly sunk into the ground and provided with either especially thick or hollow walls. Ceilings might be provided for extra insulation and ventilation was usually carefully attended to. Floors were made of stone, as indeed were the benches on which the wide shallow milk pans were placed. Because of the frequent washing that was needed to keep the inside of the dairy clean, drains might also be provided. Changes in the dairying industry, commencing with the appearance of the hand separator late in the nineteenth century, rendered such buildings no longer necessary. Nevertheless, some of these once-important structures have survived. Far less common would be the milking bails, the feed stalls and the holding yards. Because these were usually rough utilitarian features, and because they, like the dairies, have been overtaken by changing technology, there are relatively few early examples left for us to study.

Compared with Australian arable agriculture, the pastoral industry did not experience a high level of mechanization until a relatively late date. The raising and shearing of sheep, the raising and killing of beef cattle, and the raising and milking of dairy cattle, remained labour-intensive activities to which machines could at first make little contribution. It was the end of the nineteenth century before they began to do so, and it was not until the present century that they had any really significant impact. Even then it was the comparatively small dairying industry that seems to have been able to benefit most quickly from mechanization. The cream separator has already been mentioned, but there were also butterworkers, milk testers and milking machinery, and a growing tendency to remove milk-processing from the farm into increasingly mechanized dairy factories.[14]

Irrespective of whether cultivation or pastoralism was the main interest, agriculture greatly influenced the settlement pattern of rural Australia. By studying that settlement pattern, and by identifying changes in it through time, we can improve our understanding of the history of Australian agriculture. Two examples will suffice to demonstrate the sort of information that the landscape can yield. The first of these comes from the eastern Riverina district of New South Wales, where Jon Winston-Gregson discovered a string of deserted villages along the line of the present Hume Highway.[15] Two of the villages, Hillside and Little Billabong, represent the failed efforts of free selectors to survive in an area that, during the second half of the nineteenth century, was firmly in the hands of a small number of powerful graziers. Hillside seems to have been the centre of a substantial rural community for it had a hotel, a school and a graveyard that acquired over 140 burials in the 26 years between 1847 and 1873. Adjacent to this burial ground is another one, dated from documentary sources to after 1873. There are no records sufficiently detailed to indicate the extraordinary number of burials made in the earlier cemetery. Indeed, this was only revealed by a careful count of the burial plots themselves, for there are only three headstones (in the two cemeteries) to record the passing of all those people. It is an interesting demonstration of how information that is available in no other way can be collected. The other village, Little Billabong, also had a hotel and a school, and even had its own church of which the brick and granite ruin survives. Both of these villages died, victims of the power of the large landholders — two of the many examples of the failure of attempts at closer settlement for which evidence can be found in the Australian landscape.

The second example of a settlement pattern that is informative about the agricultural history of a region belongs to South Australia. Parts of the rural landscape in the Adelaide area still bear traces of the impact of groups of German settlers who arrived during the nineteenth century.[16] They came from the Prussian provinces of Brandenburg, Posen and Silesia, an area which, since 1945, has been part of western Poland. Just as the British and Irish settlers arriving in Australia brought their culture with them, they did also, but their culture was different and the differences showed. In a fascinating study of these early German settlements, Gordon Young has demonstrated how farmhouses and other rural buildings were constructed in a traditional German manner, and how the settlements themselves were laid out according to ideas that the settlers had brought with them from their homeland. Most of these German settlements in South Australia comprised farmlet-villages, or *Hufendörfer*, and some were street-villages, or *Strassendörfer*. The village of Lobethal is a good example of a settlement that originated as a *Hufendorf* and, indeed, still preserves remnants of that layout.[17] As time went on, of course, the plans of such settlements gradually changed, particularly in response to the economic necessity for larger landholdings. These German settlements introduced to part of Australia a quite distinctive pattern of land use and occupation, one that had been practised in central Europe for many centuries.

The most extensive physical impact of colonial settlement on the Australian continent has resulted from agricultural exploitation of one sort or another. The rural landscape is, indeed, an artefact of the colonial settlement of this continent, an artefact that has been in a constant state of change, reflecting not only the character of human impact on the environment but also changes in that impact as time has gone on. For these reasons the study of the archaeology of agriculture is a far more practical proposition than might appear at first sight. It is also a part of Australia's heritage that deserves far more attention than it has yet had from historical archaeologists. The problem is that the material evidence for many other aspects of our past is more obvious and more demanding of study. Slight ridges across a paddock, a rusting piece of farm machinery or a rotting woolshed fail to excite people in the way that a fine piece of architecture can. Nevertheless, they are vital components of our history, for it was the farmer and grazier who first made this country.

Notes

[1] J. Birmingham, I. Jack and D. Jeans, 1979. *Australian pioneer technology: sites and relics*, Heinemann, Richmond, Victoria, p.12.

[2] M. Walker, 1978. *Pioneer crafts of early Australia*, MacMillan, Melbourne, p.83.

[3] M. Williams, 1974. *The making of the South Australian landscape: A study in the historical geography of Australia*, Academic Press, London and New York, pp.124-77.

[4] J. Birmingham, I. Jack and D. Jeans, 1979, p.21.

[5] I. Douglas and M. Douglas, 1977. Water resources. In D.A.M. Lea, J.J.J. Pigram and L.M. Greenwood (eds), *An atlas of New England*, Vol. 2, p.102. Department of Geography, University of New England.

[6] The discussion of fences is based on J.S. Kerr, 1984. Fencing: A brief account of the development of fencing in Australia during the nineteenth century. *Australian Society for Historical Archaeology Newsletter* 14(1), pp.9-16. See also M. Walker, 1978, pp.23-32.

[7] C.R. Twidale, G.J. Forrest and J.A. Shepherd, 1971. The imprint of the plough: 'lands' in the Mt Lofty Ranges, South Australia. *Australian Geographer* 11(5), pp.492-503; C.R. Twidale, 1971. Farming by the early settlers and the making of ridges and furrows in South Australia, *Tools and tillage* 4, pp.205-23; C.R. Twidale, 1972. 'Lands' or relict strip fields in South Australia. *Agricultural History Review* 20, pp.46-60.

[8] The discussion of machines and implements is based on J. Birmingham, I. Jack and D. Jeans, 1979, pp.11-34; F. Wheelhouse, 1966. *Digging stick to rotary hoe: Men and machines in rural Australia*, Cassell, Melbourne; L. Ollif and W. Crosthwaite, 1977. *Early Australian crafts and tools*, Rigby, Adelaide.

[9] D.N. Jeans and P. Spearritt, 1980. *The open air museum: The cultural landscape of New South Wales*, Allen & Unwin, North Sydney, p.22.

[10] J. Birmingham, I. Jack and D. Jeans, 1979, pp.132-4.

[11] The discussion of woolsheds is based on H. Sowden (ed.), 1972. *Australian woolsheds*, Cassell, Melbourne, and P. Freeman, 1980. *The woolshed: A Riverina anthology*, Oxford University Press, Melbourne.

[12] M. Pearson, 1984. The excavation of the Mount Wood woolscour, Tibooburra, New South Wales. *Australian Journal of Historical Archaeology* 2, pp.38-50.

[13] See, for example: R. Roxburgh and D. Baglin, 1978. *Colonial farm buildings of New South Wales*, Rigby, Adelaide.

[14] J. Birmingham, I. Jack and D. Jeans, 1979, pp.29-30.

[15] J.H. Winston-Gregson, 1984. People in the landscape: a biography of two villages. *Australian Journal of Historical Archaeology* 2, pp.27-37.

[16] G. Young, 1985. Early German settlements in South Australia. *Australian Journal of Historical Archaeology* 3, pp.43-55.

[17] G.Young, A. Aeuckens, A. Green and S. Nikias, 1984. *Lobethal (Valley of Praise)*, South Australian Centre for Settlement Studies, Adelaide, p.5.

Chapter 8

'Out of the ground came wealth'

THE ARCHAEOLOGICAL EVIDENCE FOR MINING

If the most extensive impact of colonial settlement on the Australian landscape resulted from agriculture, then it was mining that had some of the most profound local effects. Scattered across the continent there are countless places where men have delved for payable minerals at one time or another during the last two centuries. In some instances they have merely scratched the surface, in others they have blasted their way to great depths. In all cases they have sought wealth, and in some cases they have actually found it. The archaeological record reflects one of the central facts of Australian history: the extraordinary importance of mining in the development of this nation. Geoffrey Blainey, one of the best-known historians of Australian mining and from whose writings the quotation in the title of this chapter has been taken, has described mining as 'a dynamo of Australia's growth'.[1] It is true that the dynamo has sometimes faltered, but it has never quite stopped spinning, and sometimes it has run at enormous speed. At different times it has been fuelled by a variety of minerals including gold, copper, tin, lead, silver, zinc, iron, aluminium, nickel, manganese, tungsten, uranium, coal, oil shale, oil and others. The consequences of the wealth generated by mining have been equally diverse. The first twelve years of gold mining (1851-62), for instance, saw Australia's population almost treble. Admittedly that was during the earliest period of the great gold rushes, but even in later times it was often mineral profits that stimulated expansion by providing the finance to create new industries. Indeed, so profound was the influence of mining, that 'Digger' became the colloquial form of address for several generations of Australian men.

With such an important role in Australian history, it is hardly surprising that mining has left a rich and varied archaeological record that has attracted a good deal of attention from historical archaeologists. What can the material evidence possibly tell us that we cannot learn more easily from the amazingly rich documentary sources of information that exist? Historians of Australian mining are fortunate in being able to examine a wide range of both public and private records which include such diverse materials as the reports of government mining inspectors, the prospectuses of mining companies, accounts in local newspapers and a host of personal diaries and letters. In addition, the excitement of mining, particularly the mining of gold, attracted the attention of some of Australia's earliest and most able photographers. Thus, we can see what it was actually like to be at Gulgong or Hill End in New South Wales in the 1870s, from the Holtermann Collection[2] of photographs. There, frozen in time, are the minutest details of the day-to-day activities of people long dead, presented to us with an unnerving freshness. These are far from being the earliest photographs of Australian mining; Antoine Fauchery, for instance, took superb photographs of some of the Victorian goldfields as early as 1857 (see note 2). Because of the technical limitations of nineteenth-century photography most photographs were limited to surface activities and associated settlements, but some remarkable underground pictures were also produced (Figure 8.1).

For all the richness of the documentary sources, however, they are also notable for what they do not tell us. So remote or so small-scale were some mining operations that they never got into the written records at all. Even large-scale enterprises were frequently described only in general terms with little attention to the individual components of which they

Figure 8.1 Underground at a Hillgrove gold mine in northern New South Wales, about 1895: a mine manager and some of his men. (Photograph by E.T. Kennedy; courtesy of the Armidale Folk Museum.)

consisted. This is not surprising when one remembers that some early miners were illiterate, or virtually so, and that mining, by its very nature, tends to be a secretive activity. It is this character of mining that should make us especially careful in our use of the extensive documentation that we do have. There are numerous reasons why a contemporary account might have claimed poor prospects for a particular mine when in reality it was doing very well. And there are many more reasons why such an account might have described in glowing colours a mine that was actually teetering on closure. Any documentation even remotely concerned with the sale of mining shares or the floating of mining companies must obviously be treated with particular care.

Without doubt the archaeological evidence for mining is a source of information that we cannot afford to ignore. There will even be occasions when it may provide the only chance of getting at the truth of some matter. The difficulty is that the archaeological evidence is itself beset by problems that must be fully appreciated if we are to find out the actual story. There are five circumstances that require particular comment. First, continued mining activity, whether on the surface or deep underground, has often destroyed the earlier and perhaps more interesting evidence. The more successful that a mining enterprise has been, the more likely it is that this will have happened. It is for this reason that a mine that has been relatively unsuccessful can sometimes be more informative archaeologically than one which has done well. Thus archaeologists may find themselves studying mines that were failures, or at least short-lived, rather than those that succeeded. Furthermore, even after abandonment, many mine sites have been subjected to further episodes of mining activities. They may have been reworked by frugal Chinese, by unemployed miners during economic depressions or by several generations of casual fossickers (the modern representatives of which often equip themselves with bulldozer and metal detector). The archaeologist that can make sense out of the resulting mess has to be made of stern stuff.

Second, many archaeological investigations tend to be confined to surface features which, by the nature of things, are less likely to be as well preserved as underground features. There are two main reasons for this: (1), a great deal of nineteenth-century mining consisted of shallow alluvial work or open cuts in the hard rock and (2), underground workings when present are often inaccessible and almost always dangerous. The men who originally cut the shafts, adits, drives, stopes and winzes of the deep mines must have lacked neither skill nor courage. Yet even they would surely hesitate if they were now called upon to enter some of the derelict workings to be found in parts of Australia. Rotted timbering, collapsing roofs, flooded levels, pockets of bad air; all these and other perils await anyone foolish enough to attempt underground exploration at old mine sites. It is for this reason that archaeologists writing about such sites concentrate on poppet-heads, engine houses, pit-head buildings, treatment plants, surface machinery, transport systems and mining settlements. This is a limitation that will have to be overcome eventually. After all, maritime archaeologists undertake considerable risks when diving on wreck sites, but they have been specially trained so as to minimize those risks. Similarly, if the archaeology of mining is to make real progress, it will require archaeologists with special training as mining engineers.

The remaining three problems with the archaeological evidence for mining have in common that they all involve processes of attrition after the working life of a mine has come to an end. Thus, the third problem is that mining sites have nearly always been heavily scavenged by miners, scrap dealers and others for any machinery, equipment or materials that could be re-used or recycled. At the final closure of a mine, everything of any value at all was usually auctioned. Only in the case of heavy equipment at very remote mining sites might the archaeologist find much that has been left behind, and even that is not assured. In the late 1940s a miner named Percy Kean salvaged a steel headframe and machinery from the Louisa gold mine on the Palmer River of north Queensland (Figure 8.2) and trucked them piece by piece, trip after trip, 179 kilometres through the bush to the railway at Chillagoe. From there they were railed south of Townsville to Mingela, and trucked another 40 kilometres to Totley near Ravenswood, where they were reassembled and put to use in reopening a silver mine. When the Totley mine was abandoned yet again, the re-used Louisa equipment was left there: a reminder that even if one does find gear at a mine site, it may not have originated there.[3]

The fourth problem is that mining sites have frequently been damaged by heavy erosion of the landscape, particularly after abandonment, and especially in cases where extensive shallow alluvial mining or hydraulic sluicing has been carried out. Mining has not been the only contributor to such erosion. During the life of many mines, much of their surroundings

Figure 8.2   Mining sites discussed in this chapter.

108

were denuded of trees for smelting ore, timbering underground workings or feeding diggers' campfires. In addition, the amount of human and animal traffic (horses and bullocks were the most common forms of transport) often destroyed much of the remaining vegetation, a process that was assisted in some cases by poisonous chemicals released by mining or processing. The end result is that many mining sites are now reduced to lunar landscapes of erosion in which it is difficult for the archaeologist to identify evidence of how they were actually mined.

The fifth problem consists of the almost total destruction of surviving evidence by government-sponsored 'clean-up' programmes at abandoned mine sites. The decaying shafts and adits of such sites and the surrounding eroded areas can constitute a considerable public danger, particularly if they are situated near modern centres of population. In these circumstances, it is not surprising that there is often a demand from local residents that the appropriate government department of mines or of soil conservation 'do something about' an abandoned mining site in their area. The sad result, from the archaeological point of view, is that the most frequent solution is the demolition of surviving structures, the filling or sealing of all old mine workings and the 'landscaping' of the site by extensive bulldozing. To many people this would appear to be a classic example of the public interest taking precedence over the concerns of a few impractical archaeologists and sometimes this will be the case. There are instances, however, where the public interest can be better served by the conservation and presentation of its own heritage such as that suggested for the derelict Richmond Main Colliery in the Hunter Valley of New South Wales. This area is to become an 'historic park', and may have as many as 250,000 visitors a year.[4] Sometimes imagination is more important to society than practicality.

In spite of these various problems, Australian mining has left an extraordinary amount of material evidence for the historical archaeologist to investigate. As already indicated, the features that have been given most attention have been those accessible from the surface which, for this very reason, tend to have been extensively interfered with both during the working life of the mine and since its abandonment. Nevertheless, such surface evidence can still tell us a great deal about the operation of a particular mine.[5] Some of the most remarkable surviving structures are the towering stone engine houses of Burra, Moonta and Kadina which, together with Kapunda, were the locations of South Australia's most successful early copper mines. Tall circular chimneys also survive at some of these sites and, like the engine houses, provide eloquent reminders of the contribution of Cornish miners to South Australian nineteenth-century copper mining. The mining of copper began in 1844 and pre-dates the beginning of gold mining in 1851 in New South Wales and Victoria. In contrast to the Cornish structures, the surviving 36-metre-high chimney of the nearby Port Wallaroo smelter is square, having been built and run by Welshmen, who seem to have preferred square chimneys, just as the Cornishmen preferred round ones.

Engine houses and their chimneys can still be found on mine sites in several states and show that the influence of Cornish miners was clearly spread far more widely than just South Australia. Such buildings contained steam engines which powered pumps and winding gear and were usually adjacent to a major shaft over which stood a headframe or poppet-head. Even if the shafts have collapsed or been intentionally filled, their locations can quite often be ascertained on old mine sites enabling them to be mapped by either surface survey or aerial photography (Figure 8.3). Only occasionally has the headframe survived, sometimes as a collapsed wreck but sometimes still standing. Prior to the 1880s these were always of wood, so few of them remain. Later it became usual to construct them

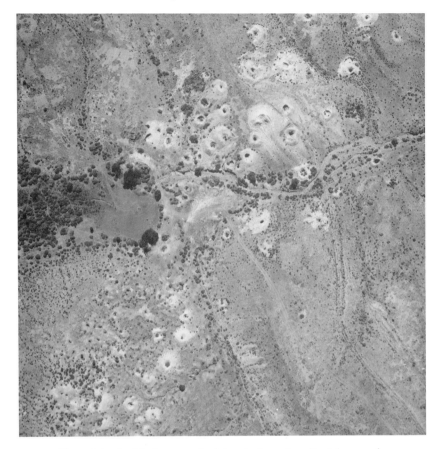

Figure 8.3   Aerial photograph of the shafts and mullock heaps of nineteenth-century gold mines taken in November 1980 at Mount Browne, near Tibooburra, New South Wales.

of steel, and these have survived at a number of places including Bendigo in Victoria, Cobar in New South Wales, and Herberton in Queensland. Nevertheless, many steel headframes have vanished, demolished because they could be sold as scrap.

Other structures that sometimes still exist on mining sites, or which might have left recognizable traces, include boiler houses, blacksmith's shops, engineering workshops, explosives stores, manager's offices and a whole host of facilities concerned with the treatment or processing of the mineral being obtained from the mine. At this point, it is necessary to emphasize that many sites, particularly if they are of mines that were engaged in deep hard-rock mining, are likely to have two sorts of evidence on them: evidence concerned with mining itself, and evidence concerned with the treatment of the ore after it has been extracted from the mine. To understand the former, the archaeologist must know something about mining, but to understand the latter, he or she must know a good deal about metallurgy. Depending on the mineral involved and the nature of the ore-body in which it occurred, pit-head locations might be equipped with a variety of structures and machinery designed to extract metal, prepare concentrates or even distil oil from shale. When in full procuction many sites would have looked like factories as well as mines.

110

Evidence of these facilities could vary enormously. At a hard-rock metalliferous mine there might be a rock-crusher, a stamp battery, shaking tables, riffle-boards, a flotation unit, a ball mill, cyanide tanks, chlorination plant, roasting kilns and perhaps even a smelter, although the latter were often at different locations. In the case of coal mining there might be coke-ovens associated with the colliery and, in the case of oil-shale mining, a refinery complete with retorts and stills would be close at hand. When it is remembered that technology changed considerably as time went on, and that some mines stayed in operation for fairly lengthy periods, it will be appreciated that a site might retain evidence of several different processes that were used at different times. At very few sites has plant remained intact, and it becomes apparent that some mine sites can be very difficult to interpret. It is for this reason that the occasional site that has survived in a complete state is so important. The Venus Gold Battery at Charters Towers, for instance, was operated from 1872 until 1972 and survives as the best-preserved battery in Queensland.[6] Such instances are rare, however, and it is more usual to have to piece together from fragmentary evidence the way in which a mine site functioned. Sometimes this can even necessitate excavation, as was the case with the investigations conducted by Christopher Davey at the site of the North British Mine at Maldon, Victoria.[7] Except for a series of quartz-roasting kilns, there was little more than foundations left at this site. Even the heavy boilers, which survive on many mining sites, had disappeared. Nevertheless, a reasonably complete plan of this gold mine site was reconstructed (Figure 8.4).

In its day, the North British Mine was a highly successful one that yielded a total of 8.3 tonnes of gold. Such a mine was provided with sophisticated and expensive equipment and was operated on a large scale. However, there were countless other mines that were far less successful or were complete failures, and which were worked on a far smaller scale by men whose inexpensive equipment was mostly made by themselves. Thus, many a shaft was topped not by a headframe with engine-driven winding gear and pumps, but by a simple hand-operated windlass, or perhaps a horse-powered whim. Such mining might also have been dispersed over a considerable area rather than being confined to a particular site. Archaeological evidence for activities of this sort tend to be limited to scattered caved-in shafts and overgrown dumps of waste rock. If any structures have survived they will usually consist only of bush timbers or of drystone walling and will probably be in an advanced state of decay and collapse. As Aedeen Cremin commented, in her report on the goldfields of Gulgong and Hargraves in New South Wales, such sites 'may be so reduced as to consist only of a hole in the ground or of a heap of discarded rock'.[8] In spite of this, both she and other archaeologists have demonstrated how much information can be got from unimpressive evidence of this sort. Geoff Tanks, for instance, has examined a singularly unremarkable part of the Rocky River Goldfield, in northern New South Wales (Figure 8.5), and, with the assistance of local historian Arnold Goode, has shown how even the most limited archaeological evidence can be made to tell us something. He has been able to suggest that the depressions and heaps at this site represent two distinct episodes of mining: a brief period of exploitation in the late 1850s and a second period of more substantial activity in the mid 1860s.[9]

The type of surface evidence available to archaeologists studying old mine sites will vary with the different sorts of mining, as well as with scale of operation. Oddly enough, it is not the differences in the minerals extracted that dictate these variations so much as the different circumstances in which the minerals can occur. Some mines can produce more than one mineral at the same time, or different ones as time goes on. The Broken Hill lode in

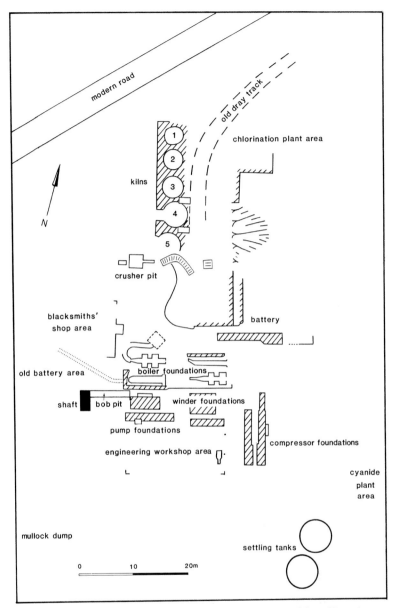

Figure 8.4 Plan of the North British Mine site at Maldon, Victoria.
(Courtesy of Christopher Davey.)

New South Wales produced silver, lead and zinc, while both the Mount Lyell mine in Tasmania, and the Mount Morgan mine in Queensland first extracted gold, but later yielded copper. More important for the type of mining that results is the fact that some metallic minerals can be found in three different ways. They can occur as ore-body lodes in hard rocks, as mineral particles in superficial alluvium or as similar particles in deeply buried ancient alluvial deposits, usually known to miners by the strange name of 'deep leads'. The occurrence of coal, oil shale and other non-metallic minerals is rather different, being

112

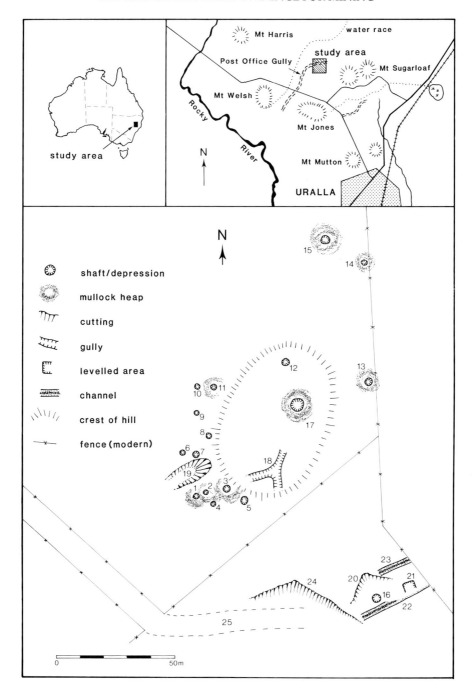

Figure 8.5 Plan of an archaeological survey of a small part of the Rocky River Goldfield, northern New South Wales. Archaeological features 1-16 are interpreted as belonging to the first period of mining and 17-25 as belonging to the second period of mining. (After Tanks 1986.)

limited to hard-rock situations. Hard-rock mining can be carried out in two ways: either by the use of the shafts, adits, drives and so on, which have already been mentioned, or by open cuts. The major determinant as to which of these two methods was used was depth; open-cut mining was only really practicable with fairly shallow deposits, although in more recent times modern machinery took the Mount Morgan open cut, for example, to a depth of 325 metres.[10] Deep-lead deposits can similarly be exploited by either underground mining or by open-cut mining, although the famous deep leads of nineteenth-century Australia, such as those of Ballarat, in Victoria, were mined by means of deep shafts or long tunnels. Deposits of superficial alluvium are different, however, involving only shallow mining that can be done in several ways. It is significant that two of nineteenth-century Australia's most important metals could occur in all three situations; these were gold and tin. It is also significant that alluvial mining could be done with little equipment, little capital and relatively little labour. Alluvial deposits were usually discovered first and, as a result, it was alluvial mining that sparked off Australia's earliest gold rushes.

The archaeologist investigating a mine site must understand its geology and the way in which mining has been done. As we have seen, the surface evidence for underground mining will consist of shaft or adit entrances and heaps of waste rock, together with traces of various facilities necessary for the running of the mine and the processing of its ore (Figure 8.6). The mining of superficial alluvium, however, will provide a very different picture, one in which whole landscapes have been turned over by shallow workings and often without the aid of facilities that will have left any substantial traces. Alluvial deposits could be exploited in a number of ways including hand-sluicing, hydraulic sluicing and dredging. The first method involved digging the paydirt from a shallow pit and washing it in a simple

Figure 8.6 Aerial photograph of a deserted mining town taken in May 1982 at Mount Cuthbert, in a remote area near Mount Isa, Queensland. This was the location of an underground copper mine with its own smelter.

device like a cradle or a Long Tom. This could be most conveniently done at the side of a creek, and fortunately alluvial deposits were often located in such situations. The second method consisted of directing a stream of water under some pressure onto the deposits and washing out the paydirt, the gold or tin was then separated out by passing the dirt over riffle-boards in a slightly tilted wooden channel. Such hydraulic sluicing needed very large quantities of water and this often meant that dams and water races had to be specially constructed, the latter sometimes over considerable distances. A great deal of care and some engineering skill was necessary to get a sufficient head of water and to be able to deliver the water with enough force at just the place that it was needed. The third method, dredging, was even more drastic. This involved the use of a suction dredge or a bucket dredge, huge boat-like contrivances that floated on a creek or river or even on flooded areas that had already been mined. They gradually ate their way through the alluvium beneath the water, separated out the gold or tin contained in it, and spewed out the waste at the other end. The dredge could be moved, so that it progressively worked its way through the available deposits. One of these dredges, suitably named *El Dorado*, has been preserved near Beechworth, in Victoria.

There was a considerable amount of alluvial mining carried out in nineteenth-century Australia and there are many mine sites of this sort. The difficulty is that they have often been worked over more than once, sometimes using different methods. This fact, plus the susceptibility of such sites to erosion, can present the archaeologist with surface evidence that is almost impossible to interpret. Fortunately, however, not all sites have been so intensively worked, and aerial photography can sometimes reveal the way in which the mining was conducted (Figure 8.7). Also, even if an area has been subjected to hydraulic sluicing, it should be possible to establish the general limits of such an operation and, more

Figure 8.7   Aerial photograph taken in September 1976 of traces of alluvial goldmining on a tributary creek of the Tia River, near Walcha, New South Wales. It would appear that hand-sluicing was the method in use.

115

importantly, there will almost certainly be the remains of a dam and a water race that will still be readily identifiable. Alluvial mining has, in some cases, left very distinctive archaeological evidence in the form of 'walls' of riverstones. These are the result of digging into the creekbeds or creekbanks and heaping up the stones along the course of the creeks. Aedeen Cremin has recorded these running for several kilometres along Clarke's Creek, south of Windeyer, on the Hargraves Goldfield of New South Wales.[11]

Another factor that can affect the sort of surface evidence found at a mine site is that the method of mining sometimes changed through time. A goldfield could commence with superficial alluvial mining, but then change to the shaft mining of deep leads. Eventually it might even turn to hard-rock mining if the parent lode could be located. Ballarat, for example, started as an alluvial field and progressed to deep-lead mining, while Bendigo, also in Victoria, commenced by working alluvial deposits and moved on to deep-quartz mining. Similarly, hard-rock mining could commence with the cutting of exploratory trenches, known by a Cornish miners' term as 'costeens'. If these were successful in producing payable ore, they might be followed by shafts and all the other trappings of underground mining. Eventually, such workings might be abandoned and the whole area exploited by making an open cut. This is the sequence of events that seems to have operated at both Kapunda and Burra, the early copper mines of South Australia.

Underground mining was only one of the types of mining for which we have archaeological evidence. It is thought by some that it was less common than alluvial mining. Nevertheless, Australia has been the scene of some remarkable underground mining, some of it very extensive and some of it very deep. For instance, the Northern Coalfield of New South Wales in the Newcastle area was first mined in 1801 and continues to produce coal. By now the area should be honeycombed with old mine workings even if they are, in general, inaccessible. Some of the gold mines of Victoria also reached considerable depths; the Magdala shaft at Stawell, for example, reaching 732 metres in 1880. In the Kalgoorlie area of Western Australia there were also shafts that went to impressive depths. It is unfortunate, therefore, that historical archaeologists have so far paid so little attention to underground evidence. Evidence which is not only likely to be less interfered with than surface evidence, but has the potential to inform us on matters for which documentary sources are often inadequate and where surface evidence is of little help.

A cautionary tale is provided by King's mine at Totley, near Ravenswood in northern Queensland. Percy Kean, who has already been referred to, reopened this silver mine in the late 1940s on the basis of a report from A.W. Wilson, a mining engineer. This report, written in 1947, was an expanded and revised version of an earlier report written by the same engineer in 1930. On neither occasion, however, was Wilson able to inspect the mine which had been closed since the early 1890s and was flooded. His report was, therefore, based on old records and reminiscences. In 1952, after Kean had dewatered the mine, T.H. Connah, a government geologist, was able to go down the mine and inspect it. Not surprisingly, T.H. Connah's report differed from Wilson's in a number of respects (Figure 8.8). As any person would agree, nothing quite equals having a look for yourself. As it was, Percy Kean's reopening of the mine does not seem to have been as successful as he had expected.[12]

It was a minor incident, in 1979, that made the writer realize the potential importance of underground evidence so far as the archaeology of Australian mining is concerned. The New South Wales Department of Main Roads was cutting into the side of Mount Beef, a hill just to the north of the small town of Uralla which stands on the edge of the nineteenth-century Rocky River Goldfield. The workmen were preparing a new route for a section of

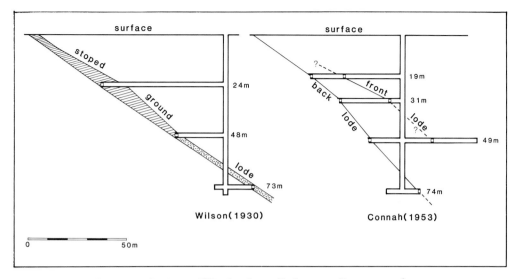

Figure 8.8 Sections of King's mine at Totley, near Ravenswood, northern Queensland. That on the left was based on old records and reminiscences, that on the right was based on an underground inspection. The differences between these two sections of the same mine emphasize the importance of underground archaeological evidence. (After Kennedy and others, 1981.)

the New England Highway in order to bypass a particularly dangerous stretch. As their graders cut down through the decomposed granite that forms the bedrock of the shoulder of the hill, they broke through the roof of an old mining tunnel (Figure 8.9). The foreman of the work was interested and kind enough to inform Lionel Gilbert, a local historian who, at that time, worked at the Armidale College of Advanced Education and he, in turn, informed the author. Together with others we visited the site and were able to enter a tunnel which ran horizontally into the hillside (Figure 8.10). At a distance of about 67 metres, fallen material from the roof and walls made further exploration unwise, although it would not have been impossible (Figure 8.11). The tunnel had been cut through very soft decomposed granite, which in places could be broken away by hand. Its level floor consisted of trampled spoil, and it had vertical walls and a rounded roof that was just high enough to allow one to stand upright. It had obviously been cut by hand, and in many places the marks of the miners' picks were still visible (Figure 8.12). The tunnel had been started from the side of the nearby Brigstock Brook gully and had apparently been driven towards the centre of the hill. There was, however, no sign of any quartz reefs — the Rocky River field had been one of alluvial and deep-lead mining. So what was the tunnel for? Local historian Arnold Goode was able to supply what is almost certainly the correct explanation. *The Uralla and Walcha Times,* of Wednesday, 20 March 1895, reported that a Dr Woods of Uralla was at that time financing a mining venture at Mount Beef. The newspaper explained that: 'it is with a view to tap the basin of this prominent peak that the doctor has decided to carry a tunnel right into the very centre of it . . . His contractor has already driven some 220ft. [67 metres] in the granite, and he expects to reach wash at about 350ft. [107 metres] from the starting point.' In other words, the tunnel seems to have been a rather speculative venture probing for a deep lead beneath the basalt hilltop. It was, to say the least, a 'long shot', and predictably it failed. By

Figure 8.9   Mount Beef, near Uralla, New South Wales: mining
tunnel as discovered during the construction of a new section of the
New England Highway in 1979. (Photograph by Shirley Dawson.)

10 July 1895, the same newspaper was reporting that the granite had dipped at such a steep angle that the removal of material from the sloping tunnel had become too difficult. The enterprise was abandoned without any deep lead being located and seems to have been forgotten by the time that the Department of Main Roads workmen rediscovered the tunnel eighty-four years later. It would have been interesting to have cleared out the fallen material from the furthest point reached in 1979 and to have inspected the leading end of the tunnel. This might have been particularly valuable if a geologist or a mining engineer could have taken part in such a inspection. Unfortunately, however, there was no time to do this before the tunnel was sealed up again, but a series of photographs was taken as a record of this unsuccessful mining venture.[13]

Although practical considerations made it impossible to do in the case of the Uralla tunnel, a detailed examination of such underground evidence would clearly have the potential to inform us on past mining methods and extent of geological knowledge. It would be interesting to use modern knowledge and expertise to assess ventures of that sort. Was Dr Woods wildly wrong, was he merely throwing his money away, or is it possible that he could have succeeded if he had been able to call on the sort of technology that now exists? Indeed, could it be that there really is a deep lead under Mount Beef, and that the failure of Dr Woods has discouraged any further search for nearly a century?

There must have been many other occasions when there have been opportunities to inspect old mine workings, but there seems to be little that has been written about them from an archaeological point of view. An exception is from Ian Jack, who, in a discussion of

Figure 8.10 Inside the Mount Beef mining tunnel, looking towards the 1979 entrance. Note the tree roots which have penetrated the decomposed granite. (Photograph by Shirley Dawson.)

Figure 8.11 One of the perils of exploring old mine workings: a rock fall inside the Mount Beef mining tunnel. The author should have been wearing a protective helmet. (Photograph by Shirley Dawson.)

Figure 8.12 Pick-marks on the wall of the Mount Beef mining
tunnel, which had obviously been cut by hand. Scale in centimetres.
(Photograph by Shirley Dawson.)

mining methods in Australian coalfields, refers to underground evidence from two mines. One is the Commonwealth No.1 mine at Lidsdale, near Lithgow in the Western Coalfield of New South Wales. This is a tunnel mine that is quite extensive and contains underground stabling for pit-ponies, some remains of rail-track and even some of the wagons that were used on it. The other mine, at Sheedy's Gully, also in the Lithgow area, is a humble affair of a single tunnel, but nevertheless contains traces of an internal tramway. One photograph from inside each of these two mines has also been published, whetting one's appetite for more.[14] Another example of an underground investigation was done by Ray Whitmore who, in 1980, was able to inspect the inside of a coal-mine, near Ipswich in Queensland, that had been sealed off since 1923.[15] Photographer Richard Stringer took a series of photographs inside this old mine and one of these is reproduced here (Figure 8.13). The underground evidence for old mining is certainly a subject to which historical archaeologists should be giving more attention. Old mines, it is true, can be extremely dangerous, but if their investigation is undertaken by people with suitable training that danger can be minimized. In Britain there are at least two old mines that are actually open to the public and have been instant successes with the tourists. One is a coal-mine, Big Pit, at Blaenavon in South Wales, which was worked from 1880 to 1980. The other is the Llechwedd slate caverns at Blaenau Ffestiniog in North Wales, most of which date from the nineteenth century. In both cases members of the public are taken on a guided underground tour which is very popular.

Apart from the on-site surface and underground evidence, there are two other sources of information to which the historical archaeologist can usefully give attention. The first of these concerns the tools, equipment and machinery used in the process of mining. With the exception of some of the heavier items, such things have often not survived at the mines

Figure 8.13 The main drive of the old Cardiff workings at Blackstone, near Ipswich, Queensland. This coal-mine had been sealed off in 1923 and it is seen here in 1980 when Rhondda Collieries Ltd broke into it. The metal plate in the foreground acted as a turntable between the wooden rails to the right and the metal rails in the main drive. (Photograph by Richard Stringer, using an exposure of approximately 4 minutes.)

themselves. There are numerous museums in Australia, however, that have preserved representative collections, particularly of smaller objects. Thus there is a great variety of hand tools and equipment for alluvial mining, but there are also larger items like winding engines, steam engines and coal-cutting machines. Collections of this sort deserve more formal investigation than has yet been carried out.

The second supplementary source of information is a rather unusual one — there exists a number of contemporary models of nineteenth-century mining activities. These are highly detailed scale models that constitute very important evidence. They were made by Carl Nordström, a Swedish professional modelmaker on the goldfields of Ballarat, Buninyong, Clunes and Bendigo between 1856 and 1859. Several of his models survive in the Science Museum of Victoria, and Murray Walker has described them as 'amongst the masterpieces of colonial folk craft' and as 'accurate models which show superbly in three dimensional form the machines and processes of which little remain today'.[16] Certainly, the Nordström models provide detailed representations of both the mining landscapes and the activities of the goldseekers. It is possible, however, that there are other contemporary models depicting aspects of past Australian mining. The only other one known that is contemporary with the equipment it portrays is a model of the waterwheel-operated battery at the Mount Bischoff tin mine in Tasmania. This is in the Zeehan Museum in the same area.[17]

In addition to the material evidence for the mining operation itself there is a great deal of other evidence for what might be called the infrastructure of mining. For example, the miners had to live somewhere, and mining by its nature was often conducted in places remote from other settlement. Some of the mining towns that sprang up were to survive and prosper even after the mines had closed or shrunk to relative insignificance. Ballarat, in Victoria, is such a case. Others, like Silverton in the far west of New South Wales, shrivelled into ghost towns when the mining died, and in the arid areas of Western Australia, the Northern Territory and Western Queensland there were settlements that disappeared off the map after the miners had left. These shrunken or deserted settlements constitute an archaeological resource of very considerable importance: the survey and excavation of sites of that type can provide us with quite detailed information about the social and economic conditions in which their inhabitants were living. Hill End, for instance, a former gold-mining town north of Bathurst in New South Wales, has been the scene of much archaeological research, although relatively little of it has been published. A far more remote mining settlement that has attracted archaeological attention is that of White Range, on the Arltunga Goldfield, northeast of Alice Springs in the Northern Territory. This site was mentioned in Chapter 6, where one aspect of the excavations by Kate Holmes was referred to. These excavations were particularly valuable for the information they yielded on the living conditions in this remote mining settlement at the beginning of the twentieth century. As is often the case in such instances, the surviving documentary records give us a substantial amount of information about the progress of mining in the area, but tell us relatively little about the conditions in which the miners were living. Archaeological survey and excavation has suggested that life must have been hard in the roughly-built huts of stone, corrugated iron and canvas. Yet even here, in a place so remote that supplies arrived only at two or three month intervals, and had to be carried in by camel or horse-teams, there were some 'home comforts'. White Range had its own store, which sold tinned and bottled commodities as well as stationery. There was also a billiard room, as was mentioned in Chapter 6, and amongst the artefacts excavated from the settlement were items that had been manufactured as far away as Paris, New York and Lincoln, in England. The last of these places had supplied one of the inhabitants with a bottle of tonic. Here, in the middle of the Never Never, somebody had needed a bottle of 'Clarke's World Famed Blood Mixture'! World famed, indeed, to travel to such a place, but some of the miners no doubt preferred bottles of stronger stuff.[18]

The archaeological investigation of deserted mining settlements can sometimes do more than merely supplement the historical record. As was explained in Chapter 1, one of the reasons that archaeologists have become interested in historical sites is because they can provide a testing ground to try out their theories and their methods. For example, archaeologists in recent years have wanted to know a lot more about how sites form so as to be able to interpret more accurately the evidence from such sites. It is for this reason that Danny Gillespie has conducted intensive surface investigations of a 1930s goldmining site in the Top End of the Northern Territory. This is at a place called Imarlkba, which is now within the Kakadu National Park and the location of a rather remote and not very successful mining venture which was abandoned by the early 1940s. Everything even remotely reusable was removed from the site, and the climate and the white ants destroyed most of what was left. All that remains are traces of mining, a boiler for a steam engine, some concrete foundations, a levelled area for one of the buildings, and a surface scatter of artefacts including bottle glass, metal containers, roofing iron, wire and fragments of ceramic. There is, however, a surprising amount of information available for the settlement from both documentary and oral sources. This information includes a small number of photographs taken at the time of greatest activity. By comparing the photograph of the store/residence with the archaeological evidence, Gillespie was able to show how the distribution of glass fragments reflected the use of different areas, and how the occupants disposed of their 'empties' by merely throwing them outside their residence. Indeed, they did not even bother to throw them at the back of the building, so that the distribution of this evidence indicated the two sides of the building adjacent to the living quarters. Those living quarters, however, were kept relatively clear of such glass containers, and the area occupied by the store mainly produced pickle containers, in contrast to the mixture of pickle, alcohol and other containers which had been tossed outside of the building (Figure 8.14). Here, therefore, is an example of how a fairly recently abandoned site, with surviving documentation, can help to explain the nature of archaeological evidence. There have been many occasions when prehistoric archaeologists have employed the distribution of different sorts of artefacts to suggest the ways in which different parts of a living site might have been used. The case of the store/residence at Imarlkba provides some indication that this can be a legitimate research strategy.[19]

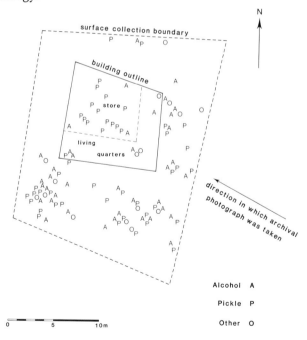

Figure 8.14 Plan of the distribution of glass fragments on and around the site of the store/residence building at Imarlkba, in the Northern Territory. This archaeological evidence reflects the ways in which the different parts of the site are known to have been used. (After Gillespie 1985.)

Another important part of the infrastructure of mining was the transport systems that linked the mines to the rest of the world. The heavier the commodity per unit value produced by a mine, the more important it was that reliable and cheap transportation be available. Thus, copper mining and particularly coal mining were greatly dependent on the availability of inexpensive transport. The very first railway constructed in Australia was opened, in 1827, by the Australian Agricultural Company to carry coal from its mine near Newcastle, in New South Wales, down to the Hunter River, where it was then loaded into boats. Between them, water transportation and railways contributed a great deal to the development of Australian mining. The early copper mines of South Australia were successful not only because of the richness of their copper ores but also because of the closeness of the mines to the sea — for at first all the ore was shipped to South Wales for smelting. In contrast, the owners of the copper and tin mines of northwest Tasmania found it necessary to create a whole series of private railways in order to provide essential transportation through a desolate and difficult landscape. Like many of the settlements, transport systems built to serve the needs of mining usually disappeared once the mining died. This leaves the historical archaeologist a variety of evidence such as the remains of wharves, or the cuttings, embankments and bridge remnants from former railways. Although some study of this type of evidence has taken place, there would seem to be a great deal of scope for its further investigation. In particular, detailed field research into the routes taken by mining railways and into the ways in which engineering problems were solved by their builders would probably extend our knowledge of a subject area where the documentation is not always as detailed as could be wished.

The remains of a multitude of mining activities make up a large part of Australia's historical archaeological evidence. Some of the mining sites are very extensive and their surviving structures can be of substantial size. This plus the innate fascination of mining, particularly of the mining of gold that was so important in nineteenth-century Australia, has meant that the physical traces of mining have attracted a great deal of attention, both from the public and from conservationists. This is as it should be, for mining sites are an important part of our heritage. They are also an extremely important subject for archaeological research, because some of the Australian sites are of world-wide significance. Items of equipment and evidence of activities can be found that, in Britain, Europe or America, have often been swept aside by later developments. Particularly in the remoter parts of Australia, the survival both of examples of nineteenth-century mining technology and of evidence of mining techniques is little short of extraordinary. The archaeology of mining is, indeed, a subject in which Australian scholars could become world leaders.

Notes

[1] G. Blainey, 1969. *The rush that never ended: A history of Australian mining* (2nd edn), Melbourne University Press, Carlton.

[2] For the Holtermann photographs see K. Burke, 1973. *Gold and silver: Photographs of Australian goldfields from the Holtermann Collection*, Penguin, Ringwood. For the Fauchery photographs see H.H. Paynting, 1970. *The James Flood book of early Australian photographs*, James Flood Charity Trust, Melbourne.

[3] K.H. Kennedy, P. Bell and C. Edmondson, 1981. *Totley: A study of the silver mines at One Mile, Ravenswood District*, Department of History, James Cook University of North Queensland.

[4] G. Brooks, 1984. The survival of a colliery — Richmond Main Historic Park. *Heritage Australia* 3(2), pp.26-30.

[5] The best introduction to this evidence will be found in J. Birmingham, I. Jack and D. Jeans, 1979. *Australian pioneer technology: sites and relics*, Heinemann, Richmond, Victoria. Separate chapters of this book deal with gold; copper, tin, silver, lead and zinc; the iron and steel industry; coal; and oil shale.

[6] J. Birmingham, I. Jack and D. Jeans, 1979, p.49. Also A. Rollinson, 1987. Saving Queensland's industrial heritage: The Venus Gold Battery. *Heritage Australia* 6(1), p.19.

[7] C.J. Davey, 1986. The history and archaeology of the North British Mine Site, Maldon, Victoria. *Australian Journal of Historical Archaeology* 4, pp.51-6.

[8] A. Cremin, 1986. Mudgee Shire industrial archaeology survey, unpublished report, p.3.

[9] G. Tanks, 1986. Report on a survey of one aspect of the Rocky River Goldfield, unpublished report forming part of coursework, Department of Archaeology and Palaeoanthropology, University of New England, Armidale.

[10] J. Kerr, 1982. *Mount Morgan: gold, copper and oil*, J.D. & R.S. Kerr, St Lucia, Queensland, p.210.

[11] A. Cremin, 1986, p.5.

[12] K.H. Kennedy, P. Bell and C. Edmondson, 1981, pp.10-16.

[13] A. Goode, 1984. Tunnel, dredge and drought: The Rocky River 1860-1900. *Armidale and District Historical Society Journal and Proceedings* 27, pp.1-22.

[14] J. Birmingham, I. Jack and D. Jeans, 1979, pp.110-11.

[15] R.L. Whitmore, 1984. Old Blackstone Mine revisited, *Queensland Government Mining Journal*, August 1984, pp.283-5.

[16] M. Walker, 1978. *Pioneer crafts of early Australia*, MacMillan, Melbourne, pp.106-9.

[17] J. Birmingham, I. Jack and D. Jeans, 1979, p.79.

[18] K. Holmes, 1983. Excavations at Arltunga, Northern Territory, *Australian Journal of Historical Archaeology* 1, pp.78-87.

[19] D.A. Gillespie, 1985. Imarlkba: Historical archaeology and a fossicking economy site in the Top End of the Northern Territory. M. Litt. thesis, Department of Prehistory and Archaeology, University of New England, Armidale.

Chapter 9

Made in Australia

INFORMATION FROM INDUSTRIAL RELICS

Many of us tend to think of the history of Australia as one of wide open spaces: of sheep and cattle raising, of grain growing, and of mines isolated in the desolation of the outback. In fact, one of the most remarkable aspects of our history is the rapidity with which secondary industry grew in a new and remote country. Manufacturing started in the very first year of settlement; bricks were being made at Brickfield Hill within months of the landing in Sydney Cove. By the middle of the following year, 1789, about 10,000 bricks per month were being produced, and tiles were being made. Bricks, of course, were only one of the many commodities that were urgently required in the new colony. Flour, beer, leather, timber, lime, salt and all sorts of ironwork: these and many other things needed to be manufactured locally in order to reduce the dependence on imports which could take so long to arrive and which entailed payments to British manufacturers. As time went by, and other colonies were founded, so the demand for local manufactures increased even though the industrial might of Britain could produce many goods, and ship them to Australia, more cheaply than they could be produced in this country. This was also in spite of the deep-seated conviction acquired by many Australians, and one that is with us still, that anything manufactured overseas must, by the very nature of things, be of superior quality to anything made in our own country. Indeed, there was a certain nationalism that spurred on some industrial entrepreneurs, even when profits eluded them. They frequently made mistakes, and their enterprises often failed, but this was all part of the learning process and should not blind us to the fact that Australian manufacturing was able to grow to impressive proportions by the end of the nineteenth century. Between 1861 and 1890, factories grew from a 4.9 per cent share in the gross domestic product to a 10.9 per cent share, having peaked at 12.7 per cent in 1882 and 1884. In the Census of 1891 there was 16.5 per cent of the Australian workforce employed in manufacturing, either working in factories or as makers-cum-dealers or home-workers. The only type of employment that exceeded this figure was the agricultural and pastoral sector, which employed 24.7 per cent of the workforce.[1]

All this manufacturing activity has left us extensive material evidence as well as a substantial documentary record. The physical traces of secondary industry, however, often suffer from some of the same problems that beset many mining sites. Thus defunct factories have often been stripped of everything that was saleable or could be re-used elsewhere. Furthermore, after initial abandonment, a factory building is quite likely to be brought back into use and usually for a completely different type of manufacturing from that for which it was originally designed. This process of abandonment and re-use can sometimes have occurred more than once before the structure has been finally allowed to fall derelict. Again, just like mining sites, old manufacturing sites are quite likely to be wiped off the face of the earth, in the public interest, during some well-meaning 'clean-up' programme. Old factories have even fewer people willing to speak up for them than old mines. There is yet another factor, however, that leads to the destruction of many manufacturing sites, a factor that is far less of a problem with mining sites. Most factories were built in or near towns or cities. With urban growth, the industrial developments of a century ago on the outskirts of Sydney, Melbourne or Perth are now occupying prime real estate near the centre of a metropolitan sprawl. In such circumstances the pressure from modern developers is likely to be so great that all evidence of the former activity will be quickly destroyed. Fortunately, this factor tends to be less important in country towns because of the economic stagnation of many of them during the present century. Thus, to some extent, the smaller the town, the more likely it is that manufacturing sites will have survived. One problem is that the factories and other installations that survive in this way may not be fully representative of those that formerly existed. For example, historical records for New South Wales, between 1877 and 1900, show that one of the biggest employers was what might be loosely called the metal industry. This included the following categories: metals, engineering; railway workshops; vehicles (coaches and wagons); and boats, ships and slips.[2] Because of the tendency for this type of industry to be concentrated in major centres, it is not as well represented in the archaeological record as some other industrial activities. Factories involved in the metal industry that were successful were eventually modernized or replaced, those that were not successful were often swept aside to make way for other activities.

Circumstance has therefore selected the material evidence that is available for study. It is the study of such evidence for past industries that has become known as 'industrial archaeology', a term that seems to have originated in Britain in the early 1950s.[3] However, industrial archaeology is but *one* aspect of Australian historical archaeology, just as maritime archaeology is another. Such a contention might not be understood by British archaeologists, but it does make sense in Australia, as it also surely does in New Zealand, America, Canada or South Africa. The point at issue is that the archaeology of past industries should not be considered in isolation but as an integral part of the whole range of material evidence available for the periods in question.

The study of Australian industrial archaeological evidence is new, extending back to the late 1960s at the earliest. As a result, the evidence that can be discussed in this chapter is further limited by the selective character of the research that has so far been conducted and adequately published. Some types of manufacturing have been quite well studied, while others have hardly been touched. The series of examples that has been chosen aims to give a cross-section of the work that has been done, although the examples given are not evenly spread geographically because of the uneven distribution of completed research work. Irrespective of these shortcomings, however, each of the examples represents a process that must be understood if we are to comprehend the often fragmentary components that have survived. In each case it is necessary to ask oneself: What went in, what was done to it, and what came out? In other words: What were the raw materials, what manufacturing processes were used, and what was the finished product?

One of colonial Australia's oldest industries was the production of whale-oil which, in the early years of settlement, was an important export because of its use as lamp-oil and for a variety of other products. The industry involved the pursuit, catching, killing and retrieving of whales that were then cut up into chunks of blubber that could be rendered down into oil in a tryworks. This could be done either on a whale ship or on a shore-station, and early European settlers in Australia engaged in both types of whaling. Whichever method was adopted, however, the technology was similar involving harpoons, lances, lines, guns, and mincing, cutting-in and trying-out equipment.[4] As might be expected there is little archaeological evidence for ship-based whaling, although the wreck of an early-nineteenth-century British whaler (possibly one named *Lively*) has been investigated off the Western Australian coast.[5] Nevertheless, the locations of a number of shore-based whaling stations are known on the coasts of New South Wales, Tasmania, South Australia and Western Australia. Identifiable features or artefacts have survived on some of these sites, but it is only in the single instance where extensive excavation has taken place that we have sufficient archaeological evidence to see how the process of whale-oil extraction was carried out.

This excavation was conducted, in 1984, at the site of Bathers Bay whaling station, in Fremantle, Western Australia.[6] The site is situated on the seaward side of Arthur Head, which forms the southern side of the entrance to Fremantle Harbour and the Swan River. Documentary sources indicated that the whaling station had operated from 1837 to around the 1860s, but its unusual urban location gave little hope that much evidence could have survived. Indeed, when Jack McIlroy excavated at this site it was then in use by the Fremantle Port Authority as a storage area for unwanted machinery and building materials. However, excavation revealed up to 3.5 metres of complex stratified deposits which covered several nineteenth-century structures, three of which had belonged to the whaling station. Deposits as deep as this are unusual on historical archaeological sites in this country and in this case they resulted from the adjacent limestone cliffs being substantially cut back on various occasions and the resulting rubble used as landfill after the abandonment of the whaling station. It was in this way that the remains of the early structures had been covered and preserved.

The excavation was not successful in locating the whaling jetty, but it did uncover part of the Station House consisting of the base of a rough limestone wall and a fragment of a rammed limestone floor. The most important discovery, however, was the remains of the tryworks, which were surprisingly well preserved (Figure 9.1). Tryworks were the means by which the whale blubber was melted down into whale-oil and therefore constituted the crucial piece of processing equipment in this particular industry. They usually consisted of two or three large cast-iron pots, set above adjacent brick-built hearths, and provided with one or more chimneys. In ship-based whaling they were situated on the deck of the whaler and had to be sufficiently stable to withstand the movement of the ship and designed in such a way as to minimize the danger of fire. On shore-stations they did not need to be so carefully built, but it was still important that they provide an efficient means of rendering down the blubber. This process of 'trying-out', as it was called, was the cause of much of the dirt and stench always associated with whaling. Not only did the blubber smell when it was being heated, but the usual practice was to fuel the fire with 'scrap', the crisp remains of the blubber after the oil had already been heated out of it. One suspects that anybody who had ever smelt a tryworks in operation never forgot it!

The tryworks at the Bathers Bay whaling station was revealed as a brick structure built against the former cliff face. It consisted of three hearths and a presumed central chimney. There was no sign of the trypots which, as valuable and movable items, would almost certainly have been removed for use elsewhere when the station finally closed down. The

Figure 9.1 The remains of the tryworks excavated at Bathers Bay, Fremantle, Western Australia. The three black oblong areas are the hearths over which the trypots were heated. Scale in 10cm divisions. (Photograph by Patrick Baker, courtesy of Jack McIlroy.)

three hearths, however, were still filled with charcoal and soot and an oily residue that seemed to be the remains of whale blubber. The bricks used in the tryworks were of two types: red ones, which were probably of local origin, and yellow ones, which had probably been imported as ships' ballast and could have come from eastern Australia or from a number of places overseas. Lime mortar held the brickwork together, and adjacent to the tryworks were the remains of a limestone and brick structure that had possibly been a boatshed and workshop. The archaeological evidence excavated at the site of the Bathers Bay whaling station is important for the clear picture that it gives of the functioning of such a station. A part of the business of the archaeologist is to show us what it was actually like to be there. In the case of Bathers Bay, this can actually be done (Figure 9.2).

Another industry that is one of colonial Australia's oldest, and for which the surviving material evidence is often more extensive and better preserved than whaling, is that of flour-milling. This was an essential and an extremely important industry. The staple food in colonial Australia was bread, to make bread one needed flour. One of the first priorities of early settlement was to be able to produce flour from locally grown wheat. This was done in a variety of ways: using human muscle power, using animal traction, harnessing the power of the wind or of running water, employing steam engines and, more recently, utilizing diesel engines or electricity. Except for the simplest methods, flour-milling required quite a lot of machinery and a substantial building. Because milling was one of the first industries to make use of the gravity principle, in which the material being processed was gradually

Figure 9.2   An artist's reconstruction of the Bathers Bay whaling station in
operation about 1838. To the left, blubber is being cut up and transported
to the tryworks seen in the background. Everything is complete, except
the smell! (Drawing by Chris Hill, courtesy of Jack McIlroy.)

moved by its own weight from the top to the bottom of a building, flour mills were usually
several storeys high and often higher than any of the buildings around them. In addition,
because the market being served was a domestic one, because everyone needed flour, and
because transport systems were poor in many areas until the railways were developed,
there were a great many flour mills. Even quite small country towns had their own flour
mill, and many towns had more than one. However, with the advent of modern transportation systems, milling is one of a number of industries that have become increasingly
centralized in a few big cities, resulting in the abandonment of facilities in rural towns. As a
consequence of these various circumstances flour-milling has left us a considerable amount
of material evidence. This evidence has been studied by a number of historical archaeologists, including Ian Jack who has provided a most useful introduction to the subject.[7]

Quite often it is the flour mill building, rather than the machinery, that has survived, even
if only as a ruin. In Chapter 5, for instance, the crankmill on Norfolk Island and the treadmill
at Port Arthur were both mentioned. These are famous instances of flour mills that were
powered by human effort, but in neither case does much more than the shell of the building
remain, although the disassembled components of the Norfolk Island crankmill machinery
do exist in storage. Similarly, only one intact example of a mill driven by animal power
survives, in this case on the central tablelands of New South Wales and dating from 1836.
Although the remains of windmills are rather more common, none of them seem to contain

their original machinery. The South Perth windmill in Western Australia, a much restored tourist attraction, does have machinery, but it is not its own having been transferred from another windmill at Busselton, in the same state. Other windmills that still stand consist of little more than the building. Neither the windmill at Wickham Terrace, Brisbane, built in 1828 and therefore the oldest surviving building in Queensland, nor the windmill at Mount Barker in South Australia, have any sails. At least their basic structures still stand, however, whereas the windmill at Cattai in New South Wales, which has been called the earliest industrial building surviving in Australia (it was built between 1806 and 1809), is now reduced to a ruined fragment. There also appears to be no trace whatever of any of the nineteen windmills that at one time existed in Sydney.

With watermills the situation is rather better. Surprisingly, in a continent that has often been described as the driest, water power was quite extensively employed in nineteenth-century Australia. Waterwheels drove crushing equipment at some of the mines, sometimes provided the power for sawmills, and were used in other ways which included flour-milling. In spite of the problems of drought and flood, there seems to have been a substantial number of water-powered flour mills. Only one of these has survived relatively intact on the Australian mainland. This is the mill built in 1860 at Bridgewater, in South Australia, which has a fine example of a cast-iron 'pitchback' waterwheel, that is to say, one that ran in the reverse direction to the flow of water that drove it from above. The wheel is 11.27 metres in diameter, was made in Glasgow in Scotland, and was imported into Australia in pieces. The place where waterwheels were most common was in Tasmania, where a more regular rainfall made them more reliable. In 1861, there were no less than fifty flour mills powered in this way. One of these, the Thorpe mill, at Bothwell, which was built around 1823 and functioned until 1906, has been restored to working order in recent years and provides a unique insight into water-powered milling technology.[8]

Thorpe watermill consists of a fine, partly three-storey brick building, with a mill-race running under its centre so that the wheel is housed at basement level. The waterwheel is 'overshot', which means that the water enters the buckets on the wheel at the top, just past its highest point. Thus the wheel is turned by the weight of the water in the buckets, rather than by the actual flow of the water. The water is led from the nearby Clyde River along a mill-race and, after turning the wheel, runs back into the river along a tail-race. The wheel produces about 4 horsepower, turning at a speed of 8 revolutions per minute which the gearing increases to 120 revolutions per minute at the millstones. It takes 2250 litres of water to grind one kilogram of flour. As well as driving the stones, the waterwheel provides power for the mill's auxiliary machinery by means of a crown wheel, pinions, pulleys and belts. The gearing between the waterwheel and the stones consists of both cast-iron and wooden cog-wheels, an arrangement that reduces both the noise and the danger of fire as well as allowing the relatively inexpensive replacement of worn wooden teeth. Thorpe mill has only one set of millstones, whereas some watermills had several sets. However, its stones are of the very best material known as French burr, consisting of a type of quartz that must have been imported from France. Because this quartz was only found in small pieces, millstones made from this material had to be built up in a composite fashion and then bound together with iron hoops. The lower stone is stationary, and the upper stone revolves close to but not quite touching it. A regulating mechanism feeds the grain through a hole in the centre of the top stone and the meal falls from between the outer edges of the stones into a wooden container, from which it escapes by a meal chute.

Thorpe watermill is particularly important because we can see how it operated and we can therefore understand the whole process whereby grain was turned into flour (Figure 9.3). Sacks of grain were unloaded from wagons at the front door of the mill. From there they were carried into the mill to the base of the sack hoist, this lifted the sacks to the top floor through trap doors that opened upwards, and fell shut, as each sack passed through. On the top floor, the grain was either dumped into large storage bins or tipped immediately into a large hopper that fed the 'smutter', or grain cleaner, on the floor below. From the smutter, the grain ran down to the next floor where it was fed by the regulating mechanism into the millstones. The wholemeal produced by the stones was then raised back to the first floor by an endless belt fitted with buckets. It was there tipped into a flour sifter which separated it into four different products: flour, middlings, bran and pollard. These were then fed by a chute to the ground floor, where they were bagged and weighed. The whole process made good use of gravity to move around a heavy and bulky commodity, and the arrangements showed sound traditional design. It is interesting to observe that Thomas

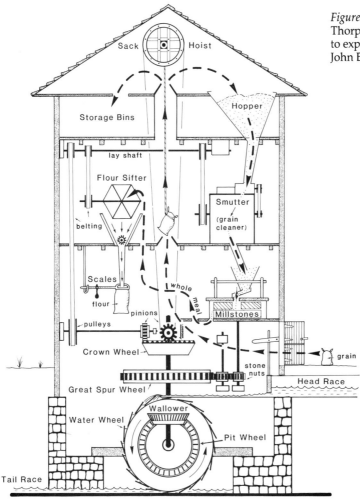

Figure 9.3 Section through Thorpe watermill, Tasmania, to explain its operation. (After John Bignell.)

Axford, the builder of the mill, only arrived in Tasmania about a year before he constructed it. He had come straight from England, and came from Abingdon in Berkshire. In the England of the early nineteenth century he would have had ample opportunity to observe many watermills in action. Not surprisingly, it was an English watermill that he built in Tasmania.

From about the 1830s, flour mills driven by steam engines became increasingly common. Some of these were specially built for the purpose, but others were former watermills that were converted to steam, just as some steam-driven mills were converted to diesel or electricity during the early part of the twentieth century. Steam engines had obvious advantages over the power sources that had previously been used for milling. Unlike wind or watermills, steam-mills could be run at any time providing there was wood for the fire-box and water for the boiler. They could also develop a great deal more power which meant that milling could be carried out on a larger scale, and they could be sited conveniently within a town, rather than being confined to a windy hilltop or a flood-prone river valley. Indeed, with the development of railways, many mills were located adjacent to the tracks so as to keep transportation costs for both raw materials and finished products to a minimum. At first the steam engines used in such mills drove stones, and the mills operated in much the same way as windmills or watermills. From the late 1870s, however, there was a gradual change to milling with rollers made either of porcelain or of chilled iron. Roller-mills were cheaper to run and produced a whiter flour, and they have remained the basis of flour-milling technology ever since.

As with other forms of flour-milling, there are very few steam-mills that have retained much of their nineteenth-century machinery. The roller-mill in Lovell Street, Young, is the only exception in New South Wales, and its machinery is of late-nineteenth-century date. Because of the decline of country milling, and the centralization of the industry in a few big cities, substantial numbers of former steam-mills stand as derelict shells or have been re-used for other purposes that have necessitated the removal of all the milling equipment. The buildings were usually large, multi-storeyed and solidly built and have, therefore, had a relatively high survival rate. A careful study of these structures can often tell us quite a lot about the milling process that was formerly conducted in them. The investigation of McCrossin's Mill, in Uralla, northern New South Wales, provides a good example of what can be done.[9]

McCrossin's Mill was built as a steam-mill in the early 1870s and functioned until the early to mid-1890s. It was then used for a variety of purposes: first, as the premises for a skin-buyer, then for an undertaking and hardware business, then as a storehouse for an adjacent grocery and produce firm, and finally, since 1979, as a local museum. At some time during the first few decades of the twentieth century the steam-engine and the milling machinery were removed, and the external boiler room and its tall chimney demolished. In 1981, Luke Godwin took on the difficult task of conducting an archaeological examination of the surviving structure and of carrying out limited excavations inside and outside the building. The mill is a large, oblong structure, three storeys high, mostly built of brick, but with the foundations and ground-floor walls on three sides constructed of solid granite masonry. The fourth side is of brick only, and excavations here revealed traces of the former boiler room in the form of the brickwork of the boiler bed and the boiler itself — which was probably a replacement of about 1883 and which had apparently been rolled off its bed and deliberately buried in the early 1960s (Figure 9.4). These excavations, which were outside of the mill building itself, also uncovered the well which had supplied water for the boiler.

Figure 9.4   Part of the boiler uncovered in the 1981 excavation at McCrossin's Mill, Uralla, New South Wales. Scale in centimetres. (Photograph by Luke Godwin.)

This is said to have been 7 metres deep and to have been filled in at some time during the fifty years before 1981. Over 4 metres of deposit was excavated from it without reaching the bottom, but in it was found a number of carefully shaped large blocks of granite which appear to have constituted the upper layer of the engine bed and to have been removed and dumped down the well when the remains of that bed were covered by a timber floor some time early this century. This floor was pulled out, and excavations beneath it revealed the lower part of the engine bed consisting of large granite blocks standing on a floor of lime mortar and crushed brick. The shape of this bed would suggest that a horizontal steam engine was in use, and it is known from historical sources that a 16-horsepower engine was installed which was capable of driving three sets of millstones.

The information gained from the excavations was complemented by that obtained from the examination of the building (Figure 9.5). Within the main part of the mill, the heavy wooden beams on the ground floor must have been the supports for the power take-off from the engine and for the millstones situated on the floor above. The stairs leading to the first and second floors still survived, as did the self-closing trap-doors which indicated the former location of the sack hoist. There was also a chute from the second floor which had presumably fed grain to the stones on the floor below. At the end of the building, furthest from the engine, was (and still is) a large, roughly built, wooden shed that is thought to have been constructed in the early 1880s for chaff-cutting. This seems to have been a rather desperate effort to attract as much trade as possible at a time when rural flour-milling was already in decline. Indeed, the abandonment of the boiler when all the other machinery was removed would suggest that it had become burnt out and useless and that the mill had closed in the mid-1890s because the owner could not afford a new one. There is one further detail of Luke Godwin's examination of this building that must be mentioned. From scorings on the wall of the engine room, where the flywheel of the engine seems occasionally to have brushed against it, Godwin was able to ascertain that the flywheel must have had a diameter of 290 centimetres. Because the horsepower of the engine is known from documentary sources, and because it is known that the velocity of the flywheel of such an engine is likely to have been 50 revolutions per minute, it was possible to calculate the approximate weight of the flywheel. It seems that it probably weighed 2.6 tonnes, and this piece of information is an eloquent demonstration of how information about machinery can be gained, even from a few scratches on a wall, in a building from which all equipment has been removed.

Another early industry in colonial Australia, and one that is still very much with us, was brewing.[10] Australian consumption of beer has long been remarkable, having risen, by the late 1970s, to about 137 litres per head of population per year. Breweries, like flour mills, could at one time be found in most rural towns, but a similar process of centralization in the big cities has led to the closure of almost all of these. In 1870, Victoria had 116 breweries in seventy different towns but, by 1954, only seven breweries were left in the whole state. Like flour mills, the process of brewing made use of gravity to move its materials around during the course of manufacture. For this reason breweries were often tall buildings, with the major brewing stages taking place on successively lower floors of a four or five-storeyed tower. Although the closure of so many breweries has led to the demolition of numerous examples of these fine industrial buildings, quite a number have survived in a disused condition or have been successfully converted to other uses. Again, like flour mills, most of these have lost all or part of their processing equipment. One of the exceptions appears to be

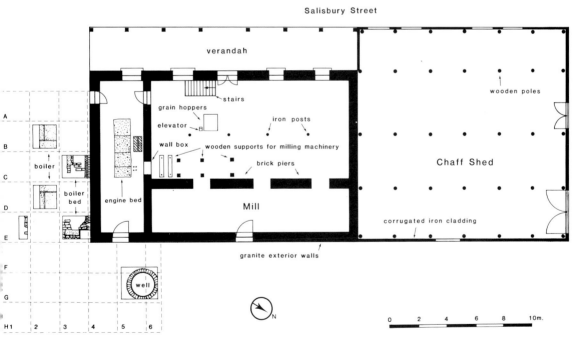

Figure 9.5 Plan of the ground floor of McCrossin's Mill in 1981, showing surviving features within the building and excavated areas outside. (Courtesy of Luke Godwin.)

135

Bradley's Goulburn Brewery, in New South Wales, but in the greater number of cases it is only the buildings and their layout which have survived for study. Nevertheless, even such limited evidence can prove quite informative, as was demonstrated by Damaris Bairstow in the case of two breweries in Newcastle, New South Wales.[11]

The Castlemaine Brewery, dating from 1876, and the Great Northern Brewery, built in 1888, have both left substantial brick structures still standing in Wood Street, Newcastle. The first of these has had a variety of uses since it ceased to be an operational brewery in 1931, and it is now to become a museum; the second had only a brief working life, and currently provides accommodation for technical students. In both cases, therefore, the material evidence is virtually limited to the structures alone. A careful examination of this evidence and of contemporary press accounts which describe the two breweries and their facilities in some detail has made it possible to understand how the different sections of these buildings were used in the brewing process. It has also made it possible to work out the rather complex structural history of the Castlemaine Brewery from 1876 to around 1914. This was the larger of the two breweries and seems to have handled every aspect of the production of beer — from the steeping and germination of barley, that was then kiln-dried into malt, to the barrelling or bottling of the end-product. Both of these Newcastle breweries are good examples of how the documentary record can be vital in the interpretation of historical sites and also of how the sites, in turn, can add to that documentary record. It is one thing to have a contemporary drawing of how the Castlemaine Brewery looked in 1878, but a study of its surviving remains can tell us a great deal about the rise and fall of its fortunes in the hundred years and more that have elapsed since then (Figures 9.6 and 9.7).

The industries of nineteenth-century Australia produced very much more than just lamp-oil, flour and beer. Of crucial importance in a new nation was a group of related activities that provided a range of building materials. Of these, it is the making of bricks that has left the most obvious evidence.[12] Because both the raw materials and the finished products were heavy, there was an established brickworks in almost every town in areas that had both suitable clays or shales and adequate fuel. Indeed, bricks would sometimes be made locally for a specific building project with manufacture ceasing as soon as that demand was met. As late as 1959 there were 150 brickworks in New South Wales alone. Like flour mills and breweries, however, economies of scale and improved transport facilities have led to an increasing centralization of the industry so that now we have only a small number of very large manufacturers and many of the rural brickworks have closed. The result of this is that evidence of former brickmaking might be found in many places, although there has often been a systematic policy of demolition and landfilling. A quarry from which the clay was dug, by now often flooded, the ruins of brick-kilns, the remnants of buildings which once housed brickmaking machinery. These are the sort of remains that one might expect from brickmaking over the last hundred years or so. Traces of earlier brickmaking would be much less substantial because clay-digging was usually on a smaller scale, bricks were often moulded by hand, and firing was frequently done in open 'clamps' or stacks rather than in specially constructed kilns. Such early brickyards might leave little evidence — only a few overgrown depressions and a scatter of broken brick. Many of the oldest of these sites have probably vanished for ever, submerged by the growth of the cities and towns on whose outskirts they were located.

In practice, it can be quite difficult to study the archaeology of brickmaking and all too easy to drift off into a technological history based on the documentary record rather than on

Figure 9.6 The Castlemaine Brewery, Newcastle, New South Wales, in 1878. This drawing was originally published in the *Illustrated Sydney News*, 13 July 1878. (By courtesy of the Mitchell Library, Sydney.)

Figure 9.7 The Castlemaine Brewery in 1988 during its restoration.

the material remains which are so often vestigial or absent. Certainly we will need that documentary record if we are to understand a complex industrial process from only fragmentary evidence. On occasions, however, there will be opportunities to apply archaeological observation to examples of industry that are still functioning in a traditional fashion or have only recently ceased to function. This is what has sometimes been called 'living archaeology', in which the archaeologist is able to compare his or her interpretation of the material evidence with what the people who actually created that evidence have to say about the activities that are responsible for it. In the case of brickmaking, a good example of such an opportunity is the brickworks at Glen Innes, in northern New South Wales, which has continued to function until recent times, although its future is now uncertain. This brickworks was studied by Don Godden, in 1985, who reported that it had undergone only minor changes in technology and organization over the previous sixty years.[13] It was, at that time, one of the longest continually operated rural brickworks in New South Wales, one of the few where the bricks were still wood-fired, and the only one in Australia that was still wholly powered by steam. Equipment for both hand-moulding and mechanical extrusion have survived at the works, but since early this century the principal activity has been the production of 'dry press' bricks, that is to say, the making of bricks by putting crushed clay with a low moisture content under great pressure. This forms the 'green' bricks which are then dried and subsequently fired within a kiln. Originally there

Figure 9.8 Foster brick press at Glen Innes Brickworks, northern New South Wales.

were three or four relatively inefficient updraft kilns but, in 1967, a downdraft kiln was built which gradually superseded them.

For anyone interested in industrial archaeology, a visit to the Glen Innes Brickworks is an exciting experience. The whole process of manufacture can be followed in great detail — from the extraction of the clay from the quarry which forms part of the site, to the removal of the finished bricks from the kiln. The visitor can see a single-cylinder, horizontal steam engine, installed in 1922, and probably made by the famous firm of Tangye of Birmingham, in England; can examine one boiler that was manufactured in Brisbane in 1932, and another that was made in Newcastle in 1948; and can inspect three brick presses and two repress units made by the three Sydney firms of Marrickville Engineering, T. Hodkinson & Co. and Foster and Sons (Figures 9.8 and 9.9). In addition there is an under-driven pan crusher, also made by Hodkinson, that grinds the clay to the required consistency. The most important thing about this site, however, is that one can see how the individual components, interesting in themselves though they may be, fit into the overall production line. They are not just pieces of equipment preserved in a museum, they are actually in use as part of a functioning system.

There were other clay products that were important to the building industry as well as bricks: drainage pipes, roofing and flooring tiles and chimney-pots were all produced in one place or another. There are several other industries that produced building materials that must be mentioned. A very important one was the burning of lime which was essential for the making of the best mortars, plasters and washes, but was also used in agriculture, mining and other industries. From the late nineteenth century onwards there was, in addition, the related industry of cement manufacturing. As mentioned in Chapter 6, shortage of lime created some problems for colonial builders, but wherever limestone (or

Figure 9.9 Maker's plate on brick press at Glen Innes Brickworks. It reads: 'T. HODKINSON & CO MAKERS NEWTOWN SYDNEY NSW'. Scale in centimetres.

sea shell) was readily available within reach of a populated area, limeburning soon got under way. This process involved the turning of limestone into quicklime (calcium oxide), a nasty substance that can burn one's skin, damage eyes and cause hair loss. The simplest way of burning lime was to heap the stone and firewood into a pit and set it alight, but the industrial production of lime necessitated the construction of special kilns which were burnt for one to three days at about 1000°C. Built of brick, or stone, or of both, these were substantial structures which have quite often left recognizable ruins such as those on Maria Island, Tasmania, or around Goulburn, in New South Wales.[14] Like the brickmaking at Glen Innes, however, our best chance of understanding the traditional process of limeburning is to observe it still being practised, and this is exactly what Michael Pearson was able to do at Wanneroo, north of Perth in Western Australia.[15] Here, as recently as 1984, Mr Jack Susac and his brother still operated a double kiln consisting of two rectangular kilns separated by a central unloading area. As it took two to three days to load a kiln, a day-and-a-half to fire it, a night to cool down, and (before mechanical unloading) several days to empty, these two kilns were formerly operated in tandem so that a constant output of lime was ensured. At the present time one kiln is kept loaded and in reserve, while the other is loaded, fired and emptied once a week, producing 36 tonnes of lime on each occasion. To achieve this, however, about 72 tonnes of limestone have to be carefully loaded into the kiln, together with about 30 tonnes of timber fuel. All the stone and fuel have to be hand-placed in alternate layers, with smaller stones in the cooler parts of the kiln and larger stones in the hotter parts. Also, the lower stones are built up in three fire-arches to facilitate the process of burning (Figure 9.10).

The Susac kilns, which were built in 1955 and 1957, are constructed of limestone blocks and lined with two or three layers of bricks that are bonded with clay mortar. They are open at the top, to which there is easy access because they are built into sloping ground. There is also an unloading door on one side of each kiln that is sealed up during firing. Each kiln has three elongated ash pits which extend from front to back across its floor, and over each of these are iron bars and a brick grate, the top of which is level with the floor. During firing, these grates are fed with fuel from three stoke-holes in the front of the kiln. Clearly, considerable skill is required in the loading and firing of these kilns, as well as in their general management. Pearson's observations of their operation make it easier to interpret the tumbled ruins that constitute the archaeological evidence for past limeburning, not only in Western Australia but in the rest of the country also.

Another vital industry in colonial Australia, on which builders depended heavily, was the sawing and milling of timber.[16] This activity, however, has left us relatively little material evidence of the sawmills themselves, many of which were dismantled and moved whenever the timber resources of a particular locality became depleted. Furthermore, the actual process of timber-getting, and such activities as sleeper-cutting, are unlikely to have left many traces that can be identified. Even the collapsed and silting depressions that mark the sites of pit-sawing can be difficult to recognize unless they are of fairly recent date. However, the timber industry has left its mark in the form of changed landscapes and damaged vegetation, while the literally millions of wooden buildings in Australia are eloquent testimony to its productive capacity. Not all sawmills could be moved; urban mills with large stationary steam engines and mills powered by waterwheels had to stay in one place. Almost none of the latter survive, although their sites can still be identified in some cases. One example of such a site is Bagot's Mill, at Ben Lomond Station, near Guyra in northern New South Wales, which has been investigated and excavated by the author.[17]

Figure 9.10 Loading limestone into one of the limekilns at Wanneroo, Western Australia, in 1984. (Photograph by Michael Pearson.)

Built in 1877 by an extraordinary Irishman, Christopher Thomas Bagot, the 9-metre-diameter waterwheel was designed to drive both a sawmill and a flour mill. It was only the sawmill that certainly functioned before Bagot was declared insolvent in 1879. The only case known of a water-powered sawmill that is still intact is one dating from early in the present century at Yallingup, in Western Australia, and the main reason for its survival is probably its relatively recent date (Figure 9.11). However, some steam-powered mills existed until only a few years ago and their ruins can sometimes be found. In some cases they are running still, although now converted to a more modern power source. Apart from these surviving sawmills, the timber industry also has one or two other types of archaeological evidence. The remains of an embankment, or the ruins of a bridge, can indicate the former existence of a logging tramway; a brick sawdust kiln may be all that is left of a busy milling site; and a logging wharf or the wreck of a 'drogher' (a specialized paddle-steamer that carried logs) can demonstrate the importance of river transportation (Figure 9.12). The archaeological study of the Australian timber industry is not easy, but it is by no means impossible.

There was one further Australian industry that played such an important part in

Figure 9.11 Overshot waterwheel at Yallingup, Western Australia. Constructed early in the present century, the wheel drove a sawmill. (Photographed by Ian Jack in 1979.)

supplying building materials that it must be mentioned. This was the manufacture of pressed metal ceilings, at first made of zinc, but later, and more commonly, made of steel. There are very large numbers of Australian houses and other buildings which contain ceilings made in this way. Imitating plasterwork, and embossed with intricate patterns that could, if desired, be highlighted with a variety of colours, these ceilings were very popular in the late nineteenth century and in the earlier part of this century. Although there were some early competitors, most pressed metal ceilings were made by Wunderlich Ltd, a remarkable firm with a factory in Redfern, Sydney, that operated from 1890 till 1969. Wunderlich also had other manufacturing plants and, at one time or another, produced a variety of pressed metal goods, terracotta roofing tiles, asbestos cement sheets, aluminium windows and even plastics. It is perhaps their ceilings for which they were best known, however. When the Redfern factory was finally demolished in 1980, there was an opportunity to conduct an archaeological investigation that included not only the recording of the buildings but also the rescue of some of the remaining machinery and of some of the more important fittings. In particular, it was possible to collect a representative series of the pressed metal panels which had been widely used throughout the factory and its administration building.[18]

In addition to those that have already been discussed, colonial Australia had a vast appetite for a wide range of other manufactured goods. Scattered across countless archaeological sites all over the continent is abundant artefactual evidence that the factories of Britain, America and elsewhere, were only too happy to supply a great variety of Australian requirements. It is not surprising that there were repeated efforts by Australian

142

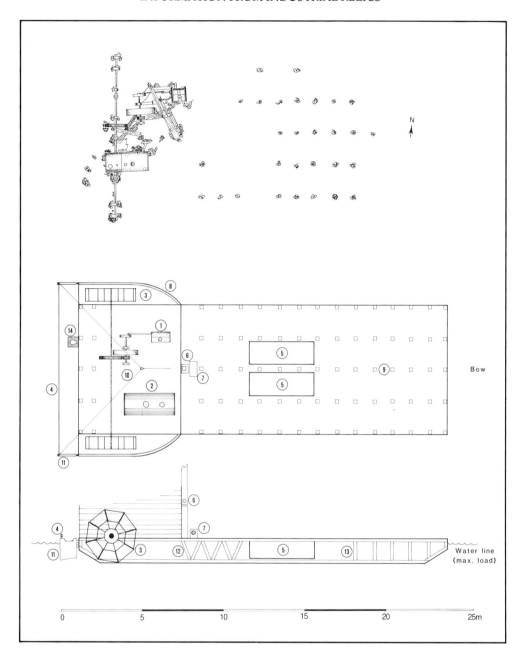

Figure 9.12   Above: Archaeological plan of the wreck of a 'drogher' on the lower Nambucca River, northern New South Wales. *Below*: Reconstructed plan and section of such a vessel, based on historical sources and oral tradition. 1: engine. 2: boiler. 3: paddle-wheel. 4: rudder bar. 5: freshwater tanks. 6: mast. 7: steam winch. 8: fairing. 9: centre spar. 10: rudder cable. 11: rudder. 12: triangular or 13: vertical spar bracing. 14: toilet seat. (By courtesy of Paul Chatenay.)

entrepreneurs to meet these demands with home production. Almost irrespective of their success or failure, and they often did fail, these ventures have left evidence that is of interest to the historical archaeologist. One of the first examples of such evidence to be investigated was the site of James King's Pottery at Irrawang, near Newcastle, in New South Wales.[19] Extensive excavations by Judy Birmingham, in the late 1960s and early 1970s, revealed much of the layout of one of Australia's earliest potteries which produced during the period 1833 to 1856. In the centre of the site was the clay pit, and around it were a crushing mill and a puddler (both horsedrawn), two kilns, a workshop, traces of an approach road and a possible well. One of the kilns was apparently circular, with four fireholes and a spiral flue under the floor. It was built of brick, and the numerous biscuit-fired and lead-glazed earthenware fragments that lay around it indicated the purpose for which it had been mainly used. In contrast, the other kiln, also of brick, was rectangular, with one firehole or perhaps two, and had more salt-glazed stoneware around it, suggesting that its use had been different. Near the circular kiln was the workshop with two brick-built flues running beneath the floor. These were probably fed with hot air from the adjacent kiln presumably to assist the drying of green pots that were stacked in the workshop as they were made. Quite a substantial amount of documentary evidence exists for King's Pottery works, particularly in the form of contemporary newspaper advertisements. From these it is apparent that his main products consisted of cheap, good, domestic earthenwares and stonewares. However, only six complete pieces of all the pottery that he made during twenty-three years are known to survive, and those are in private collections. Thus the excavations at this site were important not only for showing us its layout, but also for providing an excellent sample of its products, fragmentary though most of the sample is.

There were many other examples of Australian manufacturing enterprise covering an impressive number of activities, but it would be tedious to consider them all and many of them have not yet been adequately investigated archaeologically. A few cases will be mentioned to give some idea of the variety. For instance, in 1981, the derelict Cooerwull Woollen Mills at Bowenfels, near Lithgow in New South Wales, still provided a reminder of the development of Australia's textile industry.[20] The fine bluestone buildings towering above the Barwon River at Fyansford, near Geelong, Victoria, that functioned as the Barwon Paper Mill from 1878 to 1922, indicate that the paper-making industry in this country had already reached a sophisticated level over a century ago.[21] Again, the remains of the saltworks at Little Swanport, on the eastern coast of Tasmania,[22] the ruins of the sugar mill on St Helena Island, Queensland,[23] and the site of the Ramornie meat-canning works near Grafton, New South Wales,[24] demonstrate some of the diversity of past Australian industry. Finally, there is the most Australian of all industries: the distillation of eucalyptus oil, evidence of which can be found in South Australia, Victoria and New South Wales, and which, indeed, is still being carried out today.[25]

It would be a mistake to give the impression that Australia's early industries were confined to light manufacturing. As explained at the beginning of this chapter, the archaeological record may not be fully representative in this respect. Nevertheless, there is some surviving material evidence that serves to remind us of the important role played by heavy industry in the past. At Joadja, in the Blue Mountains of New South Wales, are the remains of a kerosine oil-shale refinery that reputedly employed over 400 people towards the end of the nineteenth century and was one of the largest of Australia's early industries. In the same general area is Newnes, the former location of another kerosine refinery, and nearby is Glen Davis, where remnants survive of a refinery which made Australia's only

144

attempt to produce petrol commercially from shale. The refinery closed in 1952, but in its day, even by world standards, it was a most unusual enterprise. Fostered by the shortages of World War II, Glen Davis proved insufficiently competitive in the years that followed the war, and has been described as a grand failure. Be this as it may, its remaining structures provide a near-unique opportunity to study a technology that might someday become important again.[26]

Real heavy industry, however, is concerned with such things as the production of iron and steel, and there is archaeological evidence of Australia's early involvement even in this activity.[27] The Fitzroy Ironworks, near Mittagong in New South Wales, which ran intermittently from 1848 to 1878, has left us only a few foundations cut into solid rock, but at Lal Lal, near Ballarat in Victoria, a blast furnace survives from 1880-1 that is one of the best examples of its sort remaining anywhere in the world. Built of stone, and lined with imported English fire-bricks, this furnace still stands to a height of 17 metres. Smelting at Lal Lal did not last long, although it was at least more successful than the other more brief attempts in Tasmania and South Australia which have also left some archaeological traces.

Figure 9.13 Ruin of the engine house at the blast-furnace site, Lithgow, New South Wales. (Photographed by Ian Jack in 1985; courtesy of Aedeen Cremin.)

It was at Lithgow, in New South Wales, that the Australian iron and steel industry at last got going properly. From 1876 to 1932, it was the location of considerable activity — involving the operation of a blast furnace from 1876 to 1883, the production of Australia's first steel in 1900, and the construction and operation of further blast furnaces from 1907 and from 1913, respectively. Nothing remains of the early ironworks nor of the later steelworks, but the site of the later blast furnaces does retain substantial structural evidence. There is an impressive ruin of the brick-built engine house, which still stands to roof-height (Figure 9.13). Foundations and slag mark the position of the blast furnaces, and areas of brickwork and concrete indicate the location of the rest of the plant.[28] From Lithgow, the iron and steel concern was moved to Port Kembla, and subsequently became a part of BHP, thus contributing to one of the great industrial success stories of modern Australia.

This is a fitting point at which to end this discussion of the archaeology of Australian industry. Limited though the examples have been, they have given some indication of the variety of industrial activity that has characterized Australia's past. The material evidence for that activity is frequently fragmentary and difficult to study. In addition, there is some indication that such evidence gives a distorted picture of industrial activity, emphasizing some things, but virtually ignoring others. This, however, is where the special character of historical archaeology comes to our rescue, for historical documentation can correct such an imbalance, just as the archaeological data, in its turn, can amplify the sometimes singularly laconic written record. The industrial archaeologist, clambering over concrete ruins and measuring disembowelled machinery, has a great deal to contribute to our better understanding of Australia's past industrial achievements. Also, as was the case with mining sites, Australia's industrial sites have a special contribution to make to international studies of nineteenth- and early-twentieth-century industrial technology. Some of the evidence that we can study has not survived anywhere else. Finally, one thing is certain, Australia has come a long way since those first bricks were made on Brickfield Hill in Sydney.

Notes

[1] G.J.R. Linge, 1979. *Industrial awakening: A geography of Australian manufacturing 1788 to 1890*, Australian National University Press, Canberra, pp.717-18.

[2] G.J.R. Linge, 1979, p.740.

[3] K. Hudson, 1979. *World industrial archaeology*, Cambridge University Press, Cambridge, p.1.

[4] M. Pearson, 1983. The technology of whaling in Australian waters in the 19th century. *Australian Journal of Historical Archaeology* 1, pp.40-54.

[5] G. Henderson, 1986. *Maritime archaeology in Australia*, University of Western Australia Press, Nedlands, pp.102-5.

[6] J. McIlroy, 1986. Bathers Bay whaling station, Fremantle, Western Australia. *Australian Journal of Historical Archaeology* 4, pp.43-50.

[7] J. Birmingham, I. Jack and D. Jeans, 1983. *Industrial archaeology in Australia: rural industry*, Heinemann, Richmond, Victoria, pp.27-52.

[8] Anonymous, 1979. Thorpe water mill: A Tasmanian restoration project. *Australian Society for Historical Archaeology Newsletter* 9(2), pp.34-7. (Based on a leaflet by J. & J. Bignell.)

[9] L. Godwin, 1983. The life and death of a flourmill: McCrossin's Mill, Uralla. *Australian Journal of Historical Archaeology* 1, pp.67-77.

[10] J. Birmingham, I. Jack and D. Jeans, 1979. *Australian pioneer technology: sites and relics*, Heinemann, Richmond, Victoria, pp.166-72.

[11] Bairstow, D. 1985. The Castlemaine and Great Northern Breweries, Newcastle, New South Wales, *Australian Journal of Historical Archaeology* 3, pp.70-8.

[12] J. Birmingham, I. Jack and D. Jeans, 1983, pp.53-74.

[13] D. Godden, 1986. The Glen Innes Brickworks. Unpublished paper read at 6th Annual Conference of the Australian Society for Historical Archaeology, University of New England, Armidale, N.S.W. Also D. Godden and others (n.d.), The Glen Innes Brickworks: History and technology, unpublished report.

[14] J. Birmingham, I. Jack and D. Jeans, 1983, pp.74-7.

[15] M. Pearson, 1986. Archaeological interpretation and ethnographic analogy: the lime industry in Western Australia. *Archaeology in Oceania* 21, pp.94-102.

[16] J. Birmingham, I. Jack and D. Jeans, 1979, pp.180-7.

[17] G. Connah, 1983. Stamp-collecting or increasing understanding?: The dilemma of historical archaeology. *Australian Journal of Historical Archaeology* 1, pp.15-21.

[18] S. Bures and B. Groom, 1980. The Wunderlich Project: An exercise in industrial archaeology. *Australian Society for Historical Archaeology Newsletter* 10(2), pp.11-17.

[19] J. Birmingham, 1976. The archaeological contribution to nineteenth-century history: some Australian case studies. *World Archaeology* 7(3), pp.306-17; and J. Birmingham, I. Jack and D. Jeans, 1983, pp.80-4.

[20] J. Birmingham, I. Jack and D. Jeans, 1979, pp.143-5; and A. Cremin and others, 1986. *Survey of historical sites Lithgow area*, Department of Environment and Planning, Sydney, pp.170-4.

[21] P. Milner, 1985. The Barwon Paper Mill, Fyansford. *Heritage Australia* 4(1), pp.18-21.

[22] J. Birmingham, I. Jack and D. Jeans, 1979, p.141.

[23] Anonymous, 1982. *Park Guide: St Helena Island National Park*, leaflet, Queensland National Parks and Wildlife Service, North Quay, Queensland.

[24] J. Birmingham, I. Jack and D. Jeans, 1979, p.136.

[25] J. Birmingham, I. Jack and D. Jeans, 1979, p.188.

[26] R. Mackay, 1986. Conservation and industrial archaeology: Recent work by the National Trust (N.S.W.). *Australian Journal of Historical Archaeology* 4, pp.9-16. Also J. Birmingham, I. Jack and D. Jeans, 1979, pp.120-30.

[27] J. Birmingham, I. Jack and D. Jeans, 1979, pp.88-98.

[28] A. Cremin and others, 1986, pp.149-59.

Chapter 10

'The glad bright days have vanished'

THE POTENTIAL OF AUSTRALIAN HISTORICAL ARCHAEOLOGY

The quotation in the title of this chapter comes again from Henry Lawson's poem *Reedy River*. Like the poem, it evokes a longing for the past and bitter sweet regret for a youth that has gone for ever. There is much in the new and growing interest in Australian heritage that is similar. The widespread fascination for family history, the numerous local historical societies and museums, the touristy 'pioneer villages', the astounding quantity of glossy, coffee-table publications on everything from old court houses to old pubs: all of these things seem to be characterized by a regret for Australia's lost youth. Yet all of us realize that the past was made up of sad and gloomy days as well as glad and bright ones. Given the choice, most of us would prefer to live with our modern comforts. Archaeologists, who tend to be rather unsentimental people, would almost certainly have no illusions on the matter. Yet they would be the first to admit that a concern for the past is an important human emotion that helps us to identify who we are. Whether we like it or not, we are as surely a product of the past, as we are architects of the future.

Whatever the character of Australia's past, has it really gone for ever; has it, as the poem says, 'vanished'? It has been the intention of this book to show that this is really not the case. It has been argued that we are surrounded by material evidence which, if we know how to read it, has the capacity to improve our understanding of the origins and development of our nation. A selection of major topics has been examined to show how such material remains can inform us about our past. We have looked at evidence of external contacts before the advent of European colonization, at evidence for the earliest settlement at Sydney, for some of the failed attempts at settlement, for the contribution of the convict population, for the development of Australian housing, for the role of agriculture, for mining, and at evidence for the growth of secondary industry. Throughout this examination the emphasis has been on things: on sites, on buildings, on ruins, on artefacts and so on. The object has been to show how useful and interesting information can be extracted from the ordinary things that we take for granted and tend to forget. There is nothing new in this, it is an archaeologist's job to do it, a job that was neatly summed up some years ago by the American archaeologist James Deetz:

> It is terribly important that the 'small things forgotten' be remembered. For in the seemingly little and insignificant things that accumulate to create a lifetime, the essence of our existence is captured. We must remember these bits and pieces, and we must use them in new and imaginative ways so that a different appreciation for what

life is today, and was in the past, can be achieved. The written document has its proper and important place, but there is also a time when we should set aside our perusal of diaries, court records, and inventories, and listen to another voice.

Don't read what we have written; look at what we have done.[1]

This, indeed, has been the aim of this book: to look at what the men and women who made Australia actually did, rather than at what they said they did. In the process of looking at the material evidence it has been continually apparent that written and oral sources both have what Deetz called their 'proper and important place'. To put it bluntly, the historical archaeologist cannot do without them. What should also have been apparent, is that the archaeological evidence has something to contribute to the historian, this is still not as widely recognized as should be the case.

The selection of topics in the previous chapters are representative of the general body of material evidence that exists for the European colonization of Australia. The sheer bulk of the available evidence and its incredible variety would make a comprehensive study impossible, even in a very much larger book than this one. To a large extent the selection has been determined by the sort of topics on which Australian historical archaeologists have published. Little use has been made of the very large amount of unpublished and inadequately published material that also exists, since the average reader would find it difficult to obtain access to it. Because Australian historical archaeology is a relatively new subject, the body of formally published material is not large and has numerous limitations. It might, therefore, be instructive to identify some of the subject areas that this book has neglected. Such subjects, after all, could be the very ones that researchers will be investigating over the next few years.

Two related subjects that have been repeatedly mentioned, but not accorded the detailed discussion that they deserve, are those of power sources and communication. Engineers have investigated the first, and historical geographers have discussed the second, but archaeologists have not yet contributed much to these fields.[2] There is little, for example, that has yet been published on the surviving evidence for water-power utilization in nineteenth-century Australia. The question of its viability in different environmental zones of the continent is one that could very well be addressed using archaeological methodology. Similarly, the subject of road-building is one to which archaeologists could make substantial contributions. Grace Karskens has already shown how this can be done with her examination of the constructional methods used on the Great North Road when it was being built in 1826-36. She has clearly demonstrated that the archaeological evidence can tell us things that we would not know from the documentary sources.[3] Archaeologists could also add to our understanding of the building of railways, particularly when lines have been abandoned or construction never completed (Figure 10.1). It might prove instructive, for instance, to compare the actual gradients and curve radii of a track with contemporary engineering records, if they exist. It would also be interesting to ascertain the extent to which the most practicable route was picked and to what extent economic and even political factors prevented this from happening. There is, indeed, only one type of transportation in which archaeologists have taken much interest as yet. This is shipping, a subject to which maritime archaeologists have been contributing in a very significant fashion. Excavations at the wreck site of the *Rapid*, on the Western Australian coast, are providing important information about early-nineteenth-century American shipbuilding, while those at the wreck site of the *William Salthouse*, in Port Phillip Bay, Victoria, are

Figure 10.1 Aerial photograph taken in April 1980 of unfinished railway line, near Guyra, northern New South Wales. This was a casualty of the 1930s slump.

particularly informative about nineteenth-century methods of stowage on sailing-ships. Maritime archaeologists have also begun to contribute to our knowledge of the power sources that were so important to the development of communications. They have, for example, raised the steam engine of the *S.S. Xantho*, which sank off the Western Australian coast in 1872, but was built in 1848.[4]

There are numerous other types of site or structure to which historical archaeologists have as yet given relatively little attention. Cemeteries have long interested local historians, genealogists and those concerned with heritage conservation. There seem to have been few attempts in Australia, however, to subject them to archaeological analysis, as has been done in some cases overseas. Not only can they yield useful demographic information (Figure 10.2) but they can also inform us about changing attitudes to death, the chronological and geographical distribution of monumental styles, the changing availability of materials, the skills of local craftsmen and so on. Considering that archaeologists studying earlier periods have paid so much attention to the subject of burial, it is a pity that the available historical evidence has been so little investigated for it could well provide a useful means of testing some of the available analytical techniques. This, of course, is not meant to suggest that the burials should in any way be disturbed, for neither law nor public opinion would allow this in the foreseeable future.

Churches and other places of worship constitute another subject area that seems to have been neglected by historical archaeologists. Architectural historians have interested themselves in some of the technically more accomplished buildings, but many of the smaller and humbler structures have not been accorded such attention. With changing settlement

Date of death (in decades)

Age at death	1840-1849	1850-1859	1860-1869	1870-1879	1880-1889	1890-1899	1900-1909	1910-1919	1920-1929	1930-1939	1940-1949	1950-1959	1960-1969	1970-1979	1980-1989	TOTALS
100 and OVER	•															1
90-99					•••••	•••	••••	•			•	•				15
80-89		•	•		•••••	••••• •••••	•••	•••••	••••	••••• ••	••	•••••				55
70-79		•	••••	••••• •••••	••••• •••••	•••••	••••• •••••	••••• •••	••••	•••••	•••	••				99
60-69		••••• •	••••• •	••••• •••••	••••• ••••• •••••	•••••	••••• •••	•••••	••••	•••						85
50-59		••••	••••	••••• •••••	••••• •••••	•••••	••••• ••	••	•••	•	•					57
40-49	••	••••• ••	••••• •	••••• •••••	••••• •••••	•••		••		••						51
30-39	•	•••	•• ••	••••• •••	••••• ••••• •	••••	•••	•••								50
20-29		••	••••• •••	••••• ••••	••••• •••	•••••	••••	•								48
10-19		••	••••• •••••	••••• •	••••• •••••	••	•					•				31
1-9	••••	••••• ••••• •••	••••• •••••	••••• ••••• •	••••• •••••	•										73
0-1	••	••	••••• ••	••••• •	••••• ••••• •	••	•									41
TOTALS	10	43	73	125	147	68	40	42	16	25	7	10				606

Figure 10.2 Changing life expectancy revealed by plotting age at death against date of death, from the tombstones of a cemetery. Based on a survey of St John's Churchyard, Ashfield, Sydney. (Courtesy of Lionel Gilbert and Bill Driscoll.)

patterns, and declining religious zeal, many of the more isolated examples (and even some in the dying centres of our cities) have been abandoned to decay and vandalism. Yet some of these buildings are quite old, display a variety of constructional techniques, and sometimes contain culturally significant fittings. Indeed, when one considers the central role that they played in the lives of those who worshipped in them and paid for them, it seems particularly unfortunate that historical archaeologists have not given them more attention. In some rural areas, they can be almost the only surviving structure from a previously flourishing community (Figure 10.3).

Hospitals have also failed to attract much interest from historical archaeologists as yet. Demolition and modernization have often destroyed many of the earlier structures or changed their interiors beyond recognition. Nevertheless, some of our older hospitals would still delight any archaeologist who is interested in the sort of structural analysis discussed in Chapter 6. Many of them consist of a variety of buildings of different dates that form structural groupings of great complexity. In other instances, we are fortunate in having buildings that have survived with relatively few changes. The Kalgoorlie District Hospital in Western Australia seems to be an example of this, while in Glen Innes, New South Wales, the hospital that was in use from 1877 to 1956, has been preserved by its adoption as the local museum.

Another very large subject area that has been neglected in this book and, to a fair extent, by historical archaeology as a whole, consists of the huge numbers of movable artefacts, of almost every possible type, that are preserved in museums and private collections all over

Figure 10.3 St Nicholas's Anglican Church, Saumarez Ponds, near Armidale, New South Wales. Constructed in 1864, this is one of the few surviving structures from a former rural settlement. (Photograph by Lionel Gilbert.)

the country. It is true that these items are divorced from their original context and, indeed, the place from which they were collected has in some instances not even been recorded by the museum concerned. Undoubtedly, such circumstances reduce the archaeological value of the material, but it still provides an important source of information about Australia's past. The problem is that relatively few analytical studies of these collections have yet been published. If the individual archaeologist is to make use of the collections, then he or she has to visit at least a representative number of them in order to collect the necessary information. As a result artefact studies have not yet received the attention from historical archaeologists that they deserve, for some aspects of Australia's past will be most readily discernible through such collections. Most of the material evidence for this country's involvement in World War I is to be found in museum collections and it is from the actual artefacts of the war that the archaeologist is likely to gain most information. The Australian War Memorial Museum in Canberra, for instance, provides an unbelievably rich resource in this respect. It is by no means the only museum that does so; at the Queensland Museum, in Brisbane, one is even privileged to see the only surviving example of a German World War I tank anywhere in the world. Its existence in Australia is easy to explain. It was captured in battle by the Australian army and very properly we have it still (Figure 10.4).

152

Some of the artefacts in museum collections are important for another reason: they indicate a particularly serious deficiency in historical archaeology as presently practised in Australia. These are such things as pots and pans and corsets and dresses; things that make one realize that, in much of the material evidence that has been discussed in this book, women are archaeologically invisible, or seem to be. It was while working on Chapter 5, about the archaeology of convictism, that this aspect began to worry the author: where was the archaeological evidence for the convict women? Almost everything seemed to be male-oriented. Once identified, indeed, the problem refused to go away in later chapters; housebuilding is surely a male activity, so is ploughing and sheep-shearing, mining, flour-milling and steel-making, and yet these are the sort of things that historical archaeologists write about and they are the sort of things with which this book has been concerned. Moreover, not only is the archaeological record male-dominated, it appears to be adult-male-dominated; there is not much evidence of children either! Obviously, something has to be done about this situation, the distortion must be at least partly in the minds of those selecting and interpreting the evidence rather than inherent in the archaeological record

Figure 10.4   The archaeology of war: the only surviving example of a German World War I tank anywhere in the world. This is on display in the Queensland Museum, Brisbane. Its height (to the top of the turret) is 3.3 metres, its width is 3.06 metres and its length is 7.35 metres. Within this space, a crew of 18 to 21 men rode into battle. The tank is seen here during Anzac Day weekend 1987, when its guns were temporarily remounted. (Photograph by Carlos Picasso, courtesy of Queensland Museum.)

itself. Some signs that topic selection is one of the problems are already evident. For example, Phyllis Murphy has written about the colonial Australian kitchen and, elsewhere, about the use of wallpaper from 1850 to 1930, both of these being subjects that are surely concerned with female rather than male activities.[5] It is a start, but clearly we still have a long way to go.

Another subject area that appears to be underrepresented in Australian historical archaeology is that of ethnic minorities. Not all the early settlers came from Britain, there was a variety of people from other places of whom Germans, Italians and Chinese were the more numerous. Something has already been said in Chapters 6 and 7 about the German settlers of South Australia and about the pioneering work of Gordon Young and his associates on that topic. The emphasis in those investigations, however, is one of architecture and historical geography. A notable exception is the study, by Noris Ioannou, of the pottery made by Johann Hoffmann, who arrived in Australia in 1845 and died in 1900. Hoffmann was a *Töpfermeister* (a master-potter) who had learnt his craft in his native Brandenburg. It is hardly surprising, therefore, that at Rowland Flat, in the Barossa Valley, he produced the traditional pottery of his native land.[6]

Early Italian settlers in Australia seem to have attracted as little interest from historical archaeologists as early German settlers, however one investigation has been conducted by Harold Boughen in Cobar, western New South Wales. Boughen set out to explain a group of stone-walled buildings of unusual design, whose ruins stand on Fort Bourke Hill just outside Cobar. These are said to have been constructed in the 1890s by a person called Towser, who rented them out to single men who were employed in the local mining industry. To the people of Cobar they are known as 'Towser's Huts', and the local tradition is that Towser was a Cornishman, but may have been German, Danish, Swedish or Baltic. In fact, Boughen's research produced documentary evidence that the builder and owner of the huts was an Italian called Antonio Tozzi, who died, aged sixty-five, in 1916. Some of the huts seem to have been already in existence by 1902, when a surveyor drew up a plan of the area, but others were probably built shortly after this time. A careful comparison of this plan with the archaeological evidence indicated that one of the earlier buildings had accidentally crossed the boundary of Portion 265, which appears to have been a Mining Tenement held for residential purposes by Mr Tozzi. Unfortunately for him, his land was surrounded by a gold lease held by The Cobar Gold Mines Ltd and it is suspected that they obliged him to demolish the offending building. To get in the way of big business was not wise, but to do so when one belonged to an ethnic minority at that time was probably very unwise indeed. However, Boughen's study of Towser's Huts, or Tozzi's Huts, as they should properly be called, has provided us with a rare glimpse of what would appear to be traditional Italian building methods used in Australia.[7]

Much more numerous than the Germans or Italians were the Chinese, who flocked to the Australian goldfields in surprisingly large numbers. As a result, there exists a substantial amount of material evidence for the Chinese presence. Best known, perhaps, are the cemetery and burning towers at Beechworth, Victoria, and the joss-house at Emu Point, Bendigo, also in Victoria.[8] There are many other Chinese sites in Australia, some of which have been investigated by historical archaeologists — the Chinese sites of northeast Tasmania, for example, have been surveyed by Helen Vivian.[9] Little has been formally published about the archaeology of Chinese sites, however, a situation that makes the work at Ah Toy's Garden all the more important. Ah Toy was one of the many Chinese who found their way to the Palmer River Goldfield, in far northern Queensland, towards the end of the nineteenth century. Born in Canton, in 1855, he survived until 1934, but, unlike most of the settlers in the Palmer River area who left when the gold gave out, Ah Toy stayed on in the area until shortly before his death. His interest was not in mining, but in a market-garden that he ran from 1900 onwards and from which he supplied the few remaining miners with fruit and vegetables. We know about Ah Toy because of the work of Ian Jack, Kate Holmes and Ruth Kerr, who carried out extensive archival research in 1982, together with a detailed archaeological examination (including some excavation) of the market-garden site.[10] A dam and a series of water races showed evidence of the well-known Chinese skill with irrigation technology. In addition, the excavation of Ah Toy's house, tool-shed and outside cooking hearth demonstrated a remarkable adaptation to the conditions of the area. The artefacts from the site were of mixed origin, but the presence of rice-bowls, opium tins and Chinese bottles indicated that Ah Toy had clearly retained his cultural identity (Figure 10.5). The archaeology of Ah Toy's Garden gives some idea of the interesting research work that could be done on other Chinese sites in Australia.

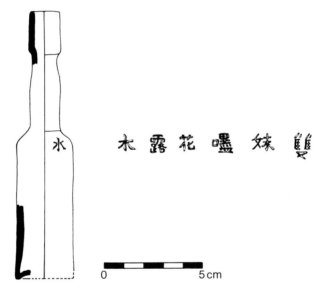

Figure 10.5   Chinese perfume bottle from Ah Toy's Garden, Palmer River Goldfield, northern Queensland. The characters read, from right to left, 'Twin Sisters brand Eau de Cologne'. (By courtesy of Ian Jack.)

There is one further subject area which has been neglected in this book and, to a large degree, by Australian historical archaeology generally. This is the very important topic of historical sites associated with Australian Aborigines, the original inhabitants of this continent. Some archaeologists have been reluctant to investigate Aboriginal sites of such a recent date, for fear of giving offence to Aboriginal communities. One might speculate, however, that the Aboriginal archaeologists of the rising generation will want to give these sites a high research priority.

Dispossessed of their land in much of the country, nineteenth-century Aborigines found themselves in a variety of acculturation roles, enduring everything from murder to paternalistic institutionalization. It is probably true to say that the less contact they had with the incoming European settlers, the luckier they were. Nevertheless, their experiences have contributed to the historical archaeological record, just as certainly as have those of the immigrant farmers or miners. Amongst the important subjects on which archaeology could provide information would be to show how the Aboriginal people altered their diet as they gradually changed from traditional foods to a diet which included introduced domestic animals and the introduced rabbit. Study of animal bones from Aboriginal sites occupied during the nineteenth century could demonstrate the extent to which this happened at different times in different places. The archaeological evidence resulting from the contact of peoples of different cultures has long interested both anthropologists and archaeologists. In the United States of America, for instance, so-called 'contact sites' have frequently attracted the attention of researchers. In Australia this has not really been the case. Prehistoric archaeologists have usually been too busy with sites of far greater antiquity; historical archaeologists have generally been so concerned with the experiences of the colonizers that they have forgotten about the colonized.

Nevertheless, some investigations have been carried out on Aboriginal-European contact sites, the most notable being one of the earlier historical archaeological projects in this country. This was the excavation, during the late 1960s and early 1970s, of part of the site of Wybalenna, which was a government settlement from 1833 to 1847 for Tasmanian Aborigines. Wybalenna is situated on the east coast of Flinders Island, the largest of the Bass Strait islands. It was established with the best intentions of caring for the remaining Tasmanian people who were then thought to be a dying race, and from 1835 to 1840 its commandant was George Augustus Robinson whom the government had appointed as a conciliator some years before. The settlement was carefully planned as a self-sufficient community and included houses for the supervising Europeans, as well as for the Tasmanians themselves. It was on the site of the latter that Judy Birmingham concentrated her excavations which were able to demonstrate that, in spite of being provided with houses of stone and brick, the Tasmanians still preferred to spend a lot of time sitting outside their front doors. In the end, however, the settlement was abandoned because of dwindling numbers, and as an archaeological site it presents us with an almost unique opportunity to investigate an historically significant institutionalized contact situation. The excavations at this site have not yet been fully published.[11] During 1984 and 1985, however, excavations were conducted at another institutionalized contact site, which, although not as famous as Wybalenna, still provides some indication of what it was like to be on the receiving end of colonization. This is the site of the Lake Condah Aboriginal Mission, in southwestern Victoria, which functioned from 1867 until it was officially closed in 1918, but it was still occupied by some Aboriginal people until the 1950s. Excavations by David Rhodes and Robyn Stocks have not only recovered structural information about the buildings, but have also shown how the artefacts that were in use reflect the process of acculturation that was taking place. The work at the Lake Condah Mission was done with the active cooperation of interested Aboriginal people.[12]

The previous paragraphs could be read as an extended apology for the present state of Australian historical archaeology. Alternatively, and more positively, they can be taken as an indication of the sort of things that some historical archaeologists might be doing during the next few decades. However, archaeologists are unlikely to accomplish much, in either old or new areas of research, without the support and assistance of the public. This is where the readers of this book come in. This book was not intended for archaeologists, but for all those other people who have an interest in the material heritage of Australian colonization. It is appropriate, therefore, to consider ways in which we can all benefit from that concern for the past that was mentioned at the beginning of this chapter. With this in mind, a Suggested Activities section has been included at the end of the book so that members of the public can pursue their own interest in historical archaeology whilst also contributing to the development of the subject itself. A second section provides a guide to further reading by listing the most significant of the publications referred to in each chapter.

In conclusion, Australia's colonial past has not totally vanished, its material remains are all around us if we have the eyes to see them. Those remains can improve our understanding of the hut that was built or of the city that was created. By such a means, we can better appreciate how it was that this nation came to be the way it is. We owe it to those who will come after us to bequeath to them that appreciation, that bitter sweet concern for things past, as expressed in Henry Lawson's poem. Australia's past is written in the site of the selector's hut, in the deserted mullock heap and in the city cottage. It is such things that make up our heritage. We would do well to cherish them. They, and what they represent, are a crucial part of the Australian identity.

Notes

[1] J. Deetz, 1977. *In small things forgotten: The archaeology of early American life*, Anchor Press/Doubleday, Garden City, New York, p.161.

[2] The best introduction to the subject of transport and communications is J. Birmingham, I. Jack and D. Jeans, 1983. *Industrial archaeology in Australia: rural industry*, Heinemann, Richmond, Victoria, pp.119-56.

[3] G. Karskens, 1985. The construction of the Great North Road, NSW, 1826-1836. *Journal of the Institution of Engineers — Multi-disciplinary* GE9 (2), pp.102-10.

[4] G. Henderson, 1986. *Maritime archaeology in Australia*, University of Western Australia Press, Nedlands, pp.105-14 for *Rapid*, pp.124-5 for *Xantho*. For *William Salthouse* see M. Staniforth and L. Vickery, 1984. *The test excavation of the* William Salthouse *wreck site: An interim report*, Australian Institute for Maritime Archaeology, Special Publication No.3.

[5] P. Murphy, 1985. The colonial kitchen. In R. Irving (ed.), *The history and design of the Australian house*, Oxford University Press, Melbourne, pp.232-47. P. Murphy, 1981. *The decorated wall: Eighty years of wallpaper in Australia c.1850-1930*, Historic Houses Trust of New South Wales, Sydney.

[6] N. Ioannou, 1986. Hoffmann: master-potter of the Barossa Valley. *Heritage Australia* 5(2), pp.14-17.

[7] H. Boughen, 1986. Towser's Huts, Cobar, New South Wales: Historic ruin or ruined history? *Australian Journal of Historical Archaeology* 4, pp.67-77.

[8] J. Birmingham, I. Jack and D. Jeans, 1979. *Australian pioneer technology: sites and relics*, Heinemann, Richmond, Victoria, p.56.

[9] H. Vivian, 1985. Tasmania's Chinese heritage: An historical record of Chinese sites in North East Tasmania. Unpublished report for the Australian Heritage Commission, Canberra, and the Queen Victoria Museum, Launceston.

[10] I. Jack, K. Holmes and R. Kerr, 1984. Ah Toy's Garden: A Chinese market-garden on the Palmer River Goldfield, North Queensland. *Australian Journal of Historical Archaeology* 2, pp.51-8.

[11] J. Birmingham, 1976. The archaeological contribution to nineteenth-century history: some Australian case studies. *World Archaeology* 7(3), pp.306-17.

[12] D. Rhodes and R. Stocks, 1985. Excavations at Lake Condah Aboriginal Mission 1984-85. *Historic Environment* 4(4), pp.4-12.

Suggested activities

Some readers of this book may wish to follow up their interest in Australian historical archaeology and I will here discuss differing levels of involvement in the protection of our heritage that can contribute to the development of the subject itself. The basic rule held by archaeologists is that nothing should be done that changes in any way the character of the evidence. Thus, nobody should ever attempt even the most minor piece of excavation on an historic site until they have had professional training and experience in archaeology and, in New South Wales, they would also need a permit from the State government. Material evidence can be irreparably damaged by any form of disturbance. Even the removal of vegetation from an overgrown ruin in order to plan it or photograph it can lead to an acceleration of decay. Furthermore, no artefacts or materials should ever be removed from a site unless it is essential to do so in order to prevent their theft, damage or destruction. When this is necessary, such items should be placed in a public museum collection and removal should only be carried out after professional archaeological opinion has been obtained. It is necessary to emphasize these things because souvenir-hunters, bottle-collectors, metal-detector enthusiasts and people scavenging building materials have done enormous damage to many of Australia's historical sites over the last few years. The first concern of readers who are really interested in Australia's heritage is to make themselves aware of these conditions and, if possible, to discourage others from damaging sites.

On a more positive level, the activities that can be undertaken will vary with the degree to which individual readers wish to become involved. At the least level of involvement, individuals can contribute to an overall public awareness of the importance of Australia's material heritage. Thus, in the community in which they live, they can support local projects aimed at preserving items of cultural heritage. More particularly, when old structures are threatened with demolition or when archaeological material is discovered accidentally, sympathetic members of the public can often fill a vital role by bringing these matters to the attention of those who may be able to do something about them. Such people may be found in a local museum, in a local historical society, in a local branch of the National Trust or in a university or State museum, in the case of readers who live near the latter. Each State also has a section of government which is responsible for heritage matters and which usually depends heavily on the goodwill of the public in bringing things of importance to its notice. In New South Wales the appropriate body is the Heritage Council, and in Victoria, it is the Victorian Archaeological Survey. Comparable arrangements exist in the other states also, and at the Commonwealth level the Heritage Commission has responsibility for such matters. All these bodies employ archaeologists who will be grateful to receive information about events in a particular area and may be able to arrange for the proper investigation or even the conservation of a threatened item of heritage.

At greater levels of involvement, there are all sorts of useful things that readers can do.

First, it is useful to establish contact with other people who have similar interests. This can be done in a number of ways. Some readers may find it helpful to join the National Trust of Australia, which is organized on a State basis but has local branches in many areas. These local branches often have active programmes of visits to sites and buildings which would not normally be accessible to the public. Some branches are also involved in the care and presentation of National Trust properties. Particularly for readers interested in houses and gardens, membership of the National Trust is an excellent way to meet others with similar enthusiasms and to extend their own appreciation. Such a membership is not costly and contributes usefully to the wellbeing of Australia's heritage while also providing pleasant social contacts.

Other readers may be fortunate in living in a place that has its own local historical society. There are many, scattered all over Australia, and in some cases they are responsible for small local museums that are totally dependent on volunteer help and support. Readers whose interests are inclined to local history and to local material culture may find membership of such a society a valuable way of developing those interests. Such membership is usually inexpensive and may prove either an alternative activity to membership of the National Trust or a useful addition to such a membership.

Those readers whose interests are more thoroughly archaeological should seriously consider joining the national organization concerned with Australian historical archaeology. This is the Australian Society for Historical Archaeology, known affectionately to its members as ASHA. This society is based in Sydney, although it has members from all over Australia and produces an annual journal in which are published papers concerned with various aspects of historical archaeology and also circulates a periodic newsletter and a research bulletin. There is also an annual conference which is usually held in a different regional centre each year, and the society organizes occasional lectures in Sydney. Its address might prove difficult to find, it is: The Secretary, Australian Society for Historical Archaeology, Box 220, Holme Building, University of Sydney, N.S.W. 2006. Membership of the society is open to all interested people, and the relatively modest subscription includes the cost of the annual journal and of the newsletters and research bulletins.

Having established contact with other people in one or several of the ways suggested, readers would be wise to obtain a copy of the legislation concerning matters of heritage in their State. It is important to be aware of the law as it applies to archaeological sites and other items of heritage. This will ensure that any activities undertaken do not unintentionally break the law. It will also make it possible to acquaint others with the legislation that exists. Furthermore, it may prove very useful to know what protective measures are available under the relevant legislation; circumstances may arise, in the individual reader's area, when the application of those measures by the appropriate authorities may be able to save a site, building or other feature from destruction.

Some readers may want to become involved in practical archaeological work. The best way to do this is to find out, through whichever societies have been joined, whether there is any heritage study or archaeological investigation being conducted in one's immediate area. Not only do archaeologists from universities undertake such work, but there are also numerous consultant archaeologists who carry out field surveys, and sometimes excavations, on behalf of government or commercial or industrial clients. If such work is being done in their area, interested readers should ask the person in charge whether they could help on a volunteer basis in their spare time. Sometimes help will not be needed, but quite often it will be welcomed, particularly by consultant archaeologists who are often working against time in the face of demolition or development. Helping on a professional project, in this way, is one of the best ways to learn. In both Britain and the United States of America, for instance, there is a long-standing tradition of volunteer involvement in professionally directed archaeological programmes. This provides interest and experience for the volunteer helpers, and is of great assistance to professional archaeologists who are often working with very limited funds. Such a volunteer participation is a relatively recent development in Australia, but it has become increasingly common in recent years.

Readers of this book who become involved at this level will also find that, to gain the maximum understanding and pleasure from their interest in historical archaeology, they will need to increase their knowledge of the subject. This can be done in a number of ways. In the Suggested Reading section will be found a list of publications on the subject discussed in each chapter to enable readers to follow up matters of particular interest. Local libraries may not have many of the publications on their shelves, but will probably be able to obtain them from other libraries, on interlibrary loan. Another way in which readers could extend their knowledge of archaeology would be to attend any adult education courses on the subject that are organized by universities in their area. These extramural courses are available in many places and are sometimes concerned with archaeology, although not only with Australian historical archaeology. Sydney University, in particular, has provided a number of such archaeological courses over the years. A third way for readers to extend their knowledge is to visit as many historical archaeological sites and museums as possible. Many of the sites mentioned in this book are on private property and cannot be visited without first obtaining permission from the landowner. An increasing number of sites, however, are in public ownership, or are at least open to the public and can be visited without difficulty. For example, Port Arthur penal settlement in Tasmania, Trial Bay Gaol in New South Wales and St Helena Island Gaol in Queensland are all accessible to the public, and are highly informative about Australia's nineteenth-century prison system. A visit to the Western Australian Maritime Museum in Fremantle, or to the Power House Museum in Sydney, can also be an enlightening experience. Singling out these examples does considerable injustice to many other sites and museums, but the enthusiastic archaeological traveller will find that local tourist offices in the various parts of Australia are usually a fund of information about items of heritage interest. There is hardly an area that does not have something to offer, and some of the small town museums in rural Australia are particularly worthy of a visit.

For those readers who would like to pursue their interest in Australian historical archaeology even further, there are several universities where it can be studied as part of a degree and where suitably qualified graduates can undertake postgraduate studies in the subject. The Department of Archaeology in Sydney University seems to have taught Australian historical archaeology longer than any other place, but it has also been taught for some years by the Department of Archaeology and Palaeoanthropology in the University of New England, at Armidale, New South Wales, and the Department of Archaeology at La Trobe University in Melbourne has introduced it in recent years. Other universities that teach archaeology are also showing an increasing interest in this branch of the discipline.

Most of these opportunities for university study are available only to those who are able to become full-time or, at least, part-time 'internal' university students. At the University of New England, however, Australian historical archaeology can be studied by 'external' students while continuing to earn a living at whatever job they do. External students of that university can major in archaeology if they wish, although the greater number of courses offered are concerned with prehistoric, not historical, archaeology. In addition, postgraduate work in historical archaeology can be undertaken by suitably qualified external students, although the university insists on a short residence period during each year of registration as is also the case with undergraduate courses. Any readers interested in university courses in archaeology should write to the universities concerned and ask for further details.

There will also be readers who, when they have gained some experience and knowledge, will want to do things on their own. Here are three main ways in which this interest can be constructively used without altering any evidence. First, carefully written descriptions, measured sketch plans and photographs of any structures or features more than fifty years old that relate to the European settlement of this continent can be of great value. Records of this sort are important, and the more ridiculous it may seem to record something, then the more likely it is that it should be recorded! The derelict cinema, the grandstand at the local footy ground, the bar in one's favourite pub: the most surprising things may be found to be part of the material evidence for the history of an area. When undertaking recording of this sort, use black and white photography in preference to colour (it keeps better), and make more than one copy of all field records. On completion of the work a copy of those records, together with copies of plans, drawings and photographs, should be sent to the National Trust, the heritage authority of the relevant State government, a local historical society or a local library. Essentially, one copy of such records should always be put in some place where it will be kept safely for the use of people in the future.

The second activity that is particularly valuable, and perhaps more attractive to those people less inclined to field projects, would be to undertake artefact studies in the nearest local museum. The museum in question might have an extensive collection of mining tools, barbed wire, lawn-mowers, women's dresses, bicycles, or of any one of some hundreds of artefact types. In Australia we seem to have very few detailed analytical studies of classes of objects in museum collections. Anyone attempting this sort of work would need to select one particular class of objects and compile a detailed catalogue of every example in the museum collection being examined. Such a person would also need to make a diligent search of available literature so as to learn as much as possible about the type of artefacts under investigation. If it was then possible to conduct a similar analysis of the same class of objects in other museum collections, it would eventually permit the construction of an important data source. For instance, it would be of great help if there was an analytical catalogue of all the early stump-jump ploughs in Australian museum collections. So far no such thing exists, and there are probably very few artefact classes that have been documented in such a way. For those interested in computers, here is a task to which they could very usefully turn their skills.

The third way in which readers might choose to assist heritage investigations is by taking an interest in the collection of archival material. Newspapers, photographs, glass negatives, picture postcards, diaries, letters, school exercise books, invoices from shops, commercial records; all these and many other types of archival material can prove to be of great value. Much material of this sort has been and is still being destroyed, usually because the owner thinks that it is unimportant junk. Too much of Australia's history has already finished up at the local garbage dump. Informed members of the public can play a vital role in saving items of archival interest; once rescued, these things should be placed in a suitable archival collection, either locally or in the nearest State capital. Archives need proper storage and care, neglect usually results in their deterioration. Local historical societies can often advise on the available archival facilities in an area and, in some instances, they themselves have built up collections concerning the history of their own region.

The foregoing suggestions are clearly not exhaustive, but it is hoped that they will help readers both to develop their own interest and to contribute to the future development of Australian historical archaeology.

Suggested reading

The following is a selection of the more important publications referred to in each of the chapters of this book. It should also be noted that the main periodical publication on this subject area is *The Australian Journal of Historical Archaeology*; Volumes 1, 2, 3 and 5 contain a detailed bibliography of over 800 references.

Chapter 1: The material heritage of Australian history

Deetz, J. 1967. *Invitation to archaeology*, Natural History Press, Garden City, New York. (A useful and readable general introduction to archaeology.)

Deetz, J.F. and Dethlefson, E.S. 1978. Death's head, cherub, urn and willow. In R.L. Schuyler (ed.), *Historical archaeology: A guide to substantive and theoretical contributions*, Baywood, Farmingdale, New York. (A classic demonstration of how historical archaeology can be used as a means of testing archaeological methods and theories.)

Denholm, D. 1979. *The Colonial Australians*, Penguin, Harmondsworth. (A study of nineteenth-century Australia from an unusual standpoint. Includes consideration of material evidence.)

Freeland, J.M. 1968. *Architecture in Australia: A history*, Cheshire, Melbourne. (A standard history of Australian architecture.)

Gilbert, L.A., Driscoll, W.P. and Sutherland, A. 1984. *History around us: An enquiry approach to local history* (2nd edition), Methuen, North Ryde. (An important book in which the authors show how material evidence can contribute to the study of local history. Written for senior school students, but a useful source of information for a far wider readership.)

Jack, R.I. 1986. *Exploring the Hawkesbury*, Kangaroo Press, Kenthurst. (A guide to the material evidence for the history of a region near Sydney.)

Jeans, D.N. (ed.) 1984. *Australian historical landscapes*, Allen & Unwin, North Sydney. (A series of studies that show how landscapes can inform us about our past.)

Jeans, D.N. and Spearritt, P. 1980. *The open air museum: The cultural landscape of New South Wales*, Allen & Unwin, North Sydney. (A useful introduction to an important part of Australia's built environment.)

Williams, M. 1974. *The making of the South Australian landscape: A study in the historical geography of Australia*, Academic Press, London and New York. (A most important book that examines the impact of European settlement on the South Australian landscape.)

Chapter 2: The historical archaeology of precolonial contact

Henderson, G. 1986. *Maritime archaeology in Australia*, University of Western Australia Press, Nedlands. (The first synthesis of this subject. Useful and readable.)

Macknight, C.C. 1976. *The voyage to Marege': Macassan trepangers in northern Australia*, Melbourne University Press, Carlton. (A major source of information on this subject and an interesting study.)

Chapter 3: Seeking the remains of early Sydney

Birmingham, J. and Liston, C. 1976. *Old Sydney Burial Ground*, Studies in Historical Archaeology No. 5, Australian Society for Historical Archaeology, University of Sydney. (A useful excavation report on an important and in some ways unique site.)

Higginbotham, E. 1987. The excavation of buildings in the early township of Parramatta, New South Wales, 1790 – 1820s. *Australian Journal of Historical Archaeology* 5, 3-20. (A detailed excavation report on a highly significant early site.)

Mulvaney, D.J. 1985. *'A good foundation': Reflections on the heritage of the First Government House, Sydney*, Australian Heritage Commission Special Australian Heritage Publication Series No. 5, Australian Government Publishing Service, Canberra. (A thoughtful discussion of the history and relevance of the First Government House, Sydney, by one of the founders of modern archaeology in Australia.)

Proudfoot, H. 1983. The First Government House, Sydney. *Heritage Australia* 2(2), 21-5. (A useful introduction to the First Government House, Sydney.)

Stanbury, P. (ed.) 1979. *10,000 years of Sydney life: A guide to archaeological discovery*, Macleay Museum, University of Sydney. (An interesting series of papers on different aspects of both prehistoric and historic archaeology in the Sydney region.)

Chapter 4: Investigating the sites of failed settlements

Allen, J. 1967. The technology of colonial expansion: A nineteenth-century military outpost on the north coast of Australia. *Industrial Archaeology* 4(2), 111-37. (A basic source of information on the site of Victoria, Port Essington.)

Coutts, P.J.F. 1981. *Victoria's first official settlement Sullivans Bay, Port Phillip*, Victoria Archaeological Survey, Albert Park. (An investigation of the history and archaeology of a short-lived settlement.)

Coutts, P.J.F. 1985. *Report on the results of archaeological investigations at the 1826 settlement site at Corinella*, Victoria Archaeological Survey, Albert Park. (A detailed report on archaeological fieldwork and excavation.)

Crosby, E. 1978. *Survey and excavation at Fort Dundas, Melville Island, Northern Territory, 1975*, Australian Society for Historical Archaeology, Occasional Paper No. 1, Sydney. (An archaeological study of an important site in a remote part of Australia.)

McGowan, A. 1985. *Archaeological investigations at Risdon Cove Historic Site: 1978-1980*, National Parks and Wildlife Service, Tasmania, Occasional Paper No. 10, Sandy Bay. (A detailed discussion of archaeological survey and excavations at Tasmania's first official European settlement.)

Chapter 5: Vestiges of the penal system

Byrne, M. 1976. *Ross Bridge, Tasmania*, Australian Society for Historical Archaeology, Studies in Historical Archaeology No. 3, Sydney. (A field study of an early convict-built structure.)

Higginbotham, E. 1983. The excavation of a brick barrel-drain at Parramatta, N.S.W.

Australian Journal of Historical Archaeology 1, 35-9. (A pioneer investigation of an early nineteenth-century drainage system.)

Karskens, G. 1984. The convict road station at Wisemans Ferry: an historical and archaeological investigation. *Australian Journal of Historical Archaeology* 2, 17-26. (A paper that examines the living conditions of some of the convict gangs that built the Great North Road from Sydney to the Hunter Valley.)

Karskens, G. 1986. Defiance, deference and diligence: three views of convicts in New South Wales road gangs. *Australian Journal of Historical Archaeology* 4, 17-28. (An examination of archaeological evidence from the Great North Road, in order to throw light on the performance of the convict gangs that built it.)

Kerr, J.S. 1984. *Design for convicts: An account of design for convict establishments in the Australian Colonies during the transportation era*, Library of Australian History, Sydney. (A detailed study, from documentary sources, of the buildings constructed for the use of convicts during the earlier part of the nineteenth century.)

Wilson, G. and Davies, M. 1983. *Norfolk Island: The archaeological survey of Kingston and Arthur's Vale* (2 vols.), Australian Government Publishing Service, Canberra. (An important source of information on the archaeological remains of Norfolk Island.)

Chapter 6: Extracting history from houses

Boyd, R. 1952. *Australia's home: Its origins, builders and occupiers*, Melbourne University Press, Carlton. (A famous study of Australian houses which although old is still well worth reading.)

Connah, G., Rowland, M. and Oppenheimer, J. 1978. *Captain Richards' house at Winterbourne: A study in historical archaeology*, Department of Prehistory and Archaeology, University of New England. (Useful as an example of a detailed study of an early homestead.)

Evans, I. 1985. *The Australian home*, Flannel Flower Press, Sydney. (A helpful introduction to the subject.)

Freeland, J.M. 1968. *Architecture in Australia: A history*, Cheshire, Melbourne. (A standard history of Australian architecture.)

Irving, R. (ed.) 1985. *The history and design of the Australian house*, Oxford University Press, Melbourne. (Highly detailed, a major source of information on the subject.)

Stapleton, M., Burton, C. and Stapleton, I. 1980. *Identifying Australian houses*, Historic Houses Trust of New South Wales, Sydney. (A small pamphlet of great use to beginners.)

Walker, M. 1978. *Pioneer crafts of early Australia*, MacMillan, Melbourne. (Contains much useful information and is well illustrated.)

Chapter 7: Reading the rural landscape

Birmingham, J., Jack, I. and Jeans, D. 1979. *Australian pioneer technology: sites and relics*, Heinemann, Richmond, Victoria. (An essential introductory text on selected aspects of Australian historical archaeology. Well illustrated.)

Freeman, P. 1980. *The woolshed: A Riverina anthology*, Oxford University Press, Melbourne. (A regional study of woolsheds containing useful plans.)

Pearson, M. 1984. The excavation of the Mount Wood woolscour, Tibooburra, New South Wales. *Australian Journal of Historical Archaeology* 2, 38-50. (A unique excavation report that examines an important aspect of the pastoral industry.)

Sowden, H. (ed.) 1972. *Australian woolsheds*, Cassell, Melbourne. (A general study that is a good introduction to the subject.)

Twidale, C.R., Forrest, G.J. and Shepherd, J.A. 1971. The imprint of the plough: 'lands' in the Mt Lofty Ranges, South Australia. *Australian Geographer* 11(5), 492-503. (A most important paper concerned with an aspect of landscape archaeology that has not yet been adequately studied in Australia.)

Walker, M. 1978. *Pioneer crafts of early Australia*, MacMillan, Melbourne. (Contains much useful information and is well illustrated.)

Wheelhouse, F. 1966. *Digging stick to rotary hoe: Men and machines in rural Australia*, Cassell, Melbourne. (A valuable introduction to the history of agricultural machinery in Australia.)

Williams, M. 1974. *The making of the South Australian landscape: A study in the historical geography of Australia*, Academic Press, London and New York. (A most important book that examines the impact of European settlement on the South Australian landscape.)

Winston-Gregson, J.H. 1984. People in the landscape: a biography of two villages. *Australian Journal of Historical Archaeology* 2, 27-37. (An interesting paper that looks at the landscape archaeology of a small area in the Riverina.)

Young, G. 1985. Early German settlements in South Australia. *Australian Journal of Historical Archaeology* 3, 43-55. (A study of village layouts and building techniques that reflect the origins of some of South Australia's German settlers.)

Chapter 8: The archaeological evidence for mining

Birmingham, J., Jack, I. and Jeans, D. 1979. *Australian pioneer technology: sites and relics*, Heinemann, Richmond, Victoria. (An essential introductory text on selected aspects of Australian historical archaeology. Well illustrated.)

Blainey, G. 1969. *The rush that never ended: A history of Australian mining* (2nd edition), Melbourne University Press, Carlton. (A classic study of Australian mining history. Readable and useful.)

Burke, K. 1973. *Gold and silver: Photographs of Australian goldfields from the Holtermann Collection*, Penguin, Ringwood. (Difficult to put down: provides an intriguing insight into conditions on some of the goldfields.)

Davey, C.J. 1986. The history and archaeology of the North British Mine Site, Maldon, Victoria. *Australian Journal of Historical Archaeology* 4, 51-6. (A report on the survey and partial excavation of the remains of a Victorian gold mine.)

Kennedy, K.H., Bell, P. and Edmondson, C. 1981. *Totley: A study of the silver mines at One Mile, Ravenswood District*, Department of History, James Cook University of North Queensland. (A good example of an historical and archaeological study of mining evidence.)

Walker, M. 1978. *Pioneer crafts of early Australia*, MacMillan, Melbourne. (Contains much useful information and is well illustrated.)

Chapter 9: Information from industrial relics

Bairstow, D. 1985. The Castlemaine and Great Northern Breweries, Newcastle, New South Wales. *Australian Journal of Historical Archaeology* 3, 70-8. (An historical and archaeological study of two major industrial structures.)

Birmingham, J. 1976. The archaeological contribution to nineteenth-century history: some

Australian case studies. *World Archaeology* 7(3), 306-17. (An important paper that examines the historical value of historical archaeology in Australia.)

Birmingham, J., Jack, I. and Jeans, D. 1979. *Australian pioneer technology: sites and relics*, Heinemann, Richmond, Victoria. (An essential introductory text on selected aspects of Australian historical archaeology. Well illustrated.)

Birmingham, J., Jack, I. and Jeans, D. 1983. *Industrial archaeology in Australia: rural industry*, Heinemann, Richmond, Victoria. (Like the 1979 book by the same authors, this is an essential text that introduces selected aspects of Australian historical archaeology. Well illustrated.)

Godwin, L. 1983. The life and death of a flourmill: McCrossin's Mill, Uralla. *Australian Journal of Historical Archaeology* 1, 67-77. (A good demonstration of the information that can be extracted from rather limited evidence.)

Linge, G.J.R. 1979. *Industrial awakening: A geography of Australian manufacturing 1788 to 1890*, Australian National University Press, Canberra. (An essential background book for any archaeological study of industrial evidence.)

McIlroy, J. 1986. Bathers Bay whaling station, Fremantle, Western Australia. *Australian Journal of Historical Archaeology* 4, 43-50. (An account of the excavation of a whaling station.)

Pearson, M. 1983. The technology of whaling in Australian waters in the 19th century. *Australian Journal of Historical Archaeology* 1, 40-54. (A very useful paper for gaining an understanding of the conduct of whaling during the nineteenth century.)

Pearson, M. 1986. Archaeological interpretation and ethnographic analogy: the lime industry in Western Australia. *Archaeology in Oceania* 21, 94-102. (A paper that provides useful insight into an industry that has been little studied.)

Chapter 10: The potential of Australian historical archaeology

Birmingham, J., Jack, I. and Jeans, D. 1983. *Industrial archaeology in Australia: rural industry*, Heinemann, Richmond, Victoria. (Like the 1979 book by the same authors, this is an essential text that introduces selected aspects of Australian historical archaeology. Well illustrated.)

Boughen, H. 1986. Towser's Huts, Cobar, New South Wales: Historic ruin or ruined history? *Australian Journal of Historical Archaeology* 4, 67-77. (Discusses the investigation of the ruins of stone huts built by an Italian settler.)

Deetz, J. 1977. *In small things forgotten: The archaeology of early American life*, Anchor Press/Doubleday, Garden City, New York. (A stimulating and readable introduction to American historical archaeology.)

Henderson, G. 1986. *Maritime archaeology in Australia*, University of Western Australia Press, Nedlands. (The first synthesis of this subject. Useful and readable.)

Jack, I., Holmes, K. and Kerr, R. 1984. Ah Toy's Garden: A Chinese market-garden on the Palmer River Goldfield, North Queensland. *Australian Journal of Historical Archaeology* 2, 51-8. (Report on the survey and excavation of a remote Chinese site.)

Karskens, G. 1985. The construction of the Great North Road, NSW, 1826-1836. *Journal of the Institution of Engineers — Multi-disciplinary* GE9 (2), 102-10. (A discussion of the construction techniques used for one of Australia's earliest roads.)

Murphy, P. 1981. *The decorated wall: Eighty years of wallpaper in Australia c.1850-1930*, Historic Houses Trust of New South Wales, Sydney. (A useful introduction to a most important subject.)

Index